UNVEILING TREASURES

The Attic Guide to the
Published Works of Irish Women
Literary Writers
Drama, Fiction, Poetry

by

Ann Owens Weekes

Attic Press
Dublin

First Published in Ireland in 1993 by
Attic Press
4 Upper Mount Street
Dublin 2

British Library Cataloguing in Publication Data
Owens, Ann Weekes
    Unveiling Treasures: Attic Guide to Irish Women Literary
        Writers
    I. Title
    820.989287

ISBN 1-855940-671 pb
ISBN 1-855940-728 hb

Cover Illustration: *Running 11* by Jill Teck
Cover Design: Syd Bluett
Origination: Sinéad Bevan, Attic Press
Printing: Guernsey Press

This book is published with the assistance of The Arts
Council/An Chomairle Ealaíon and Bord na Gaeilge.

Acknowledgements

I thank all the people who have helped me to prepare this *Attic Guide*: in the first place, the women whose writing inspired this work, and the many who talked to me of their writing and that of others; the editors who contributed texts and information, much of which was unavailable elsewhere, in particular Pádraig O Snodaigh, Dermot Bolger, and Jessie Lendennie; the colleagues who shared their knowledge; Siobhán Ní Fhoghlú who researched, wrote, and advised on many writers in Irish; Gail Nic Eoghain and Stephen Fennell who translated Irish poetry; my family in Ireland for their constant prompting with gifts of Irish books. Eileen de Lauer and Kelly Barber of the Humanities Programme in the United States of America/Ireland transactions. I wish also to thank the staff of Attic Press for their cheerful assistance: in particular Gráinne Healy and Róisín Conroy for their tireless work in checking out new names and additional information, and for their superb willingness to add and change entries as new information became available to us. Finally, I wish to thank my husband Trevor – this book would never have been written without his encouragement; perhaps equally important was his expertise and usually willing assistance with word-processing.

The publisher wishes to thank the following for assisting in the compilation of the *Attic Guide* – Bríona Nic Dhiarmada, Professor Lorna Reynolds, Gerardine Meaney, Emma O'Donoghue, Anna Birch, Colette O'Daly, Deirdre Davitt and Siobhán Ní Fhoghlú. Thank you also to Breeda Mooney and WAG for all their assistance in selecting the illustration for the cover of the *Attic Guide* and to Michael McMonagle, Mount Charles, Co Donegal, the owner of *Running 11*, by Jill Teck, for his kind permission.

To my Mother

Introduction

'In fields I hear them sing'
Jo Slade

What is a Guide to Irish Women Writers, and why compile one? This *Attic Guide* is intended to be a collection of bibliographical and biographical information on Irish women who have published a volume of poetry, fiction, or drama from the eighteenth century until the present time. It is intended as an introduction for the general reader and as a reference tool for scholars. Descriptions of and quotations from many writers' work are included, allowing the reader to sample a variety that ranges from the eighteenth-century English prose of Mary Davys to the 1990s Irish poetry of Nuala Ní Dhómhnaill.

The *Attic Guide* aims to collect rather than evaluate; thus, it is inclusive with respect to writers' work and to details of nationality. The designation 'Irish' is not limited to women born in Ireland to Irish parents, but to women who identify themselves or their work with Ireland. Nuala Archer, for example, born to Irish parents in the United States of America and brought up in Central America, is included because she adopted Ireland as one of her mother-countries. Also included are the Israeli-born Ronit Lentin and many other foreign-born women who make their homes in Ireland, and women, such as Iris Murdoch and Edna O'Brien, born in Ireland but living elsewhere, who see themselves as connected to Ireland, or whose work is shaped by their Irish background. The works listed are written in the Irish and English languages. No distinction is made between the popular and the literary.

There are many reasons to compile such a guide. In the first place, the *Attic Guide* is an effort to make public both the numbers of women writers and the quality of their published work over the centuries. The briefest review of

5

Irish Literature anthologies shows male writers overwhelmingly outnumber female writers. Yes, some women are acclaimed, and many more – like their brothers – are acclaimed and forgotten. In the past, women's work was not published at the same rate as men's so there was some justification for the imbalance. Today, however, Irish women and men are publishing at a comparable rate, and, thus, one would expect the number of women to increase in the anthologies. This is not the case, as the recent crop of Irish poetry anthologies testifies. I can think of three possible explanations. Firstly, that Irish women writers do not publish the same quality work as Irish men. Secondly, that women's work is different, and that this difference somehow excludes their work from anthologies; or, thirdly, that some unrecognised force – a pooka with a hearty appetite – in the publishing business devours their work. My response to these points follows; the *Attic Guide* will allow scholars and general readers to begin their own assessment.

My bias is toward Irish women writers; I see no qualitative difference between the best work of Irish women and the best work of Irish men. Like many another girl growing up in the pre-television Ireland of the 1950s, I was an insatiable reader. Our diet was rich in nineteenth-century British novelists and the ubiquitous British school-girl sagas; Yeats, a small taste of Joyce, Seán O'Faoláin and Frank O'Connor were the home-grown ingredients. Not a bad feast for the imagination. Yet enjoyment was often tinged with a sense of unease I could not articulate, an Irish Catholic enchanted by the experiences of British Protestants, an Irish girl excluded from a world of and for Irish men: I was not 'at home' in fiction.

The first Irish woman writer to breach my teenage exile was Mary Lavin; the collection of stories was *At Sallygap*. I did not like Annie and Manny in the eponymous story, but I knew that something extraordinary had occurred in my world. In a fever of excitement, afraid that this elusive, unnameable thing might disappear, I sought and read every

Lavin text I could find. Here were people like those I knew, people whose stories could have come from my own village. As such, they fed a void barely sensed till then and changed my perception about the world I lived in. With the force of revelation I saw that my life and the apparently dull lives of those around me were as valuable and as worth exploring as the lives of the more privileged. Further, their stories, their lives, however dreary, were transformed by the artist's hand into something beautiful in itself, literature.

When the weak Manny in 'At Sallygap', escaped from the stifling confines of his wife's hatred to the Dublin hills, Mary Lavin wrote, a 'rare recklessness' came over him:

> He walked along, looking from side to side, and in his heart the night's potent beauty was beginning to have effect. But he felt confused. The dark hills and the pale sky and the city pricking out its shape upon the sea with starry lights filled him with strangely mingled feelings of sadness and joy. And when the sky flowered into a thousand stars of forget-me-not blue he was strangled by the need to know what had come over him, and having no other way to stem the tide of desolating joy within him, he started to run the way he used to run on the roads as a young lad. And as he ran he laughed out loud to think that he, Manny Ryan, was running along a country road in the dark, not knowing but he'd run into a hedge or a ditch.

Manny could only laugh; Mary Lavin revealed the beauty of his emotion.

Not only did she voice the emotion of the inarticulate, she also allowed us to understand the creation of bonds by the embittered. The hardened Annie — cheated, she thinks of vibrant life by a spineless husband — fashions bonds that bind herself and Manny, bonds which she no longer knows how to unlock. Waiting for Manny, assuming an accident must have delayed her timid husband, she retreats into her dark kitchen:

... the evening was so fair and so serene, so green and gilt, it threatened to rob her of all her dreads and to soothe her fears. It was better to sit by the whitening fire and imagine that the city outside was dark and vicious as she had often felt it to be, crossing it late on winter nights; ... She did not know which of her black forebodings she felt to be the more likely, but the ones that brought terror without robbing her entirely of the object of her terror were the ones that most appealed to her. And so she more or less expected a living Manny to be brought home to her, but one in whom some latent mutinous instinct had at last set up a twanging of chords that would echo throughout the rest of their lives and put reality into their relationship. She waited for his coming with more eagerness than when he was coming to court her.'[1]

Lavin prompted this young reader to delve into the works of Kate O'Brien, Somerville and Ross, Maria Edgeworth, to discover that Elizabeth Bowen was Irish, to hasten to the feast Edna O'Brien, Julia O'Faolain, Jennifer Johnston, Clare Boylan, Molly Keane, Christina Reid, and so many others were preparing. Many more — too many to name — had begun to assemble original and beautiful dishes. And then came the poets: Eithne Strong, Eavan Boland, and Eiléan Ní Chuilleanáin led the procession, followed by an ever-growing, variously robed party. Finally, the poets who write in Irish; inexcusable the reader's delay in reading these voices which 'comfort and disturb/the clay part of the heart':[2] Máire Mhac an tSaoi, Nuala Ní Dhómhnaill, Biddy Jenkinson, Aine Ní Ghlinn, Rita Kelly, Eithne Strong again, and again many more.

The 'territories of the voice' explored by contemporary Irish women are vast and changing. From the villages of Romania to the recesses of the psyche, women delve for evidence of their mothers and grandmothers. In the streets of northern Ireland they hide from dangers more destructive than bullets, or partake of them. Some delight in their sexuality with men, some with women. Some find their ancestral homes in the English language, others become threaders of 'double-stranded words,' as shades of Irish surface in their English, and still others linger in the speech of their Gaelic ancestors, asking with Nuala Ní Dhómhnaill, 'Is cé hiad patrúin bhunaidh/na laoch is na bhfathach/munar thusa is mise?' (And who are the original patterns/of the heroes and giants/if not me and you?)[3]

A believer in the excellence, originality, and delights in Irish women's writing, I decided to compile this volume in response to American students' questions on Irish literature. I live and work in Arizona, and students — detecting my Irish accent — often approach to tell of the wonderful course they took on Irish Literature. Invariably, they read Yeats, Joyce, Beckett, and a sampling of Synge, O'Casey, O'Connor, O'Faolain (Seán), Heaney, etc. Embarrassed when I ask them what women they have read, they eventually ask for a list of Irish women writers. After writing perhaps fifty such lists, I decided something needed to be done. The first publisher I consulted was Attic Press, who agreed at once on the value of this project.

Now to address the second possible reason for the exclusion of women from anthologies of Irish writing: difference. One must read the works, of course, before deciding whether women write differently and/or of different subjects than men. In quoting from many of the writers, however, this *Attic Guide* allows readers to hypothesise at least. Difference is neither superior nor inferior, but neutral. Yet all difference is worth charting. As noted earlier, as a young reader I found the works of Irish women writers different from those of British women writers and of Irish men writers. 'Still in fields I hear them sing,' those strange and familiar voices, the dark women, the hags, the witches, the mothers, the daughters, the lovers, the loved, the unloved, the angry, the serene: 'Across grass their shadows linger'.[4] Toni Morrison once said that she wrote strange and different books because they were the kind of books she wished to read. Alice Walker, noting the threat of oblivion that faced black folklore and that continues to threaten women's lives and work, goes further: 'I write all the things I should have read.'[5]

I leave 'the pooka in the publishing house' to readers. But there is another reason to compile a Guide: the *Attic Guide* presents many personal accounts of the making of a writer. Interesting in themselves, these accounts also suggest patterns beneficial or otherwise. Many contemporary writers, for example, got their first opportunity to publish in David Marcus's New Irish Writing page in the *Irish Press*, or in Caroline Walsh's page in *The Irish Times*. Publicity, and the encouragement it brought, prompted them to persevere. Others cite publishers such as Arlen House, and editors such as Catherine Rose, Dermot Bolger, Pádraigh O Snodaigh, Jessie Lendennie, and Ailbhe Smyth. Others again note the importance of writing groups in providing encouragement and advice. Arts Council bursaries help, also literary prizes and awards. The number of prizes won by the writers in this *Attic Guide*, in drama, fiction, and poetry contests, is impressive.

This, the largest collection of data on Irish women writers ever published, will introduce scholars, students, and general readers to the numbers and varieties of Irish women writers. The majority of entries list birth dates and places, death dates, education, and works, describe and quote from texts, and many present the writers' own accounts of how they became writers. In some cases, the writers wished to preserve their privacy and the work is the sole focus of the entry. In other instances, information on the writers and/or their work was unavailable; length of entry is thus not always a measure of the writers' importance. When the information was available, works were classified as poetry, novels, short stories or plays. The *Attic Guide* covers work published from the beginning of the eighteenth century through to works published in early 1993. Though aware of some excellent forthcoming work by writers such as Briget O'Connor or Emma Donohue, that their work has not yet been published, causes them to be excluded.

Economic and cultural conditions limited the number of women who published in English in the eighteenth and nineteenth centuries; publication in Irish was even more difficult. I am indebted to Siobhán Ní Fhoghlú for information on the consequent difference between the Irish and other oral traditions: literature as well as folk tales circulated in manuscript and in oral form in nineteenth-century Ireland. This literature, for example the poetry of Máire Bhuidhe Ní Laoghaire, was first published after the authors' deaths, in Ní Laoghaire's case, in 1931, almost one hundred years after her death, by editors working from early twentieth-century manuscripts. The distinction between written and oral tradition is thus not so clear as in many other languages. Peig Sayers appears as the Irish oral tradition is being replaced by the written; she is included because her stories, strictly-speaking not fiction, but coloured or fictionalised autobiography, form an important bridge between the two traditions. I wish also to thank Siobhán for — at a very late date — researching and presenting information on many of the writers in Irish. Thanks also to Gail Nic Eoghain and Stephen Fennell whose knowledge of the Irish language, unlike my own, revealed the rich ambiguities and ironies often hidden beneath traditional dress. We did not, however, publish translations unless these were already available in print. While the intention was and is to compile information on all Irish women who have published a volume of poetry, fiction, or drama, I have not been able to collect information on all the writers. Many of the nineteenth-century Irish writers in English, for example, are still unrecognised, their work recorded in the British Museum Catalogue, but not their country. Scholars are working at the moment on unearthing Irish writers, and I invite them to send me information for a future extended issue of this *Attic Guide*. I also request information on writers in Irish and contemporary writers and am grateful in advance to those who send the missing pieces: birth dates and places, death dates, titles, and publishers.

The cooperation I invite is in line with that received while working on the *Attic Guide*. Attempting to compile a comprehensive list of Irish women writers, I turned first to the volumes on Irish fiction, poetry, and drama; the entries on women in these texts are dishearteningly small. Next, I turned to two bibliographies: *Dictionary of Irish Literature* (1979), edited by Robert Hogan, and *A Biographical Dictionary of Irish Writers* (1985), edited by Anne M Brady and Brian Cleeve; *Pillars of the House* (1988), edited by A A Kelly, an anthology of Irish women's poetry from 1690 to the 1980s, is an excellent source of information on poets, past and present; thanks to all these editors. The catalogues of the National Library of Ireland, Trinity College Dublin, and the British Museum entice and repulse; they are either incomplete or fail to identify writers by country.

Friends and colleagues working on nineteenth-century writers supplied many names. Irish publishers were very helpful with contemporary writers: Pádraig O Snodaigh, Dermot Bolger, and Jessie Lendennie, of Coiscéim, Raven, and Salmon Publishing, respectively, deserve special thanks for cheerfully providing texts and information. Poolbeg, Wolfhound, and Blackstaff were generous with their texts and assistance. The 'Irish Writers' and 'New Writers' shelves of Dublin booksellers proved a rich source also.

Personal contacts with writers and colleagues were very rewarding. Especially gratifying was the eagerness of writers to contribute the names, phone numbers and/or addresses of other writers, and their pleasure in explaining the riches in another writer's works. Women searched their memories for names of writers they had read, or heard of, in the past: Mary Brigid Pearse's name, her novel apparently forgotten by all but one writer, turned up in such a search.

Finally, I should note that space and time constraints limited this *Attic Guide*. Excluded are the many excellent Irish women journalists, such as Nell McCafferty, whose research and writing has done so much in recent years to awaken readers to conditions, not only in Ireland, but also in the wider world. Biographers, historians, literary critics and editors of volumes are also excluded. Irish women have won well-deserved awards and praise in these areas recently; my decisions were based only on an attempt to be consistent and coherent. Also excluded are women whose poetry, drama, or short stories appear only in the pages of journals, newspapers, or collections, or where work has been performed, but not published. Their voices will certainly be heard in the future, but to include the writers distributed through many papers, journals, and collections was virtually impossible. Also, the *Attic Guide's* principal value is as a reference tool to direct readers to the original work. Much of the work published in papers and journals is not retained in libraries and the reader would thus be unable to access it.

A second final note: writers born in any county in Ireland are noted in the introductory lines as being born in Ireland; the text which follows gives the particular place of birth. I use the word 'Ireland' to refer to the whole island and not as a political designation.

Saving the lives that are their own, their mothers', or their grandmothers', these Irish women writers refuse to remain 'Outside History', refuse to leave their stories untold. Their words can no more be recalled than can the new language through which the old one pours, as Medbh McGuckian says in 'The Dream-Language of Fergus':

No text can return the honey
In its path of light from a jar,
Only a seed-fund, a pendulum,
Pressing out the diasporic snow. (57)

This *Attic Guide* seeks to ensure that the words spread in chaotic and disciplined liberation will not be poured and forgotten.

Notes

1. *The Stories of Mary Lavin* (London: Constable, 1974), 33; 39.
2. Moya Cannon, 'Listening Clay', in *Oar* (Galway: Salmon Publishing, 1990), 25.
3. Moya Cannon, 'Taom', in *Oar*, 13; Medbh McGuckian, 'The Dream-Language of Fergus', in *On Ballycastle Beach* (Oxford: Oxford University Press, 1988), 57; Nuala Ní Dhómnhaill, 'Ag Cothú Linbh', ('Feeding a Child',) in *Selected Poems: Rogha Dánta* (Dublin: Raven Arts Press, 1991), 88, 89.
4. Jo Slade, 'In Fields I Hear Them Sing', in *In Fields I hear Them Sing* (Galway: Salmon Publishing, 1989), 23.
5. Alice Walker, 'Saving the Life that is Your Own: The Importance of Models in the Artist's Life', in *The Third Woman*, Dexter Fisher, ed. (Boston: Houghton Mifflin, 1980), 154, 157.

Ann Owens Weekes
Humanities Programme
University of Arizona

— A —

Anderson, Linda
Born: Ireland, 1949
Educated: Ireland.

Linda Anderson was born in Belfast, the third of five children born into a working-class Protestant family. Her father was a Belfast man, her mother Canadian. She was educated at a girls' grammar school and at Queen's University, Belfast, where she graduated in French and Philosophy, and took a postgraduate Diploma of Education. She believes she escaped bigotry because she had a Catholic friend. 'Although I wasn't politically aware at that point, a divergence of view was always appearing over things like the history we were learning in our respective schools. My heroes were my friend's villains.'[1] At Queen's, she explored history for herself: 'This was the beginning of a whole lot of secret, subversive reading which was very important for me, to grow up, get free and not feel isolated.'[2] In 1968, she joined the Civil Rights Movement in northern Ireland, but left Ireland for England, in 1972, disillusioned at the lack of change.

In England, she worked as a teacher, and later at several low-paying jobs in order to have time to write. She thinks she would have been a writer anyway because of her 'love of language, but my experiences in northern Ireland have certainly been very shaping, decisive, and mobilising in my writing life'[3]. She writes novels, short stories, and drama; her first novel, *To Stay Alive*, was published in Britain in 1984, to very good reviews. It was also published in the USA, shortlisted for prizes, and as a result she received two Arts Council Grants and was able to take time off work to write her second novel, *Cuckoo* (1986). Her short stories have appeared in anthologies and magazines; 'The Beast' was runner-up in the Cosmopolitan/Master Blend Short Story Competition in 1989, and her play, *Charmed Lives*, won second prize in the drama category of Wandsworth All London Competition in 1988.

'A recurring obsession in my work,' she notes, 'is the link between public and private kinds of violence. The way "public" violence seeps and deforms and creates what a man says to a woman in bed, for example, and the reverse situation, too. The way all our "privacies" create the mutilating world.'[4]

To Stay Alive is the story of a young couple's attempt to stay alive and humane in the ghetto of Belfast, ruled by the Provisional IRA and beset by British troops. Violence and murder is everywhere and though Dan and Rosaleen try to stay out of it, they are forced to take sides. The relationship of Dan and Rosaleen is finely portrayed. In an ambiguous encounter with McGuire, a 'Fixit-man' with Provo connections, Dan, a medical student who needs money for his wife and baby, is asked to 'preserve life' by offering his medical services to wounded Provos. Frightened that he has revealed himself to McGuire, Dan tries to dismiss his fears, telling Rosaleen that seeing McGuire was a waste of time.

> 'Don't worry about that. He's a person of no consequence.'
>
> He laughed at the sudden deflation of McGuire's Machiavellian image, then broke into a dry tearless sobbing.
>
> 'You're so lonely,' Rosaleen said. She came and held him.
>
> 'Never mind him. We'll be all right, you'll see ...'[5]

Cuckoo tells the story of Fran McDowell who has left the bigotry and violence of northern Ireland for London, of her friendships, and continued politicisation by the Greenham Common Protests.

Works:

To Stay Alive. London: Bodley Head, 1984; London: Futura, 1985; In USA as *We Can't All Be Heroes, You Know*. New York: Ticknor and Fields, 1985. Novel.

Cuckoo. London: Bodley Head, 1986; Dingle: Brandon, 1988. Novel.

Notes

1. Personal communication.
2. 'Linda Anderson: An Audacious Talent', *Cosmopolitan*, 1986, 112.
3. Personal communication.
4. Personal communication.
5. *To Stay Alive*, 66.

Archer, Nuala
Born: USA c̲ 20th century
Educated: Central America, USA.

Born in the USA and brought up in Central America, Nuala Archer is the daughter of parents who left Ireland in the 'brain-drain' of the 1950s, 'with medical degrees as passports'. Her relationship to Ireland is complex. As a child, she notes, she thought 'Spanish, with its tropical cadences,' was her mother tongue, but her own name frequently demanded explanations, which invariably involved her Irish heritage. Later, when a visit to Ireland 'shapeshifted into a stay of years and a house in Dublin,' she experienced a sense of rendezvous. Her first volume of poems, *Whale on the Line* (1981), won the Kavanagh Award, and she responded both to the poetry and the friendship of Irish women poets. Her dissertation completed for the University of Wisconsin, she left Ireland in 1984 to teach poetry in Oklahoma State University. She kept in touch with Irish writers, however, and in 1986 edited a special

issue of Irish women's writing for the *Midland Review*.[1]
This excellent issue won Irish women writers of poetry and
fiction a wide American audience. Two collections of her
own poetry have been published to date, a third volume,
Two Women, Two Shores (1989), presents poetry of Nuala
Archer and Medbh McGuckian, and a fourth is ready for
publication.

Archer's poetry often wings into exuberance, remarking
the wonderful and strange in the ordinary. Rejecting the
tedious in 'Flaneurs', the persona and her friend take
imaginary flight to the food, clothes, and countries of their
fantasies, playing with that most difficult of notions,
identity.

> Spiralling
>   into
>   the attic's
>   ear,
>   fossicking through Freya's
> old trunks of clothes and Olive's books,
> boxes of letters and Irish canvases,
>   floating
>   into another time
>   and timeless linens
>   and silk
>   we let ourselves go
>   looney
>   and with every thread Leigh says,
>   smell this. [2]

Poems from *Whale on the Line* and *Two Women, Two Shores*
probe distance and echoes, as well as identity. 'You can't
hear me dialling your number,' 'Whale on the Line' opens,
'because a whale is tangled/in the telephone cables on the
ocean floor.'[3] 'Who is the mother of these words?' Archer's
first poem in the collaborative volume *Two Women, Two
Shores*, asks:

Nonsense syllables
leaping up between Swilly and Sewanee. Three
thousand miles of ocean: *O, bring back, bring*

back: Lovers crossing over: winging the never-
forever gap, the Atlantic assemblage: her mother
and my mother and myself'.[4]

Language becomes liberating delirium, 'a zany confluence'
which ultimately unites Archer's mobile home in
Oklahoma with McGuckian's 'Blue Farm' in Belfast, the
poet with mother and history, reason with imagination,
and ourselves with our would-be-selves.[5]

Works:
Whale on the Line. Dublin: Gallery Books, 1981. Poetry.
Two Women, Two Shores: poems by Medbh McGuckian and
    Nuala Archer. Baltimore: The New Poets Series, 1989. Poetry.
The Hour of Pan/Ama. Galway: Salmon Publishing, 1992. Poetry.

Notes
1. 'Introduction', *Midland Review*, xiv.
2. In *The Hour of Pan/Ama*, 43-44.
3. In *Whale on the Line*, 18.
4. 'Between Swilly and Sewanee', *Two Women, Two Shores*, 38.
5. The phrase is from 'Between Swilly and Sewanee', but the
    conclusion is mine.

Armitage, Marigold
Born: England c 20th century
Educated: England.

Marigold Armitage, the eldest daughter of Sir Arthur
Harris, was born on an RAF station in Lincolnshire. She
worked as an ambulance driver and despatch rider during
World War II. She moved to Ireland after her marriage,
and lived in Tipperary and Limerick, where she wrote *A
Long Way to Go*, described as an Anglo-Irish near tragedy.
She lives in England.[1]

The reader is introduced to an eccentric Anglo-Irish family in *A Long Way to Go*, as Anthony Kavanagh returns to the family home, Knockmoree, after a six-year absence: Aunt Emmy, dressed in ill-assorted garments, but exuding charm; Mother, 'like a pansy the least bit frost-bitten'; and the ubiquitous Nanny, disapproving of foreign places and still solicitous for the welfare of her erstwhile charge. Dressed for dinner, Gillian, Anthony's girl-friend, acts as a foil to Aunt Emmy, 'who had arranged herself quite normally in a dowager gown of black velvet, but had omitted to remove the knitted garment she had worn all day ("in case would me rheumatism creep on") which now poked up wilfully above her semi-décolletage; do what she would to poke it down. "I thought me amber would hide it," she explained. "Never mind, Aunt Emmy, it's madly fashionable, Dior is mixing wool and velvet like anything at this very moment,"' Gillian assures her.[2]

As we might expect, horses are Aunt Emmy's prime interest. She offers Anthony a mare for the next day's hunt, assuring him that 'she's a great ride, only for her little habit of not rising at her walls.' The story is told through Anthony's affectionate but skeptical eyes. He responds to Emmy's offer in typical fashion: 'That's a little habit I should find very unattractive' (32).

Selected Works:
A Long Way to Go. 1952; rpt. London: Robin Clark, 1989. Novel.

Notes
1. Author Introduction, *A Long Way to Go*, Clark edition.
2. *A Long Way to Go*, 28-29.

— *B* —

Bannister, Ivy
Born: USA, 1951
Educated: USA, Ireland.

Ivy Bannister was born in New York City where she attended the Lenox School; she took her Bachelor of Arts at Smith College, Massachusetts, and her PhD at Trinity College, Dublin. She decided to be a writer at thirteen while reading Daphne du Maurier's *Rebecca*, but spent the next 'twenty years avoiding the hard work of actually writing', by 'doing degrees, and working part-time in theatre and at the *New Yorker* magazine'. 'At the age of nineteen,' she writes, 'I came to live in Ireland, because as a small child, I'd met an Irish workman who used language much more vividly than ordinary mortals, and I looked forward to meeting the intelligentsia of such an eloquent nation!'[1]

Although she has written poetry and short stories, she may be best-known as a playwright. Three of her plays received rehearsed readings at the Peacock Theatre and the Project Arts Centre, *The Wilde Circus Show*, *The Rebel Countess*, and *Errol Flynn had the Body of a Tired Old Man*. RTE Radio produced two of her plays in 1991, *Love Nest* and *The Road to Revolution*. *The Wilde Circus Show* was published by Proscenium Press in 1990, and her scripts received the O Z Whitehead Award in 1986, the Listowel Award in 1987, and the P J O'Connor award in 1991.

Her poetry and short stories have been published in many magazines and have also received awards: the

21

Hennessy (1988); *IT*/Mills and Boon (1988); *Image*/ Maxwell House (1988, 1990); Image/Bord na Móna (1992); and the Francis MacManus (1990; 1991).

Works:
The Wilde Circus Show. Newark, Delaware: Proscenium Press, 1990. Play.

Notes
1. Personal communication.

Barber, Mary

Born: c.1690; Died: 1757
Educated: Ireland.
Mary Barber is believed to have begun writing poetry to enliven her four children's lessons.[1] She married Jonathan Barber, an English-born draper of Capel Street, Dublin. Certainly, many of her poems are written for her children, 'Written for my Son, and spoken by him in school, upon his master's bringing in a rod', for example, and 'A letter Written for my Daughter, to a lady who had presented her with a cap'.[2] Swift admired her work and helped her to publish *Poems on Several Occasions* (1734), transcribed again by Bernard Tucker, in 1992, and edited from the 1734 edition. The poems were well received, but did not bring in sufficient funds for Barber to care for her family — her husband is rarely mentioned in letters of the period or in the poetry. Barber again turned to Swift for help; he allowed her to publish his *Polite Conversations* (1738), which were more successful financially.

In common with her eighteenth-century contemporaries, Barber wrote poetry to commemorate an occasion or a patron; her subjects, however, are domestic rather than the public subjects of her male counterparts. An early poem, 'Written for my Son, and spoken by him at his first putting on breeches', satirises men's clothing during a century when poets enjoyed ridiculing women's:

> What is it our Mammas bewitches,
> To plague us little Boys with breeches?
> To Tyrant *Custom* we must yield,
> Whilst vanguish'd *Reason* flies the Field.
> Our Legs must suffer by Ligation,
> To keep the Blood from Circulation;
> And then our Feet, tho' young and tender,
> We to the Shoemaker surrender;
> Who often makes our Shoes so strait,
> Our growing Feet they cramp and fret:
> Whilst with Contrivance most profound,
> Across our Insteps we are bound;
> Which is the Cause, I make no Doubt,
> Why thousands suffer in the Gout. (72-73)

Works:
The Poetry of Mary Barber. Bernard Tucker, ed. 1734; rpt. New York/Ontario: The Edwin Mellen Press, 1992. Poetry.

Notes:
1. *The Poetry of Mary Barber*, Introduction, 3.
2. In *The Poetry of Mary Barber*, 86, 97.

Bardwell, Leland (*née* Hone)
Born: India, 1928
Educated: Ireland, England.

Leland Bardwell was born to Irish parents in India and grew up in Co. Kildare, where she devoured all the books in the Foyles Lending Library. At sixteen, she had to leave school, Alexandra College in Dublin, to look after her dying mother. Then followed a stint in London, a more extensive library, several jobs, and being bombed out of her flat in 1945. She married and had three children with Michael Bardwell, lived in a cottage near Kilkenny, and attempted to study Ancient History in London University. After separating from her husband, she lived alone in London with her three children until 1959 when she moved to Wexford with Finton Mclachlan, with whom she had three sons. When she split up with Mclachlan, she again lived with her children, and now lives alone in Co. Sligo.

Despite this busy life, she found time to write poetry; indeed, she wrote from the time she was seven, but began publishing when she was thirty. Patrick Kavanagh encouraged her early work, which is full of humour. Along with co-poets Eiléan Ní Chuilleanáin, Macdara Woods and Pearse Hutchinson, she began the literary magazine *Cyphers*. She admires the work of these poets, of Paul Durcan and Rita Anne Higgins, and believes 'there is a mass of first class poetry coming out of Ireland at the moment, North and South.' She has written plays for Radio Telefís Éireann and the BBC, a musical based on the life of Edith Piaf, poetry, short stories, and several novels.

'The abiding influence in all my books is the fact that I was brought up Protestant, the minority religion in the South and this theme recurs again and again in all my novels,' she notes.[1] I would agree: her characters are usually Protestant lower middle-class, and their views sometimes appear strange to the point of madness. But the reader is brought to a stage where she recognises and understands the perspective. 'Different Kinds of Love' – in the short story collection of that title – is a sensitive and unusual portrayal of the love, anguish, and attention which a middle-aged, 'fuddy-duddy dry-as-dust solicitor' bestows on the stroke-victim he once loved passionately. This unsentimental story quietly observes very ordinary, routine, male sexuality and the unromantic helplessness of the stroke-victim, and unites the two finally in a moment of precious human sympathy. Another story in this collection, 'Night Rider', takes us into the mind of the

24

simple Patrick Gallagher, whose desire to ride the big horse suggests primitive and enduring human needs. The 'extinct creature', Patrick, differs from those around him by his straight-forward rather than disguised responses.[2]

Leland Bardwell turned from poetry to prose, hoping to make more money to take care of her children. She still considers herself primarily a poet. Her most recent collection of poetry, *Dostoevsky's Grave* (1991), confirms her opinion. She brings the same low-key sympathy to her poems and prose. 'Them's Your Mother's Pills' pictures the women 'in this strange forgotten world/of video and valium,' the new housing estate, lonely beyond sanity.

Fragile as needles the women wander forth/ laddered with kids, the unborn one ahead/ to forge the mile through mud and rut/ where mulish earth-removers rest, a crazy sculpture/[3]

Refusing to ignore the unpalatable, or to exaggerate, Leland Bardwell turns a clear eye on often ignored areas of human, particularly Irish, experience. Not least of her gifts is the clarity of her prose, a clarity which she uses ironically and often to depict the conflicting, confusing, and ambiguous nature of human desires.

Works:
The Mad Cyclist. Dublin: New Writers Press, 1970. Poetry.
Girl on a Bicycle. Dublin: Co-Op Books, 1977. Novel.
That London Winter. Dublin: Co-Op Books, 1981. Novel.
The House. Kerry: Brandon, 1984. Novel.
The Fly and the Bed Bug. Dublin: Beaver Row Press, 1984. Poetry.
Different Kinds of Love. Dublin: Attic Press, 1987. Short Stories.
Berlin: Verlag Ullstein: 1991. Translated Ilse Bessen Berger. Novel.
There We Have Been. Dublin: Attic Press, 1989. Novel.
Dostoevsky's Grave. New and Selected Poems. Dublin: Dedalus, 1991. Poetry.

Notes
1. Personal communication.
2. All in *Different Kinds of Love.*
3. In *Wildish Things*, Ailbhe Smyth ed. (Dublin, Attic Press, 1984),
   37.

Barlow, Jane
Born: Ireland, 1857; Died: 1917
Educated: Ireland.

Jane Barlow was born in Clontarf, Co. Dublin. Her father
was the Reverend James Barlow, a future vice-provost of
Trinity College, Dublin. Her narrative poems and stories of
Irish life were very popular and were published in several
editions.

Barlow attempts to represent the dialect and accent of
Irish peasants as she recounts the everyday happenings of
ordinary people. Her stories often contain small ironic
twists, humour, and insights into social conventions.
Tommy Finucane's efforts to replace his mistress's 'lost'
cactus and Mrs Kelly's envious spirit lead to an ironic
comedy of errors in 'A Cream-Coloured Cactus', as
Tommy 'borrows' the Kelly cactus, only to be confronted
by a repentant Mrs Kelly who offers it to him. The rivalry
of the two widows, Mrs Kelly and Mrs Finucane, is nicely
portrayed when Mrs Finucane calls to show Mrs Kelly the
'flat-iron' and 'zinc bucket' she purchased at the auction for
'nothing at all'.[1] Mrs Kelly informs her that her son Bob
was also at the auction, but Mrs Finucane says she never
saw him.

> 'Sure he'd nothin' to be bringin' him into the house
> where you was, ma'am,' Mrs Kelly replied suavely. 'It's
> there you'd go, I should suppose, if you was a-wantin'
> of *kitchen* articles and such — 'Deed that's a very good
> strong bucket you've got, ma'am; the ones I seen
> hangin' outside of Graham's in Talbot Street wasn't

much better, to say, and they're maybe dearer. And that's a handy iron, too, when you have to be makin' up. I don't throuble meself wid messin' over much washin' these times. Bob won't let me take in a bit, tho' I do be tellin' him I'm as well able for it as ever I was; och no, never a let he'll let me, good or bad. But 'twasn't them descripshin of things he went lookin' after; the notion he had was to get somethin' tasty in the way of a windy-plant.'

Mrs Finucane is a worthy opponent: 'Ah tub be sure, the most of yours looks to be dyin' on you.' (32-33)

Works:

Bog-Land Studies. London: Unwin, 1892. Poetry.
Irish Idylls. London: Hodder and Stoughton, 1892. Stories.
The End of Elfintown. London: Macmillan, 1894. Poetry.
Kerrigan's Quality. London: Hodder and Stoughton, 1894. Novel.
Maureen's Fairing and Other Stories. London: Dent, 1895; New York: Books for Libraries Press, 1972. Stories.
Strangers at Lisconnel, A Second Series of Irish Idylls. London: Hodder and Stoughton, 1895. Stories.
Mrs Martin's Company and Other Stories. London: J M Dent, 1896. Stories.
A Creel of Irish Stories. London; Methuen, 1897. Stories.
From the East unto the West. London: Methuen, 1898. Stories.
From the Land of the Shamrock. New York: Dodd, Mead, 1900. Stories.
Ghost-Bereft. London: Smith, Elder, 1901. Narrative Poetry.
At the Back of Beyond. New York: Dodd, Mead, 1902. Stories.
The Founding of Fortunes. London: Methuen, 1902. Novel.
By Beach and Bog-Land. London: Unwin, 1905. Stories.
Irish Neighbours. London: Hutchinson, 1907. Stories.
The Mockers and Other Verses. London: G Allen, 1908. Poetry.
Irish Ways. London: G Allen, 1909. Stories.
Flaws. London: Hutchinson, 1911. Novel.
Mac's Adventures. London: Hutchinson, 1911. Stories.
Doings and Dealings. London: Hutchinson, 1913.
Between Doubting and Daring. Oxford: B H Blackwell, 1916. Poetry.
In Mio's Youth. London: Hutchinson, 1917. Novel.

Notes
1. 'A Cream-Coloured Cactus', *Maureen's Fairing and Other Stories*, 31, New York edition.

Barrington, Margaret
Born: Ireland, 1896; Died: 1982
Educated: Ireland.

Margaret Barrington was born in Donegal. She went to schools in Donegal, Kerry, and Dublin, and attended Trinity College, Dublin. The daughter of a district inspector of police in the Royal Irish Constabulary (RIC), she married the historian Edmund Curtis in 1922. The marriage was dissolved, and she married the novelist Liam O'Flaherty in 1926. She had one child with O'Flaherty before they separated. During the 1930s she moved to England, where she wrote her novel, *My Cousin Justin* (1939), and contributed to the woman's page in the *Tribune*. Politically active, she helped refugees from nazi Germany and organised support for the republican side in the Spanish civil war. When war broke out, she moved to west Cork and wrote short stories. A volume of her short stories, with an introduction by William Trevor, was published in 1982.[1]

My Cousin Justin is a story of life in Ireland before World War I. The narrator, Anne-Louise, and her cousin Justin grow up in a golden country where their grandfather teaches them lessons, and their Aunt Molly allows them to live a carefree life. Although Protestants, the children play freely with Catholic children, unaware of bigotry and class divisions, until Anne-Louise's mother arrives, and, disliking the child's wild appearance and Irish accent, removes her from the care of her aunt.

The Ulster Volunteer Movement begins when Anne-Louise is at school. The Movement, she notes, 'sprang out of double fear, fear of the native Catholic Irish, oppressed for centuries and now since the days of Parnell asserting themselves more and more, and the more tangible fear of the workers. As usual it was the less real fear that was emphasised. The factory-owners, the ship-builders, the newspapers and the bourgeoisie declared with every breath they took that Home Rule was Rome Rule, and the worker was for the hundredth time deceived.'[2] Barrington introduces feminist concerns: Anne-Louise wishes to go to college, but her mother objects; Justin comforts her before he goes to war in 1914, 'We're lucky to have known Aunt Molly, Lou. She helps us to forgive our families.' (92)

Works:
My Cousin Justin. London: Jonathan Cape, 1939; rpt. Belfast: Blackstaff, 1990. Novel.
David's Daughter, Tamar. Dublin: Wolfhound, 1982. Short Stories.

Notes
1. Author Introduction in *David's Daughter, Tamar*.
2. *My Cousin Justin*, 78-79.

Beckett, Mary
Born: Ireland, 1926
Educated: Ireland.

Mary Beckett lived in Belfast for the first thirty years of her life, attending St Columban's National School, St Dominic's High School, and St Mary's Teacher Training College. She worked as a primary teacher in Holy Cross, Ardoyne, for eleven years. Married in 1956, she moved to Dublin, where she still lives. She has five children. Her short stories were published in the 1950s in *The Bell* and other journals and in the 'New Irish Writing' section of the *Irish Press*. She has published one collection of short stories, *A Belfast Woman* (1980), and five novels.

'All the short stories I wrote before *A Belfast Woman* deal with the loneliness of someone who feels excluded,' she notes. 'Perhaps this is due to my upbringing in a strongly nationalist family in a unionist part of Belfast.' Many of her stories are set in Belfast or the northern countryside, and she focuses on the routine difficulties – as well as terrors – for women raising families in the midst of the 'Troubles' in the North. She also presents vivid, uncomfortably recognisable, portraits of mother-daughter relationships, their tensions and bitternesses, as well as their joys. *Give Them Stones* (1987), her first novel, and *A Belfast Woman*, 'came from the necessity I felt to enlighten my middle-class Dublin friends who could not understand why there was an upheaval in the North'. *A Literary Woman* (1990), *Orla was Six* (1989), and *Orla at School* (1991), were written out of the experience of rearing a family, of being a little girl once, and of teaching and mothering girls.[1]

Beckett's insights are especially sharp when she examines family relationships from a woman's perspective. 'Heaven' for Hilary, the persona in the short story of this title, 'was an empty house'. Always appearing as the perfect 'devoted mother', Hilary's joy was in polished prams, immaculate pillows, pink-and-white faces. Even when her children were at home, Hilary looked forward to hours of solitude, free from disturbance of husband and children. When her husband retires, however, his very 'breathing banished silence from the house'. His presence impinges so much that she offers to baby-sit her grandchildren in the afternoons, thinking thus to divert her husband. The plan backfires as the husband refuses to become involved with the children. Her solitude lost, Hilary can only catch glimpses of heaven: 'calm corridors and vaulted roofs all soundless'.[2]

Give Them Stones is an elderly woman's low-key presentation of her sixty years of life in Belfast, years that cover the 'troubles' of 1935 and of the 1970s. One scene – which suggests the outsider-status of the nationalist child growing up in Stormont/Belfast – also suggests the lot of many Irish children in the 1940s and 1950s who found little in the books they read that paralleled their own experience. Recalling the books of her youth, the narrator remembers: 'They were like reading fairy stories, everything was in such order. There was the big house, the vicarage, the church, the doctor and the villagers. They all worked together in such unity I could only laugh. And of course they were every one Protestants. Until I was grown up I never came across any book that mentioned Catholics. In spite of learning in the catechism that the Church was universal I felt always that Catholics were only fit for backstreets and boglands and if by any chance you penetrated into the Protestant world they would no more mention your strange religion than they would draw attention to a disfiguring birthmark.' The same voice leads readers through the horrors of life in a Belfast where nationalists, unionists, and British soldiers are all prepared to destroy homes and families to gain political points.[3]

Works:
A Belfast Woman. Dublin: Poolbeg, 1980; New York: William Morrow, 1989. Stories.
Give Them Stones. London: Bloomsbury, 1987; New York: William Morrow, 1988; New York: Harper and Row, 1989. Novel.
A Literary Woman. London: Bloomsbury, 1990, 1991. Novel.
Orla was Six. Dublin: Poolbeg, 1989, 1992. Children's Novel.
Orla at School. Dublin: Poolbeg, 1991. Children's Novel.
A Family Tree. Dublin: Poolbeg, 1992. Children's Novel.

Notes
1. Personal communication.
2. In *Wildish Things*, Ailbhe Smyth, ed. (Dublin: Attic Press, 1989), 29-36.
3. *Give Them Stones*, 46.

Bennett, Louie

Born: Ireland, 1870; Died: 1956
Educated: Ireland.

Louie Bennett was born to prosperous parents in Blackrock, Co. Dublin. Attracted at a young age to the heroines of Jane Austen, Charles Dickens, George Eliot and Henrik Ibsen, she determined to become a writer. She wrote two romantic novels, *The Proving of Priscilla* (1902), and *A Prisoner of his Word* (1908), but is remembered chiefly for her work in the women's suffrage, pacifist and trade union movements. She worked alongside Helen Chenevix, 'life-long friend and co-worker with Louie.' [1]

A pacifist all her life, she did not condemn the militant route of the suffragettes, but helped to form the Irish Women's Suffrage Federation and the Irish Women's Reform League. The Federation helped the many Irish suffrage societies coordinate their efforts and was in touch with suffrage societies in Europe and the USA; the Reform League attempted to bring feminism to bear on women's social and labour issues. She was not involved in the Irish Women Workers' Union (IWWU) initially because she saw women's and workers' issues as international. Following the aftermath of the Easter Rising, however, she saw affinities between the lot of women and that of the Irish people and began the reorganisation of the Irish Women Workers' Union. She insisted on the need for a separate union for women, because she saw that women's concerns would always be secondary to men's. She encouraged women to join trade unions and saw their memberships increase from 20,000 in 1930 to 55,000 in 1950. [2]

Works:

The Proving of Priscilla. London & New York: Harper, 1902. Novel.

A Prisoner of his Word. Dublin: Maunsel, 1908. Novel.

Notes

1. *Louie Bennett, Her Life and Times.* R M Fox, Dublin: Talbot Press, 1957.

2. For a short account of her life, see Medb Ruane, 'Louie Bennett', in *Ten Dublin Women* (Dublin: Women's Commemoration and Celebration Committee, 1991). For more detail, Rosemary Cullen Owens, *Smashing Times: A History of the Irish Women's Suffrage Movement 1889-1922* (Dublin: Attic Press, 1984), *Did Your Granny Have A Hammer???* (Dublin: Attic Press, 1985).

Berkeley, Sara B
Born: Ireland, 1967
Educated: Ireland, USA, Britain.

Sara Berkeley began writing poetry at nine; by the time she was sixteen her poems won the admiration of Dermot Bolger, the editor of Raven Arts Press. Raven published her first two volumes of poems, the first while she was still a student at Trinity College, Dublin. She attributes her early interest in writing to a houseful of avid readers, a television-free childhood home, and an encouraging English teacher at her secondary school, Manor House in Raheny, Dublin. She took a degree in English Literature and German at Trinity, spent a year at the University of California at Berkeley, and then took an MSc in Technical Writing at South Bank Polytechnic in London. She lives in London at the moment, but plans to return to California and to Dublin.

Writing answers an 'insatiable need', she notes; 'it defines, comforts, excites, and fulfills me.' 'I write from a close observation of people and the things they do — it is as simple as that. The great thing about writing is your material crowds itself upon you from the moment you wake in the morning until the moment you sleep at night. If I am in the mood to see the stories/vignettes/poems that present themselves to me, I can come home exhausted by the flights my imagination has taken me on.' She has published two volumes of poetry, *Penn* (1986) and *Home-*

Movie Nights (1989), and one of short stories, *The Swimmer in the Deep Blue Dream* (1991).

As for subjects, 'relationships I have had have fuelled a lot of my poetry: I find a sense of loss or betrayal particularly "writable". Often I have written my happiest work when most miserable, and *vice versa*, as though imagination really is a physical and mental stepping out of whatever condition I am in ... I can never help writing of the changes of season, of different lights, particular colours; and I will never stop attempting the impossible task of putting words on human moods and their transience.'[1]

She does not feel particularly Irish as she writes, nor is she a 'feminist or politically motivated'. Her poems reflect tremendous identification with nature, the persona often assuming a female voice in nature. 'Seeding', for example, sees afresh the woman who waits 'tight limbed,/ Time-dried for her babies to begin' as harmonising with the circles of seasons, waves, flowers, and vegetables. Ironically the poem suggests fertility despite the images of fallowness, dryness, and winter.[2] Berkeley's images work richly and suggestively, without sacrificing a sense of modern idiom. The 'Fault' 'sniggers' beneath the highway in 'Valley Poem 1' (surely a Californian poem), 'cracks her knuckles publicly/But keeps apart her joy/Narrow and deep'. One day, however, the poem warns, 'She will burst her corset of rock/And take the air'.[3] The 'strange harmony of lunacy and reason' entrances the poet; her work, 'Crossing 1', for example, reverberates with this beauty, images of which will continue to haunt the reader long after the precise words are forgotten.[4]

The deceptive riches beneath the innocent word, the sharp insight around the corner of a sentence, the practices of Emily Dickinson are also those of Sara Berkeley, so it is fitting that the younger poet pays tribute in the poem addressed to her literary predecessor.

Then the Alice-like fall
Swings from dull thud to thud of her hitting earth.

In her long descent did she howl?
I worry about that sound
And watch how her own nouns
Jostle her now she is down,
Her thoughts are an empty train, doors open,
And no-one getting in.[5]

Works:

Penn. Dublin: Raven Arts Press; Saskatchewan: Thistledown Press, 1986. Poetry.

Home-Movie Nights. Dublin: Raven Arts Press; Saskatchewan: Thistledown Press, 1989. Poetry.

The Swimmer in the Deep Blue Dream. Dublin: Raven Arts Press; Saskatchewan: Thistledown Press, 1991. Stories.

Notes

1. Personal communication.
2. In *Penn*, 27.
3. In *Wildish Things*, Ailbhe Smyth. ed. (Dublin: Attic Press, 1989), 127.
4. In *Penn*, 11.
5. In *Home-Movie Nights*, 36.

Binchy, Maeve
Born: Ireland, 1940
Educated: Ireland.

Maeve Binchy was born in Dublin, and grew up in Dun Laoghaire and Dalkey. She attended the convent of the Order of the Holy Child in Killiney, and took her BA and Higher Diploma in Education in University College, Dublin. She was a teacher for eight years until she became a columnist with *The Irish Times*. Her funny-sad columns, the incidents of everyday life seen from a humorous angle, are eagerly awaited by *Irish Times* readers every Saturday morning. She has written several plays; her television play *Deeply Regretted By*, won two Jacob Awards and the Best Script Award at the Prague Film Festival. Although she first wrote short stories, she has concentrated recently on novels and has a very large – Irish and international – readership. Her stories and novels have been reprinted several times. She is married and lives in London.

In *A Portrait of the Artist as a Young Girl* (1986), she tells of a very happy childhood and her great love for Dalkey. Her father, a barrister, encouraged the children to read and to study for exams; her mother, a nurse, 'thought *people* were all important.'[1] Despite her initial disappointment at the birth of her sister, 'I would have preferred a rabbit!' she, her sisters, and brother are the best of friends. (3) Her big childhood ambition was to be a saint, not the kind who saw visions, however, for she knew they usually ended as martyrs. Thus, as she awaited God's call, she kept her 'eyes down on the road', fearing to catch sight of the Virgin in a tree. Visions, she knew from the Fatima story, appeared in trees! (9) Her first literary effort, a story for the nuns' missionary magazine, won a competition; she remembers her father telling her on the way home from school that day, 'When you become a writer, you will always be able to say *this* was your first work.' (8)

Often set in Dublin during the time when she herself was growing up and at university, Binchy's stories and novels give a detailed and very faithful picture of those days. Maeve Binchy's *Dublin 4* (1982), short stories of fashionable Dublin, are revealing and humorous glimpses of the joys and fears of contemporary Dublin socialites. *Light a Penny Candle* (1982), her first novel, introduces readers to an unsure Ireland, where the middle-class hold tightly to their few privileges and have scant charity to offer the less-fortunate. Irish readers will recognise the snobbery and the desire of the doctor's wife to keep her upward-bound son out of the 'clutches' of the daughter of the huckster shop. Those who attended university in the late 1950s and 1960s enjoy the reliving of those days: the clothes, the dances, the coffee-houses, the Green, the old college itself on Earlsfort Terrace.

A recent novel, *Circle of Friends* (1990), also presents a group of young men and women at university in Dublin in the late 1950s. The characters, as always, are finely detailed. The concerns are authentic concerns of the 1950s: the class rift, poor addresses so carefully concealed; the city-country mode of living, weekdays spent at college or working, weekends at home with the family; the frightening fear of pregnancy, and the equally frightening social fear of not having a boyfriend. Among the many fine characters are Benny, the fat girl, everyone's pal but no one's girl-friend, the clown who bleeds internally, who agonises about her size and her parents; Jack, the charmer who makes every girl feel special, but who commits to no one; Benny's parents, who cherish and over-protect the only child of their later years.

Works:
Central Line. Dublin: Ward River Press, 1977. Short Stories.
Maeve's Diary: From Maeve Binchy's Column in *The Irish Times*. Dublin: *The Irish Times*, nd *Times Columns*.
Victoria Line. Dublin: Ward River Press, 1980. Short Stories.
Maeve Binchy's Dublin 4. Dublin: Ward River Press, 1982. Short Stories.
Light a Penny Candle. London: Century Publishing, 1982. Novel.
The Lilac Bus. Dublin: Ward River Press, 1984. Short Stories.
Echoes. London: Century Publishing, 1985. Novel.
Firefly Summer. London: Century Hutchinson, 1987. Novel.
Silver Wedding. London: Century Hutchinson, 1988. Novel.
Circle of Friends. London: Random Century Group, 1990. Novel.
The Copper Beech. London: Orion, 1992. Novel.

Notes
1. *A Portrait of the Artist as a Young Girl*, John Quinn, ed. (London: Methuen), 1986, 4.

Blackwood, Caroline
Born: Ireland, 1931
Educated: England.

Caroline Blackwood was born in northern Ireland in 1931, the daughter of the fourth marquis of Dufferin and Ava.

Her mother was a Guinness and her father a descendant of Richard Brinsley Sheridan. She was educated in English boarding schools, and married three times: to Lucian Freud, the artist and grandson of Sigmund, to the American composer, Israel Citkovitz, with whom she lived in New York, and to Robert Lowell, with whom she lived in the USA and Britain.

Blackwood writes short stories and novels, as well as journalistic pieces. She often focuses on decay: of ideals, marriages, and Big Houses, ultimately seeing deterioration as the human situation, much enlivened by eccentric or mysterious characters. Her first novel, *The Stepdaughter* (1976), won the David Higham Prize for fiction. A series of letters imagined but never written by an attractive but discarded woman living in an expensive apartment in New York, the novel records the callous brutality of this woman, her ex-husband and his new wife to Renata, the stepdaughter of the title. Personally and physically unattractive, Renata is sensitive, frightened, and honest; her passivity to mistreatment is hauntingly and realistically written. Shockingly, however, the reader understands how the adults could so abuse the poor girl. The portrait of the wife, analyst of her own callousness but unwilling to redress it, fountain of inexhaustible inertia, is humorous and perceptive.

Great Granny Webster (1977), a best-selling novella and runner-up for the Booker Prize, reveals more of Blackwood's sharp wit than the first novel. The decay of the Big House is recorded through three generations, all restricted or 'interred' by the parsimony of Granny Webster. Excellent characterisations and an amused, detached view suggest the comedy rather than tragedy of the human condition. *The Fate of Mary Rose* (1981) is a disturbing and ambiguous story of rape and neglect. *Corrigan* (1984) explores the surprising development and flowering into poetry and the good life of the lonely widow Devina Blunt after the arrival of the mysterious Corrigan, the charity collector who becomes her lodger.

Blackwood's keen, quick perceptions and dry humour are perfectly suited to the short story. *In Good Night Sweet Ladies* (1983), for example, Blackwood presents brief, decisive portraits of self-deceiving characters. A few well-placed lines reveal what seems to be the defining character trait, so further exploration is unnecessary. Taft of 'Taft's Wife', a passively promiscuous man, invents a much-loved dead wife to save him from the logical sequels to his sexual adventures. Indeed, the sardonic narrator notes, this dead 'wife' 'helped to disentangle him from so many relationships which he saw as a threat to the astringently lonely existence he had chosen for himself, that in a sense it was true, he did love her.'[1]

Works:
For All That I Found There. London: Duckworth, 1974; New York: Braziller, 1974. Short Stories and Articles.
The Stepdaughter. London: Duckworth, 1976; New York: Scribners, 1977. Novel.
Great Granny Webster. London: Duckworth, 1977; New York: Scribners, 1977. Novel.
The Fate of Mary Rose. London: Cape, 1981; New York: Summit, 1981. Novel.
Good Night Sweet Ladies. London: Heinemann, 1983. Stories.
Corrigan. London: Heinemann, 1984. Stories.

Notes
1. In *Good Night Sweet Ladies*, 45.

Boland, Bridget
Born: England, 1913; Died: 1988
Educated: England.

Bridget Boland was born in London, the daughter of an Irish barrister, John Pius Boland, and an Australian mother. Her father was Member of Parliament for South Kerry from 1900-18, and the family moved between London and Kerry in those years. Bridget attended the

Sacred Heart School in Roehampton and graduated from Oxford in 1935. She was a successful screen writer and playwright, published three novels, a book on gardening and a memoir. She visited France often and lived several years in Italy.[1]

The Wild Geese (1938) is told through the letters of the Kinross family. The Wild Geese are young Irish Catholic men who join the armies of foreign countries, countries in which they have often been educated; they are denied education in Ireland because of their religion. On their return to Ireland, these men are outlaws, and through the letters we hear of Brandan Kinross's attempt to regain his land; of Maurice Kinross's love for Mary Ahearne, wife of Thomas Ahearne, a Kinross cousin, who immorally but legally took Brandan's land; and of Catherine Kinross's love for Roderick O'Byrne, a soldier recruiting for Irish regiments in France. Brandan covets the land Ahearne has taken; his brother Maurice covets the wife Ahearne has taken.[2]

Works:
The Wild Geese. London: Heinemann, 1938; rpt; London: Virago, 1988. Novel.
Portrait of a Lady in Love. London: Heinemann, 1942. Novel.
Caterina. London: Souvenir Press, 1975. Novel.
At My Mother's Knee. London: Bodley Head, 1978. Memoir.

Notes
1. Introduction. *The Wild Geese.*
2. *The Wild Geese*, 219.

Boland, Eavan
Born: Ireland, 1944
Educated: Britain, USA, Ireland.

Eavan Boland is one of Ireland's best-known contemporary poets. The daughter of the diplomat Frederick Boland and the painter Frances Kelly, she moved, as a child, with her family from Dublin to live in London, and later New York. She received a First Class Honours degree in English in Trinity College, Dublin and was a junior lecturer there, 1967-78.

Eavan Boland also writes stimulating critical essays, such as *A Kind of Scar: The Woman Poet in a National Tradition* which demand a re-thinking of national and literary assumptions. Well received and published widely in the USA and Europe, her poetry has received much recognition. She cites the 'placelessness' of her childhood as a large influence on her work, recalling one poignant incident. As a seven-year-old in a British convent school, she refused to conform, saying, 'I am'nt going to do this.' The teacher's response, 'You're not in Ireland now,' established the sense of exile. 'The sharpness and bleakness of her remark highlighted (probably mostly in retrospect) the way that language can be a storehouse for inflexions of exile.' The second influence she remarks, 'my very emphatic sense of place, living here in this suburb in my own home,' has probably 'been enriched — however painfully — by that first experience of displacement.'[1]

Readers will agree with Boland's assessment of her influences. The child's loneliness and sense of difference emerge in many of the poems, as does the woman's very rich sense of home. The poetry thoroughly and consistently explores the world of Irish child, woman, daughter, mother, wife. She is, as she says herself, a lyric poet who works with 'time and perceptions of loss and just common down-to-earth disappointments or irretrievable segments of human experience.' 'I don't think of myself as writing in the voice of a woman. I am a woman and I write in terms of what defines me.'[2] Sometimes, naturally, the situations are uniquely female: 'The Gorgon Child' expresses the experience of many mothers, 'the bitter truth/that giving birth/was our division'. So little has been written on the experience of birth that women lack the words to speak it; Boland speaks it for us, as she remarks to the child, 'from now our meetings/would be mere re-unions' and learns too 'how by separations/love survives/its own stone hour,/its gorgon birth.'[3] 'Anorexic' imagines the woman who hates her own body so much that she wishes to return to man's, become the original rib: 'I will slip/back into him again/as if I had never been away.'[4]

Subjects are often memories of the past, released by the sight of a photograph, an unfamiliar object, or an activity or aroma unchanged through time: the photograph on her father's desk, the shadow doll, and the 'cut-throat sweetness' of the 'stephanotis', all in her latest collection, *Outside History*. Boland's poetry also moves beyond the home to the situation of woman defined or simplified by myth, history, and/or tradition. 'Mise Éire', from *The Journey*, brings the female persona's concrete presence, contradictions, and complexities to revising the traditional sentimental portrait of Ireland as woman beloved by nineteenth and early twentieth-century poets and rebels. The twelve-poem sequence *Outside History* again addresses the need to celebrate a woman's being beyond the simplified and limited roles of sentiment. 'The Making of an Irish Goddess' sees 'the marks of childbirth' and 'the stitched, healed blemish of a scar' as 'accurate inscription' of the 'agony' of this 'making.[5] The poet announces:

> Out of myth into history I move to be
> part of that ordeal
> whose darkness is
>
> only now reaching me from those fields,
> those rivers, those roads clotted as
> firmaments with the dead.
>
> How slowly they die
> as we kneel beside them, whisper in their ear.
> And we are too late. We are always too late.[6]

The history is this time, this place, the 'March evening/at the foothills of the Dublin mountains.'[7]

Works:

New Territory. Dublin: Allen Figgis, 1969. Poetry.

The War Horse. London: Gollancz, 1975. Poetry.

In Her Own Image. Dublin: Arlen House, 1980. Poetry.

Night Feed. Dublin: Arlen House, 1982. Poetry.

The Journey. Dublin: Arlen House; London: Carcanet, 1987. Poetry.

Selected Poems. Dublin: Arlen House; London: Carcanet, 1990. Poetry.

Outside History. London: Carcanet, 1990; New York: Norton, 1991. Poetry.

A Kind of Scar: The Woman Poet in a National Tradition. Dublin: Attic Press, 1990. Prose.

Notes

1. Personal communication.
2. In *Sleeping with Monsters*, Gillean Somerville-Arjat and Rebecca E Wilson, eds. (Dublin: Wolfhound Press, 1990), 81, 80.
3. In *Pillars of the House.* A A Kelly, ed. (Dublin: Wolfhound Press, 1988), 140, 141.
4. In *Sleeping with Monsters*, 89.
5. In *Outside History*, 38. Norton edition.
6. In *Outside History*, 50. Norton edition.
7. In *Outside History*, 39. Norton edition.

Boland, Rosita

Born: Ireland, 1965
Educated: Ireland.

Rosita Boland was born in Ennis, Co. Clare, and received her BA in English and History from Trinity College, Dublin. After university, she spent a year travelling around Australia; this experience, she notes, made her aware of 'landscape and of place'. She worked in publishing in London for two years, spent three months hitching around the coast of Ireland, and completed a travel book based on that experience.[1] Her poetry has been included in many anthologies, and her translations from Irish appear in *The Bright Wave/An Tonn Gheal*.

Her first volume of poetry, *Muscle Creek* (1991), covers a lot of ground: growing up in Ireland, enjoying the poetry of Sylvia Plath and Philip Larkin, feeling bruised, absorbing the Australian landscape, and reflecting on history. Exuberant delight in nature is expressed in memorable, original and exact images. Her language is sensuous and exciting. The poet imagines, for example, city trees forcing themselves up through the cement pavements to stagger down streets, 'a corset of wire around their waists'; a warm day becomes 'a jungle pool/When I dived into the cool green shadiness/That rushed above my head'; after snow, 'The leaves are rinsed from the trees.'[2] Last year's Christmas tree is 'shedding tears of needle-green'; 'fireworks blow open/In huge, coloured dandelion puffs'; and 'the ornamented stones [of Newgrange]/ Necklace the mound."[3]

Celebrating Plath and Larkin, she sounds like these poets:

Reading Sylvia Plath
Is like treading on the edge of the razorblade
That you wrote your poetry with.[4]

To 'Mr Larkin,' she complains: 'You seem to have said it all, you bastard.'

Many of your poems have sunk in whole
So that to think of ambulances or high windows
Is to feel whole poems shiver and reverberate.[5]

Her own work also shivers and reverberates. In 'The Woman and the Knife-Thrower', she writes:

All day, he sits on the caravan steps
And polishes knives.
He watches me
In the reflection of their cruel blades.

Night after night,
I entrust my body to him.

44

We mark each other, eye to eye,
And the knives come like the words
He will never speak.

They brush against my flesh, glittering
With the brightness of unshed tears.[6]

Works:
Muscle Creek. Dublin: Raven Arts Press, 1991. Poetry.
Sea Legs. Dublin: New Island Books, 1992. Travel Book.

Notes
1. Personal communication.
2. 'Earth', 19; 'Gathering Wildflowers on a Warm Day,' 13; 'Landscapes', 21, in *Muscle Creek.*
3. 'Aftertaste', 23; 'Fireworks,' 24; 'Exploring Newgrange', 61, in *Muscle Creek.*
4. 'Reading Sylvia Plath', 36, in *Muscle Creek.*
5. In *Muscle Creek*, 37.
6. In *Muscle Creek*, 32.

Bowen, Elizabeth
Born: Ireland, 1899; Died: 1973
Educated: England.

Elizabeth Bowen was born in Dublin and spent her first seven years between Dublin and the Bowen family home, Bowen's Court, in Cork. When her father, Henry Bowen, became ill, Elizabeth and her mother were advised to visit relatives in England, as their presence was deemed upsetting. She records her joy on finally returning to her beloved Bowen's Court, the visit to England having extended to six years. When her father died in 1928, she inherited the house, and she and her husband, Alan Charles Cameron, used it as a holiday residence. When her husband died in 1952, she returned to live in Bowen's Court but, unable to cope with the upkeep, sold the house and returned to England in 1960.

An only child, she was often lonely, as she notes in the essay 'Out of a Book'. This loneliness, however, contributed to the artist's sensitivity, as the child peopled her life with the characters and events of fiction. Bowen also notes her sensitivity to place, a sensitivity that emerges in her novels in appreciation of the countryside, the gardens, and the beautiful drawingrooms of Big Houses. The title of her history of the Bowen family in Ireland, *Bowen's Court* (1942), suggests the importance of *this* place in the shaping of her ancestors and of herself.

Bowen wrote ten novels and many short stories and scholarly essays as well as this history. Her style is poetic, suggestive rather than definite, and rich in implication and ambiguity. Her protagonists are usually young orphaned women, possibly reflections of herself. Her second novel, *The Last September* (1929), is set in a Big House in Ireland during the troubles of the 1920s. The military conflict which backgrounds the novel is mirrored by the emotional conflict of the Naylor family, as they witness, but refuse to acknowledge, the end of their particular 'eden'. Miltonic echoes abound, as Bowen charts the apparently inevitable expulsion from the garden, an expulsion symbolised by the burning of the Big House, Danielstown, one that also opens wider avenues to the young woman protagonist, Lois Farquahar, a Naylor niece. An exchange between Laurence, the Naylor nephew from Oxford, and the British officer Gerald Lesworth, reveals Bowen's ironic humour. Laurence challenges Gerald, 'What do you, personally, think about all this?'

Well, the situation's rotten. But right is right.
Why?
Well ... from the point of view of civilisation. Also you see they don't fight clean.
Oh, there's no public school spirit in Ireland. But do tell me — what do you mean by the point of view of civilisation?
Oh — ours.

Gerald tries to explain, 'I mean, looking back on history —
not that I'm intellectual — we do seem the only people.'
Laurence will not let up:

Difficulty being to make them see it?
— And that we are giving them what they really want ...
Though of course the more one thinks of it all, the
smaller, personally, it makes one feel.
— I don't feel small in that way. But I'm not English.
— Oh, no — I beg your pardon.
— Thank God!
— Don't understand?
— God May. [1]

While she sensitively explores young women's emotions,
Bowen simultaneously criticises the culture and education
that prepares them only for love. *The Death of the Heart*
(1936), often seen as her best novel, pictures the
expectations of a naïve and sensitive young woman and
the disappointments that await her. The lesbian episodes
in *The Hotel, Friends and Relations, To The North* and *The
Little Girls* are worth mentioning, plus the impassioned
friendships between women in *The Last September*.

Bowen's novels remain very popular today. Harold
Pinter wrote the screen-play for a successful television
adaptation of *The Heat of the Day*.

Selected Works:
Encounters. London: Sidgwick and Jackson, 1923; New York:
    Boni and Liveright, 1925; republished in *Early Stories*. New
    York: Alfred A Knopf, 1950. Stories.
Ann Lee's and Other Stories. London: Sidgwick and Jackson, 1926;
    New York: Boni and Liveright, 1926; also republished in *Early
    Stories*. Stories.
The Hotel. London: Constable, 1927; New York: Dial, 1928. Novel.
Joining Charles. London: Constable, 1929; New York: Dial, 1929.
    Stories.
The Last September. London: Constable, 1929; New York: Dial,
    1929; New York: Avon, 1952. Novel.
Friends and Relations. London: Constable, 1931; New York: Dial,
    1931. Novel.

To the North. London: Constable, 1932; New York: Alfred A Knopf, 1933. Novel.

The Cat Jumps. London: Victor Gollancz, 1934. Stories.

The House in Paris. London: Victor Gollancz, 1934; New York: Alfred A Knopf, 1936. Novel.

The Death of the Heart. London: Gollancz, 1936; New York: Alfred A Knopf, 1936. Novel.

Look at All Those Roses. London: Victor Gollancz, 1941; New York: Alfred A Knopf, 1941. Stories.

Bowen's Court. London: Longmans, Green, 1942; New York: Alfred A Knopf, 1942. Second Edition, 1964. History.

The Demon Lover. London: Jonathan Cape, 1945; In USA, *Ivy Gripped the Steps*. New York: Alfred A Knopf, 1946. Stories.

The Heat of the Day. London: Jonathan Cape, 1949; New York: Alfred A Knopf, 1949. Novel.

A World of Love. London: Jonathan Cape, 1955; New York: Alfred A Knopf, 1955. Novel.

Stories by Elizabeth Bowen. New York: Alfred A Knopf, 1959. Stories.

The Little Girls. London: Jonathan Cape, 1964; New York: Alfred A Knopf, 1964. Novel.

A Day in the Dark and Other Stories. London: Jonathan Cape, 1965. Stories.

Eva Trout. New York: Alfred A Knopf, 1968; London: Jonathan Cape, 1969. Novel.

Notes

1. *The Last September*, 114. Avon edition.

Boylan, Clare
Born: Ireland, 1948
Educated: Ireland.

Clare Boylan was born in Dublin and has worked as a journalist on newspapers, magazines, TV, and radio. She received the Benson and Hedges Award for outstanding journalism in 1974 and served as judge for several literary prizes, including the Booker McConnell Prize. During her successful tenure as editor of *Image* magazine, she attracted many notable writers to its pages. Her stories have appeared in magazines in Britain, Denmark, Sweden, Norway, the Netherlands, New Zealand, Australia, Japan, and the USA; some have been broadcast on BBC Radio 3 and RTE. *Making Waves*, the film version of 'Retired Ladies on a Tour' was adapted by Jenny Wilkes and directed by Annie Wingate. *Making Waves* was nominated for an Oscar in 1988 – 'the only short art movie produced by an all-woman team, and the only non-American nomination in the category'.

Clare Boylan did not attend university, something she regrets; with the success of her first novel, *Holy Pictures*, however, she was asked to review many books and that has been an education in itself. She is well versed in twentieth-century writers, particularly women. She also writes literary criticism, book reviews, and the dining-out column in *Image*. She lives in Wicklow with her husband, who is also a journalist.[1]

Boylan's novels and short stories were immediate successes, their originality, as well as the author's wry sense of humour, economy, and elegance of style, winning critical acclaim. The largely autobiographical first novel, *Holy Pictures* (1983), introduces a child's view of a Dublin where holy pictures compete with moving pictures. Her work is not confined to Dublin life, however, though *Black Baby* (1988) takes us there again, as Dinah – the black baby Alice had 'bought' on her first Communion day – seems to come to town.

Boylan romps through time and space in *Concerning Virgins* (1989), taking us now to 1899, now to Siena, with a humour and energy that doesn't dwell on, but never ignores, hard realities. 'A Little Girl, Never Out Before', the first story, gives us the twelve-year-old's perspective on the hard world of service in a boarding house in 1899, the cold, the miserly portions of poor food and poor pay, the hard work, the abuse of the mistress. Frankie, the little girl, thinks longingly of her mother: 'They were a hopeless pair, she and her ma', loving and desiring brand new babies so much that they forgot the hurts and the hunger in happiness to have another in their over-crowded house. [2]

'The Little Madonna' swings between laughter and sorrow, as we move from the persona's delightfully fresh views to the grim facts of teenage motherhood. Appalled at the story in *The Sun* about the sixteen-year-old mother whose devotion to her little daughter prompted the neighbours to christen her the little madonna, and who leaves her baby out in the snow to freeze to death, the narrator wonders how anyone would trust a sixteen-year-old with a baby. 'And it comes to me, quite suddenly, sprouting out of the scrap-heap of my middle-aged head – God did. God the Father! He gave His only son to a girl of fifteen.' (101) Reflections on women and mothering highlight the problems of motherhood evident in all the scandal sheets: 'For a mother to learn that she can have no more children is for a surgeon to have his hands cut off. What can she do?' (100) The programming of women seems universal as the narrator reflects back to her own parents and on to her daughter.

The final story in the volume, 'Concerning Virgins', reads as economically as a fable. The vicious old man who has kept his daughters locked up awaiting suitable suitors finally decides he needs to marry, not for companionship or sex, but to beget a son to inherit his property in place of his 'unclaimed daughters'. His first advertisement he thinks modest, 'Handsome, landed gent of considerable means seeks virgin bride of childbearing age', but it receives no replies. The wise woman he visits laughs, however, 'God bless you, sir, and saving your presence, you black-hearted oul' blackguard – with curs like yourself around, where do you expect to find a virgin?' (195) When he threatens to have her head, she says, why not, 'since you had my maidenhead more than fifty years ago.' (195) Nevertheless, his next advertisement asks only for 'maiden lady in desperate circumstances'. (195) He receives two replies, both of which are grasped in his dead fists when his daughters find him. Boylan concludes briefly: 'They stooped solicitously to their father's corpse. With barely a glance at one another and only the mildest of sighs, they retrieved their very private correspondence.'(196)

Works:

Holy Pictures. London: Hamish Hamilton, 1983; New York: Simon and Schuster, 1983; London: Penguin Books, 1984. Novel.

A Nail on the Head. London: Hamish Hamilton,1983; New York: Penguin Viking, 1985; London: Penguin Books, 1985. Stories.

Last Resorts. London: Hamish Hamilton, 1984; New York: Simon and Schuster, 1986; London: Penguin Books, 1986. Novel.

Black Baby. London: Hamish Hamilton, 1988; New York: Doubleday, 1989; London: Penguin Books, 1989. Novel.

Concerning Virgins. London: Hamish Hamilton, 1989; New York: Doubleday, 1990; London: Penguin Books, 1990. Stories.

Home Rule. London: Hamish Hamilton, 1992. Novel.

Notes
1. Personal communication.
2. *Concerning Virgins*, 7.

Brady (*née* Cannon), Anne M
Born: Ireland, 1926
Educated: Ireland.

Anne M Brady (*née* Cannon), was born in Dublin and reluctantly moved to Kildare at the age of six, when her father became county surgeon there. A rather solitary childhood — one brother, no sisters — probably helped form a voracious reading habit. She attended boarding school at Loreto Abbey, Rathfarnham, and took her Bachelor of Arts Degree at University College, Dublin, in 1947. She married David Brady in 1957 and has four children. She lived for four years in Canada, where she worked in Carleton University library for some time.

She always wanted to be a writer and published her first story in her school magazine, but at college and during the early years of her marriage, she believed she needed 'to know more about life' before she could write seriously. Her first stories appeared in the *Irish Messenger*, later stories in women's magazines. Researching for a historical fiction writer, she 'became fascinated by the past and the fact that human emotions never change,' and decided that the sixteenth century was the one she wished to write about. 'Its robustness appealed to me and the fact that already one could see signs of the world as we know it today.'[1]

An interest in the Spanish Armada led to the writing of *The Winds of God* (1985), the story of Ralph Paulet's ordeals as he attempts to find his lost love. Ralph loves the Catholic Una, but Ralph, though born a Catholic, was reared a Protestant. Lured to Spain and the arms of the Inquisition, Ralph must choose between fighting in the Armada against his own country or giving up all hope of finding Una. The next novel, *Honey off Thorns* (1988), also charts the conflict of human emotions and historical events. Interested in the position of women in convents in the sixteenth century, Brady explores the fate of Isobel, who entered for the 'wrong reasons', falls in love, becomes pregnant, is branded traitor and whore, and must leave England. Isobel's love is Robert FitzHugh, who attempts to warn the abbot of Wolden Abbey in Yorkshire that Henry VIII's forces are intent on its plunder. The title is from a thirteenth-century homily which says: 'Love is a licking of honey off thorns.'[2]

Besides fiction, Brady also researches Irish writers and is listed as co-author with Brian Cleeve of *Biographical Dictionary of Irish Writers* (1985), an expanded version of his own earlier *Dictionary of Irish Writers*.

Works:
The Winds of God. London: Century, 1985. Novel.
Honey off Thorns. London: Severn House, 1988. Novel.
A Biographical Dictionary of Irish Writers. With Brian Cleeve. Mullingar: Lilliput Press, 1985. Reference.

1. Personal communication.
2. Personal communication.

Brennan, Deirdre
Born: Ireland, 1934
Educated: Ireland.

Deirdre Brennan was born in Dublin and raised in Co. Tipperary, where she attended schools in Clonmel and Thurles. She studied English and Latin at University College, Dublin, and followed her degree with the Higher Diploma in Education. Her parents came from the north of Ireland, where they had no opportunity to learn Irish. They always told their children this, and encouraged them to learn and love their own language. Many years after college, when she took her own writing seriously, the language Deirdre Brennan selected for her poems was and is Irish. More recently, she has written short stories in both Irish and English.

She taught in a Dublin secondary school from the time she received her Higher Diploma in Education until her marriage in 1959. She moved to Carlow then, where she and her husband raised their five children, and where she still lives. At the moment, she divides her time between writing, lecturing in English at St Patrick's College in Carlow, and running a writers' workshop in the town. Although she started writing poetry in her teens, she stopped while at university, 'overawed' by the work of Clarke, Eliot, and Pound. She regrets this now. Later, she found 'other excuses'. Her first four children were born in five years, and the fifth five years after, which meant extended child-caring years. 'Over those years ideas continued to niggle at me. Lines would come into my head and I almost guiltily brushed them aside as a form of self

53

indulgence. In retrospect I realise that this was quite ridiculous but a very real attitude of women at the time.'

In 1980 when her youngest daughter was ten years old, she notes: 'I knew then that I couldn't hide behind being a mother, that I had a lot of poetry inside of me and that time was running out.' The mini-Gaeltacht of Carlow being nearby, she found it natural to write in Irish. Writing in English is easier, but 'one language complements the other. As time goes on I feel the need to express myself in both languages since both are an integral part of my whole person.' At first, she wrote only poetry, but she completed two plays recently, found herself very attracted to the form, and hopes to write more. Her 1989 collection, *Scothanna Geala*, (*Bright Blossoms*) was a Poetry Ireland Choice of the year.[1]

The voice in Brennan's poetry is a magic one. The well, suggesting the magic wells of Irish myth and the well from which the Samarian woman gave Christ the refreshing water, lures mythical and contemporary figures in the poem of that name. '[T]he enchanted hind' hears the 'whispering' and comes to slake its thirst; 'the golden girl of the well/The lonely sorceress of night' lures men so her 'thirst may be satisfied'. The 'barefooted child,' 'Who comes with an enamel bucket/To draw water' finds a 'frog', her 'prince there before' her. And finally the poet – our magician/priest– comes, to 'taste from cupped hands/The music of your vitality/On my tongue/And the pulse of your sacrament/In my mouth.'[2]

A similar magic is at work in 'Sculpture'. Here 'in the ocean of my mind,' the persona says she loses herself, swimming toward 'the ghost of my beginning,' where 'The scales of flesh shatter/And plummet like shells/To the ancient bed of memory.' The voice of *Bright Blossoms* is both that of the flowers and of human beings. The desire to break out, to shatter the 'binding pots', and to protect the 'resurrection' seeds of flower and heart against the 'icy winter clay'.[3]

A few lines from 'Maidin' give us the music of the poetry in the original Irish:

An lá mar shiosúr
Ag gearradh ár ndlúthachta,
Sleabhcaimid roimh a faobhar
Go mbíonn an scaradh glan,
Míne is gaireacht oíche
Curtha chun báis
I ngairbheacht mhaidine.[4]

Works:
I Reilig na mBan Rialta. Baile Atha Cliath: Coiscéim, 1984. Poetry.
Scothanna Geala. Baile Atha Cliath: Coiscéim, 1989. Poetry.

Notes
1. Personal communication.
2. In *Wildish Things,* Ailbhe Smyth, ed. (Dublin: Attic Press, 1989), 78.
3. In *Wildish Things,* 79, 81.
4. In *I Reilig na mBan Rialta.*

Brennan, Elizabeth
Born: Ireland, 1907
Educated: Ireland.

Elizabeth Brennan was born and educated in Dublin, and lived in England and Sligo. She wrote plays and many novels, several of which were translated into other languages. *Girl on an Island* won an Irish Countrywomen's Association (ICA) Award in 1984.[1]

Brennan's books are full of mystery, adventure, and romance. *Innocent in Eden* (1971) is set in the lovely countryside around Lough Gill, for example, and features castles full of trap doors and wondrous antiques.

Works:
Out of the Darkness. Dublin: Metropolitan, 1945. Novel.

The Wind Fairies. Dublin, London: Metropolitan, 1946. Children's Stories.

Am I my Brother's Keeper? Dublin & London: Metropolitan, 1946. Novel.

Whispering Walls. Dublin: Metropolitan, 1948. Novel.

The Wind Fairies Again. Dublin, London; Metropolitan, 1948. Children's Stories.

Wind Over the Bogs. Dublin: Metropolitan, 1950. Poetry.

Children's Book of Irish Saints. London: Harrap, 1963. Children's Stories.

His Glamorous Cousin. London: Hale, 1963. Novel.

Her Lucky Mistake. London: Hale, 1966. Novel.

Retreat from Love. London: Hale, 1967. Novel.

Patrick's Woman. London: Hale, 1969. Novel.

Mountain of Desire. London: Hale, 1970. Novel.

Innocent in Eden. London: Hale, 1971. Novel.

No Roses for Jo. London: Hale, 1972. Novel.

Love's Loom. London: Hale, 1973. Novel.

A Girl Called Debbie. London: Hale, 1975. Novel.

Sweet Love of Youth. London: Hale, 1978. Novel.

Girl on an Island. London: Hale, 1984. Novel.

Notes

1. *A Biographical Dictionary of Irish Writers*, Anne M Brady and Brian Cleeve, eds. (Mullingar: The Lilliput Press, 1985), 19.

Brett, Heather
Born: Newfoundland, 1956
Educated: Ireland.

Heather Brett was born in Newfoundland, and brought to Co. Antrim, Ireland, by her adoptive parents when she was three. She attended the local grammar school, and trained as a fashion designer in York Street Art College, Belfast. In 1979, she married and has two children with whom she has lived since her divorce in 1982. She lived for six years in Tallaght, Co. Dublin, joined the local writers' class in Tallaght Priory, under the direction of Leland Bardwell, who introduced her to contemporary poetry.

This was an exciting time, when she met poets, attended poetry readings, read, and wrote, devouring magazines like *Cyphers* and *Salmon Publishing* which published new poets. Her first volume of poetry, *Abigail Brown* (1991), won the second Brendan Behan Memorial Prize, and her work has been included in anthologies, journals, and collections of poetry.

The implications of mother and individual are explored in several poems. In 'Elegy on a Saturday', the two are contrasted:

Some days, I live to be a mother, gather my children
to me and give; We go and eat hamburgers and look
at toys in illuminated city store windows.

And somedays I'm just by myself, reading or writing
to unseen hosts of ones; Those days are silent
and translucent,

perfect pockets, into which I drop
each gone minute, done day and every last
used second of being.[1]

'No Vacancies' reflects the autonomous, independent mother, Brett's 'strong woman'.

There is only one chair by the fire,
my chair; the children play on the floor
or the sofa, soles upwards, and there is
a lack of family portraits.

The poem concludes:

We have no space left, no empty
drawers or anywhere where another might make himself
at home: There are no candles burning in the windows.[2]

Works:
Abigail Brown. Galway: Salmon Publishing, 1991. Poetry.

Notes
1. In *Abigail Brown*, 27.
2. In *Abigail Brown*, 44-45.

Brooke, Charlotte

Born: c 18th century; Died: 1793
Educated: Ireland.

Charlotte Brooke was a poet and translator. When translating, and she often did so anonymously, she concerned herself with not only words and genre but cultural contexts. She paid for the publication of her work *Reliques of Irish Poetry* (1789). She also wrote *Belisaiou*: a Tragedy, which is lost.

Works:
Reliques of Irish Poetry. Bonham, Dublin: 1789. Poetry
Belisaiou: as tragedy. np, nd. Novel.

Brophy, Catherine

Born: Ireland c 20th century
Educated: Ireland.

Catherine Brophy was born in Dublin and took her Bachelor's Degree in University College, Dublin. As a child she adored Patricia Lynch and Lewis Carroll, identifying so much with Alice that she once attempted to fly Alice-like down the stairs: unfortunately, 'I crashed through the window at the bottom and cut my arm.' She credits seeing Brendan Behan's *The Quare Fella* in the Abbey Theatre with the revision of her traditional assumptions about justice, reading Ivan Illich's 'Deschooling Society' with confirming her unarticulated belief about the educational system, and reading Ishtak Bentov's *Stalking the Wild Pendulum* with awakening her to the wonder of the universe.[1]

She hitch-hiked over much of Europe while at college, and has since spent time in Mexico, Thailand, and Africa. Her experiences in these countries gave her insight into tolerance, racism, and 'first-world' arrogance. She also worked with children who suffered from hearing losses, and describes the script for a Radio Telefís Éireann soap, *Fair City*, as the hardest work she has ever done.[2]

The Liberation of Margaret McCabe (1985), Brophy's first novel (published in Polish in 1992), is the story of Margaret, a teacher in a school for difficult children, who finally leaves her home at the the age of thirty-four to live with her lover. Thinking she has achieved liberation, she eventually discovers what the reader knows from the start: she has merely exchanged benevolent for selfish paternalism. The self-concern of Oliver, Margaret's lover — while sometimes comically exaggerated — is grating. He persuades her to live with him, for example, because she disturbs his sleep by leaving his bed to go home in the small hours to her parents' house. But the novel is also filled with fine and funny character sketches: Sister Magdalen, for example, who manipulates the teachers ruthlessly, and the girls themselves. When Margaret takes the under-privileged city girls hiking in the country, they can't believe there's no road. 'You mean we're going to have to climb through all that muck with no path or anything?' they ask. 'That's why I told you that your pink, high-heeled ankle boots wouldn't do,' Margaret replies. 'Jaysus,' the girls conclude, 'it's no wonder culchies are thick.'[3]

Brophy's second novel, *Dark Paradise* (1991), is an event in Irish publishing history — science fiction from a woman's perspective. The story of Zintilla, the crystal planet covered with coweling to preserve it from the chaos of nature, suggests several ironic parallels with the contemporary world. The coweling allows old streets to be replaced with corridors of polished crystal; in turn floaters are developed to save the crystal from scuffing. The floaters make lower limbs redundant, which leads to the evolutionary program that eliminates legs, the reproductive and digestive systems. When a citizen reaches 100 years, she or he submits to crystallisation or death, and at that point, the child of her/his life is taken from the pool of life to be reared by a selected pair of co-creators. Physical union is replaced by mind-fusion.

Fendan and Joquah mind-fuse to celebrate their new daughter:

> Now his eyes were enlarging, his rainbow hues shone straight into hers, hers beamed back to him. Their colours combined, glowed deeper and brighter, kaleidoscoping the room, enfolding them both in a spiral of colour. ... She drew his eyes deep into hers and he drew hers back into his. Deeper they went and much deeper. Then their changing began. ...
>
> Over and over they changed it in ecstatic union until the whirling colours locked suddenly in phase, intensified and exploded in a blinding brilliance.[4]

Works:
The Liberation of Margaret McCabe. Dublin: Wolfhound Press, 1985. Novel.
Dark Paradise. Dublin: Wolfhound, 1991. Novel.

Notes
1. Personal communication.
2. Personal communication.
3. *The Liberation of Margaret McCabe*, 89.
4. *Dark Paradise*, 40-41.

Browne, Frances
Born: Ireland, 1816; Died: 1879
Educated: Ireland.

Frances Browne, 'the blind poetess of Donegal', was born in Stranolar, Co. Donegal and — despite her blindness — earned her living by writing novels, poems, and children's stories. She left Ireland for Britain in 1847, where she was granted a pension. Her best-known work is a collection of fairy stories, *Granny's Wonderful Chair and the Stories It Told* (1857), which Frances Hodgson Burnett enjoyed so much that she published her own version, *Stories from the Lost Fairy Book as Retold by the Child Who Read Them* (1877).

Burnett's success resulted in the recovery and republishing of several editions of Browne's book.[1]

Selected Works:
Granny's Wonderful Chair and the Stories It Told. London: Griffith & Farran, 1857. Stories.

Notes
1. *Dictionary of Irish Literature*, Robert Hogan, ed. (Westport, Conn.: Greenwood Press, 1979) 127-28. Also see Hogan for a full listing of Browne's work.

Bunbury, Selina
Born: Ireland, 1803; Died: 1882
Educated: England.

Selina Bunbury was born in Ireland and lived there until 1830. The family were devout Methodists and poor because of the father's bankruptcy. Her work supported the family, but she wrote in secret because of her mother's disapproval. She published about thirty books, and many tracts and pamphlets.[1] In the following quotation from *The Abbey of Innismoyle*, the knowledgeable narrator comments on another character:

Mrs Raymond's mind, it has been said, had sunk under the repeated strokes of sorrow, and unsupported by the power that sustained the humble curate of Innismoyle, her proud heart, which would not bend, had broken: She passed from careless gaiety to gloomy superstition, and gave up a naturally strong understanding to the control, and submitted her judgement, faith, reason and practice, to the direction of her priest. Having seen the heir of the family, just as he got beyond boyhood, drop into the tomb, and her children one by one, in infancy or in childhood, follow him, she had hardly ventured to think the child of her old age her own; — like Hannah, if she was given to her, she was ready to devote her to the Lord; — and so she gave up her surviving child to be educated and guided by her priest. [2]

Selected Works:
The Abbey of Innismoyle: A Story of Another Century. Dublin: Curry, 1828. Novel.
Tales of My Country. Dublin: Curry, 1833. Memoir.
The Star of the Court, or The Maid of Honor and Queen of England, Anne Boleyn. London: Grant, 1844. Biography.
Russia After the War: The Narrative of a Visit to that Country in 1856. London: Hurst and Blackett, 1857. Memoir.
Coombe Abbey. 8 vol. London: Lea, 1857. Novel.
Sir Guy d'Esterre. 2 vol. London: Routledge, 1858. Novel.

Notes
1. Riana O'Dwyer, Department of English, University College, Galway; Personal communication.
2. *The Abbey of Innismoyle*, 58.

Burke, Helen Lucy
Born: Ireland, c 20th century
Educated: Ireland.

Born in Dublin, Helen Lucy Burke now works as a freelance journalist and has also worked in local government. Her short stories have been published in the *Irish Press*, and in many journals and anthologies. The story, 'Trio', won the Irish PEN Award in 1970. She has published one novel and one collection of short stories.

Helen Lucy Burke's work is filled with sharp, incisive vignettes of Irish family and social life. Sometimes cynical, sometimes caricatured, her scenes are always very funny. Her novel, *Close Connections* (1979), has been compared to *The Ginger Man*, but in terms of Irish traditions, Burke's novel is the more subversive. The travails of Brigid Hickey, a plain girl disfigured with a facial birthmark, who blossoms into an enticing sex goddess, are the central focus. Brigid's opportunity comes through her affair with the middle-aged, balding, fat Frank Leahy, who is aided by her panderer-brother. The Hickey family and petty respectability, particularly the sickly piety of Agnes Leahy and Mrs Hickey, are the targets of Burke's ridicule. As husband and daughter attempt to speed up the pace of Mrs Leahy's pre-breakfast prayer, the narrator remarks, 'Mrs Leahy did not think that a prayer stood any chance of reaching the Sacred Ears unless the words dripped out, thick, slow and glutinous, like turtle soup.'[1] Mrs Hickey's sanctimony appears in facial expressions: 'She made the Sign of the Cross with unction, turning her eyes up towards Heaven so that the pupils disappeared under her upper lids and she seemed to have two shelled hard boiled eggs in her sockets. Years before she had practised this in the convent, and the nuns had said she looked like St Rose of Lima.' (24) Mrs Hickey's religion is peculiarly twisted: she adores her son, the panderer, has only harsh admonitions for her plain daughter, and viciously champions sexual ignorance.

Depicting the resentments and traps of intimate family relationships, Burke does not ignore the underlying, often motivating, love. One of her best stories, 'A season for Mothers', tells of a widowed Irish Catholic mother's visit to her unmarried, only daughter in Rome. Although pretending to visit under duress, the old lady hopes to live out her lonely life in Rome, and fantasises about her new position after the Holy Father notices and elevates the humble, pious Irishwoman: 'You can cook, daughter? We have need of you.'[2] How she'll gloat over the 'old cronies' on her visits home, perhaps dropping hints as to what 'He' said to her. Or, she wonders, 'would it be more effective to shake her head and purse her lips at enquirers?' (13) Told from the daughter's perspective, the story reveals Martha's impotent resentment at her mother's manipulations, but also the daughter's awareness of the sadness and limitations of her mother's life. Despite the fun, the story ends with Martha's depressed resignation, as she suddenly realises that her mother not only intends to spend the rest of her life cramping her daughter's life, but will load her with an alcoholic priest too — access to any priest being a plus in the Irish mother's eyes.

Works:
Close Connections. Dublin: Poolbeg, 1979. Novel.
A Season For Mothers. Dublin: Poolbeg, 1980. Stories.

Notes
1. *Close Connections*, 28.
2. *Close Connections*, 13.

Byron, Catherine
Born: England, 1947
Educated: Ireland, England.

Born to an English father and an Irish mother from Galway, Catherine Byron lives in England where she teaches creative writing and, works as a freelance writer. Her first collection of poetry, *Settlements* (1985), was followed by *Samhain*, a sequence based on *The Only Jealousy of Emer*, broadcast by Radio Telefís Éireann in 1986 and published in 1987. Byron renders the eroticism of the myths beautifully as these lines from 'Emer Asks Cuchulain To Return To Her' show:

Emer: You were a lance of burning
                      in my hearth
              a heathland fire to take me.
              We lived to a fierce tune once
                      and can again.

Cuc: Fand [new partner] is the earth I'll rest in
                      when I die
              the peace that whiles away winter.
              She is the waiting hernel
                    of sun's return.

Emer: You were a plunging salmon
                in my well
          a river in spate about me.
          My love, we could live so again
                did I still please you.

Cuc: Fand is the trench of milk
                That cures all wounds
          but you are the love of my youth
                and of my winning
          I look on your face in sorrow.
          You please me still and will
                as long as you live.[1]

Works:
Settlements. Durham: Taxus, 1985. Poetry.
Samhain. Durham: Taxus/Aril Chapbook, 1987. Poetry.
Out of Step: Pursuing Seamus Heaney to Purgatory. London:
    Lexwood Stonleigh, 1993. Non-fiction.

Notes
1. In *Samhain*, no page numbers.

— *C* —

Callaghan, Mary Rose
Born: Ireland, 1944
Educated: Ireland.

Mary Rose Callaghan was born in Dublin and attended Sacred Heart Convents at Mount Anville and Monkstown, and Loreto Abbey, Rathfarnham She attended University College, Dublin, from 1964-68. With her husband, she now lives half the year in Wicklow, and the other half in the USA, where she writes and teaches part time.

She always wanted to be a writer, but thought this was as impractical as wanting to be a spacewoman. She started her first novel when she went to the USA in 1975, and has been writing since. While her novels may have a starting point in real life, they are not autobiographical; her characters are all inventions. She does not see herself as a feminist writer, and thinks such categorisations limiting. *Confessions of a Prodigal Daughter* (1985), for instance, explores mental illness, as well as a young woman's growth.[1]

Uncertain as to what events influenced her writing, she does credit her parents' story-telling abilities, also her husband for his support, and her sisters for companionship. Writing is a lonely occupation, she notes, and this support is valuable. There were no writing groups when she started, but she has herself assisted in many, helping younger writers. She counts herself lucky to have met Angus Wilson at the University of Delaware, and Catherine Rose, 'an innovator for women's writing in Ireland'. Rose's work was instrumental in involving women in writing, especially the setting up of Arlen House Publishing Company, the Maxwell House Short Story Competition, and the Women's Educational Bureau (WEB).[2] Especially attracted to Chekhov, Mary Rose Callaghan prefers the writing of contemporary Irish women to that of men, which she finds very gloomy.

Besides many stories, book reviews, articles and entries in the *Dictionary of Irish Literature*, she has published four novels, one of them a novel for young adults, a biography of Kitty O'Shea, and a play. She is currently working on an American novel and would like to write more work for young adults and for the stage. Her play was runner-up in the O Z Whitehead competition, one of her stories won an Irish competition, and several have been read on BBC radio.

Mothers (1982), her first novel, was a very successful exploration of the lives of three generations of unmarried mothers. This was followed by *Confessions of a Prodigal Daughter* (1985), and most recently *The Awkward Girl* (1990). All of the novels have broken new ground in the Irish novel, and the latter continues by examining the relationships of a verbally clumsy and incompetent woman – Sally Ann – with her father, lovers, and friends. Sometimes the point of view is Sally Ann's first-person, sometimes that of friends in third-person, a device that allows us to see the frustration Sally Ann causes friends and family. We never lose sympathy with the awkward heroine, however, as she moves from one self-centred lover to another. During her first sexual encounter, she tells of her disappointment that 'nothing happened'. 'Then as he pulled out of me, I felt wavy sensations.' But Sally Ann's delight with orgasm is short lived as the police break into the abandoned house she and her 'Maoist' revolutionary lover occupy. Her lover deserts her when she breaks her ankle in the escape, the first of a series of such let-downs. She ruins the next romantic encounter by serving her would-be lover fish ensemble – fish complete with guts.[3]

Works:

Mothers. Dublin: Arlen House, 1982; New York: Marion Boyars, 1984. Novel.

Confessions of a Prodigal Daughter. London and New York: Marion Boyars, 1985. Novel.

Kitty O'Shea: A Life of Katharine Parnell. London: Pandora Press, 1989. Biography.

The Awkward Girl. Dublin: Attic Press, 1990. Novel.

Has Anyone Seen Heather? Dublin: Attic Press, 1990. Novel for young adults.

A House for Fools. Journal of Irish Literature, 12, 3, September, 1983. Play.

Notes

1. Personal communication.
2. Personal communication.
3. *The Awkward Girl*, 43, 87.

Cannon, Moya

Born: Ireland, 1956
Educated: Ireland, England.

Moya Cannon was born in Dunfanaghy, Co. Donegal. She studied history and politics at University College, Dublin, and at Corpus Christi College, Cambridge. She now lives in Galway, where she teaches the children of travellers.

Her first volume of poetry, *Oar* (1990), was acclaimed immediately and won the Brendan Behan Award for a First Collection. She has given readings in Ireland, England, Scotland, Germany and Austria; her poems have appeared in international poetry journals and anthologies and have been broadcast on RTE radio and television and on BBC Radio 4. A number of them have been set to music by composers Jane O'Leary, Philip Martin, and Ellen Crannitch.[1]

The voice in *Oar* is extraordinarily strong and confident. Although the poems are grounded in the particulars of the Burren (Co. Clare) and Galway landscape, they rise above the particular to an almost impersonal universal. The individual and the ordinary things of life are not ignored or sentimentalised, but dignified as part of a timeless pattern. Traces of human history are read in the fragile limestone and 'moody Atlantic' of the first eleven poems: the oratory of Colman, 'the dove saint,' remains under the high cliff eagle's haunt; human memory turns the 'death's doors' dolmens into 'beds/of lovers'; and 'Ithaca was Carna' on 'bright days' to the long-gone sailors on the Atlantic.[2] The miracle is nature itself, as in 'Holy Well':

> Images of old fertilities
> testify to nothing more, perhaps,
> than the necessary miracle
> of water trapped and stored
> in a valley where water is fugitive.
>
> A chipped and tilted Mary
> grows green among rags and sticks.
> Her trade dwindles –
> bad chests, rheumatic pains,
> the supplications, mostly, and the confidences of
> old age.
>
> Yet sometimes,
> swimming out in waters
> that were blessed in the hill's labyrinthine heart,
> the eel flashes past.[3]

Although nature seems unchanging in contrast to the brevity of human life, the poems also imply an enduring human history, sometimes linking Greek and Irish myth, sometimes the prehistoric past with the present. 'Oar', 'Thalassa', 'Taom', and 'Listening Clay' are just four of the poems where the past reverberates into the present, suggesting a kind of continuity. In 'Listening Clay', for example, the sound of 'a gale in the trees,/the soft click of stones, where the tide falls back,/a baby crying in the night' are

> Endlessly repeated,
> immutable,
> they are sounds without a history.
> They comfort and disturb
> the clay part of the heart.[4]

The anthropomorphic images of nature are at once memorable and strangely alien as in 'The Foot of Muckish':

> But one evening, coming down off Muckish
> when I was ten, a clumsy, dark-hearted child,
> I came over the last shoulder
> and the small black mountain opposite
> rose up in a cliff
> and rocked a lake between its ankles.[5]

Works:
Oar. Galway: Salmon Publishing, 1990. Poetry.

Notes
1. Personal communication.
2. 'Eagles' Rock', 'Diarmuid and Gráinne's Beds', 'Turf Boats', in *Oar*, 3-4, 8, 16.
3. In *Oar*, 7.
4. In *Oar*, 25.
5. 'The Foot of Muckish', 24, in *Oar*.

Carbery, Ethna
Born: Ireland, 1866; Died: 1911
Educated: Ireland.

Ethna Carbery, pen name of Anna MacManus *(née* Johnston), was born in Ballymena, Co. Antrim. She edited *The Shan Van Vocht*, a Belfast magazine from 1896-99. She wrote many poems and short stories for patriotic magazines, was a friend of the poet Alice Milligan, and married Seamas MacManus, another poet. Her poetry consists of mythic songs, ballads, and patriotic verse. The following lines are from her most famous ballad, 'Roddy Mc Corley'.

Oh, Ireland, Mother Ireland,
You love them still the best,
The fearless brave who fighting fall
Upon your hapless breast.[1]

Works:
The Four Winds of Éirinn. Dublin: Gill, 1902. Poems.
The Passionate Hearts. Dublin: Gill, 1903. Stories.
In the Celtic Past. Dublin: Gill, 1904. Stories.
We Sang for Ireland. Poems of Ethna Carbery, Seamas MacManus,
    Alice Milligan. Dublin: Gill, 1950. Poetry.

Notes
1. In *We Sang for Ireland*, 41.

Casey, Elizabeth Owens Blackburne

Born: 1848; Died: 1982;
Educated: Ireland.
Elizabeth Owens Blackburne was born in Slane, Co Meath. As a child she lost her sight which was later restored after an operation by Sir William Wilde (Father of Oscar Wilde). By 1873 she had decided to make a literary career for herself and against a lot of opposition finally succeeded with many publications.

Selected Works:
A Bunch of Shamrocks. London: Newman, 1879. Stories.
The Heart of Erin. np, Sampson Law, 1882. Novel.

Casey, Juanita
Born: England, 1925
Educated: England.

Juanita Casey was born in England to Annie Maloney, an Irish Traveller, and Jobey Smith, an English Romany. Her mother died when she was born, and her father abandoned her on a farm a year later. She spent her childhood on the farm and in four private boarding schools. She left school at thirteen and worked with horses — she would eventually train many horses and zebras, and a love of the circus and of animals, particularly horses, permeates much of her work. She was married three times, the first time to a farmer whom she rescued after a fall from his horse; the second time to a Swedish poet, sculptor, and artist; and the third time to a journalist, Fergus Casey, who helped her train her last zebra. She had a child with each husband.[1]

Casey's prose and poetry is rich and lyrical. Her first collection of short stories, *Hath the Rain a Father?* (1966) reads like fable, sometimes dark and often mysterious. A volume of verse followed, *Horse by the River* (1968), and in 1971 her highly praised novel, *The Horse of Selene*. Miceal, an Aranchilla islander, in this novel, is ruled by the repressive priest's tirades on sex, but attracted to the liberated Selene who visits the island. Selene wishes to catch and ride the wonderful speckled horse who stands out in the bands of wild horses. Her friend, Ran, calls Selene herself a horse. She is also happy to make love with Miceal, but he is filled with remorse and finally rejects her. When Selene and her friends leave the island, Miceal works in a group of island men to round up some of the wild horses. Miceal attempts to capture the speckled horse:

> He came up to the stallion, feeling the rope gritty in his sweating hand. He had to pull his feet out of the wet sand, heavy as a Clydesdale's in the hot boots. The horse still watched him, carved, motionless. Careful now, Miceal, or he'll have yeh guts for garters. Somehow he was Selene's. This horse. He felt he was

trespassing, yet with a right. When you stand at someone's back door, and they not in. He shook out the cow's string halter, and slid it up over the queer, still head of the horse. I'd be happier on his other side, he thought. He's the unlucky eye on him. He tightened the knot by the horse's veined cheek. He smells lion hot. God, he knew that woman. He was looking up into the blue eye, and he saw her face and knew her as the horse flung him over with a butt from his bony head. He saw the black circle of men flying like crows at gunshot, the bluestone eye over him hard set like silver. The stars were roaring, he saw them black in the white sky and the sun spinning like an orange pip as the horse cracked him, like an eggshell, against the rock.[2]

The most recent collection of poems, *Eternity Smith* (1985), extends the range of Casey's interests and skills. 'Eternity Smith' is the story of the gypsy who made the nails for Christ's crucifixion, the same gypsy whose wife had once befriended Mary. The daughter of the smith remembers the night of the birth: 'What's his name, Missus,/I said, and she smiled/ ... And smoothed my hair back out of my eyes./And suddenly I wanted to give the baby/Something for luck, like we do./How well I remember it./And had nothing, only an old nail in one pocket,/Off a mule's shoe./Take it Lady, I said, it's for luck.'[3]

The opening poem of this volume—and several others— nods to Yeats.

Yeats would have that Horseman
End the song.
When I die,
You will see no sidhe nor shade
Pass by,
But fearless,
bear the accolade
Of the stallion's eye.[4]

Works:

Hath the Rain a Father? London: Phoenix House, 1966. Short Stories.

Horse by the River. Dublin: Dolmen Press, 1968. Poetry.

The Horse of Selene. Dublin: Dolmen Press; London: Calder and Boyars, 1971; New York: Grossman, 1972. Novel.

The Circus. Dublin: Dolmen, 1974; Nantucket, Mass: Longship Press, 1978. Novel.

Eternity Smith. Dublin: Dolmen, 1985. Poetry.

Notes

1. Freda Brown Jackson, 'Juanita Casey,' in *Dictionary of Literary Biography* (Detroit: Bruccoli Clark Book, 1983).
2. *The Horse of Selene*, 174-175.
3. *Eternity Smith*, 26.
4. *Eternity Smith*, 7.

Cavanagh, Maeve

Born: Ireland, c̲ 19th century
Educated: Ireland.

An Irish poet at the beginning of the twentieth-century, Maeve Cavanagh urged rebellion and celebrated Irish patriotism. In *Sheaves of Revolt*, published in 1914, for example, Cavanagh's persona, Ireland, praises Ireland's 'ancient glory', presses for freedom for the green, white, and orange flag, and berates Irish men who would fight for England, 'whose ruthless hand has maimed me oft'.[1] Cavanagh makes much of English difficulty as Ireland's opportunity: Ireland's message, here and elsewhere in Cavanagh, is the militant demand, 'Who'd serve me true must serve me now.'(3)

Works:

Sheaves of Revolt. Dublin: City Printing Works, 1914. Poetry.

A Voice of Insurgency. Dublin: (np), 1916. Poetry.

Passion Flowers. Dublin: Printed for the Author, 1917. Poetry.

Soil and Clay. Dublin: West, 1917. Poetry.

Ireland to Germany. Dublin: Shan-Van-Vocht, nd. Poetry.

A Ballad for Rebels. Dublin: (np), nd. Poetry.
Thomas Ashe. Dublin: (np), nd. Poetry.

Notes
1. *Sheaves of Revolt*, 31.

Coghill, Rhoda Sinclair

Born: Ireland, 1903
Educated: Ireland.
Rhoda Coghill was born in Dublin and educated at Alexandra College and Read Pianoforte School. A concert pianist, she started writing poetry after an illness.[1]

Works:
The Bright Hillside. Dublin: Hodges Figgis, 1948. Poetry.
Time is a Squirrel. Dublin: Dolmen Press, published for the author, 1956. Poetry.

Notes:
1. See *Pillars of the House*, A A Kelly, ed. (Dublin: Wolfhound Press, 1988), 101-103.

Concannon, Helena

Born: Ireland, 1878; Died: 1952
Educated: Ireland.
Born in Co. Derry this writer and politician was prominent in the Gaelic League. Helena was elected to Dáil Éireann in 1933 and became a Senator in 1938. She contributed to the nationalist magazines of the day and also wrote religious articles for the *Irish Messenger*. Her many works include *Irish Nuns in Penal Days* (1931) and *Poems* (1953).

Works:
Irish Nuns in Penal Days. Dublin: Sands, 1931. Non-fiction.
Poems. Dublin: Gill, 1953. Poetry.

Conlon, Evelyn
Born: Ireland, 1952
Educated: Ireland.

Evelyn Conlon was born in rural Monaghan, educated at St Louis Convent in Monaghan, and travelled for several years in Australia, New Zealand, Asia, and the Soviet Union. She published her first short story when she was eighteen, in 'New Irish Writing' in the *Irish Press*, and has published many in collections, newspapers, and journals since. After her travels, she took a Bachelor's Degree and Higher Diploma in Education in St Patrick's College, Maynooth. She joined Irishwomen United, was a founder member of Rape Crisis Centre, and believes that the 'most important political action' of her life was founding a crèche at Maynooth College.[1] Her second child was born during her second year in college; she was separated from her husband during her third year. After two years' teaching English at Leaving Certificate level, she returned to writing short stories. She has also written one play, one novel, many critical essays and numerous book reviews. In 1988, she was awarded an Arts Council Bursary for Literature; in 1989 she won a European Script Award and Arts Council Award for an original script commissioned by film director Pat Murphy. [1] She has two children and lives in Dublin.

Conlon's fiction focuses on the dark side of women's lives, usually married women and mothers, but also single mothers and women in heterosexual relationships. Mothers of many children in Conlon's work lose their individuality and personalities through the mindless on-going routine of their work, the depersonalising ravages on their bodies, and the neglect or disinterest of their husbands. *My Head is Opening* (1987), the title of her first volume of short stories, aptly describes the desperation of many mothers in the volume who plunge into depression, mental homes, or imagined worlds, which, however bleak, seem at some level preferable to the world they inhabit.

The men and women who uphold, or are upheld by, social conventions contribute to the misery of individualistic women in Conlon's work. The single mother Rose, in 'The Day She Lost the Last of Her Friends', is not welcome in the couple-world of her 'friends' or in the world of other single women who want either mothers or better company. Unable to talk to her uncommunicative, judgmental husband, Louise, in 'My Head is Opening', dreams of travel to lovely faraway places, Florence, Venice, Paris, but goes to Lourdes, a trip to Lourdes being easier for her husband to understand. Maisie Ryan in 'Transition' is dismissed by Manus O'Brien, the married member of Dáil Éireann whose child she carries: 'I will support you in whatever you want to do. I will get you the money tomorrow.'[2] Before she leaves for England, where she will have and keep her baby daughter, Maisie calls Manus's office, to enquire his position on abortion, supposedly for a fictional survey. 'Miss, whatever your name is — Mr O'Brien is naturally opposed to abortion,' the voice of Mrs O'Brien answers. (55)

Despite the serious and widespread nature of the misery she presents, Conlon can also be humorous. The reader roots for Mona in 'In Reply to Florence' when she finally takes her crutch to Michelangelo's great David, angered by the erasure of all women's productions. In 'Once Upon a Time', God finally listens to a woman's side of the marriage story, and shows his favour explicitly when a bully in a big car tries to force his way past her.

Insights into and sympathy for women's behaviour pervade Conlon's work. The resentment and love of the young girl for the all-powerful figure of her mother is nicely balanced in *Stars in the Daytime* (1989). An only child in a Catholic household, Rose is viewed by her mother Phyllis as anomaly rather than gift. A survivor, however, Rose escapes both the confused emotions of her home and the claustrophobic nature of the small Irish town.

Works:

Where Did I Come From? Dublin: Ardbui, 1982. Sex education book for children.

My Head is Opening. Dublin: Attic Press, 1987. Short Stories.

Stars in the Daytime. Dublin: Attic Press, 1989. Novel.

Taking Scarlet as a Real Colour. Belfast: Blackstaff Press, 1993. Short stories.

Notes

1. Personal communication.
2. 'Transition', in *My Head is Opening*, 52.

Coogan, Beatrice;

Born: Ireland, 1906
Educated: Ireland.

Beatrice Coogan's father was a civil servant and she was raised in Dublin in the early years of this century. She wrote historical and romantic fiction.

Beatrice acted in the Abbey Theatre for a short while where she met with many literary figues of the day, including Seán O'Casey. She published some articles in *The Irish Times* in her youth but abandoned writing for a time. She had three children, one of whom is Tim Pat Coogan, writer and ex-editor of the *Irish Press*. In the 1950s she returned to writing.

Her novel *The Big Wind* was originally published in 1969 and won her the Author of the Year Award at the Frankfurt bookfair.[1]

Works:

The Big Wind. London: Michael Joseph, 1969, rpt 1992.

Notes:

1. *The Irish Times*, March 1993, Victoria White.

Cooke, Emma
Born: Ireland, 1934
Educated: Ireland.

Born in Ireland, Emma Cooke attended school at Alexandra College, Dublin, and took a Diploma in Philosophy at Mary Immaculate Training College in Limerick. Active in writers' workshops, the Listowel Writers' Week, Limerick Adult Education Institute, she serves as co-ordinator and/or judge in many literary competitions, and is currently involved in promoting and organising the Killaloe Writers' Group. She is also a member of the Arts Council's Writers in Schools programme.

As a writer, she notes, her 'energies and interests are pretty much concentrated on contemporary life and modern Irish lifestyles'. Her novel, *Eve's Apple* (1985), is recommended by a Travel Guide as an excellent introduction for women travellers to Ireland.[1] A keen observer of modern life, she moves quickly and quietly from character to character, insight to insight. Her low-key, economical approach allows the reader to supply the outline, consider the response. The suggestiveness embodied in Cooke's fiction reminds one of Elizabeth Bowen or Jennifer Johnston. There is always much more that could be said; richer because unsaid, this 'much more' is positively charged with potential and implication.

In her first collection of short stories, *Female Forms* (1981), Cooke enters the consciousness of a variety of women, American and English visitors to Ireland, as well as the Irish themselves, at home and as visitors to the continent. Vignettes are connected by associations and memories, reflecting a variety of female thought patterns and concerns. In 'Cousins', the first story in the volume, small anxieties and irritations intrude when the cousins, American Molly and Irish Geraldine finally visit in Ireland. Molly typifies the Irish-American who treasures every detail of the town from the memories her mother bequeathed her. The Irish/American relationship is evoked in the memories of the packages of clothing sent from North America to the Irish relatives in the fifties and sixties: the 'black chiffon gown with a tiered skirt and no back' − useless surely in the climate and economic situation of Ireland in the post-war years − might illustrate the cultural and communication gap. Irony prevails also, as Molly discovers that the tablecloth, with its 'rich hues of purple and green [which] looked so traditional and Irish that she could have sworn it was an example of local handcraft,' is actually a factory-made product sent by her own mother from Chicago.[2]

Lack of communication, or misread communications, bedevil most of Cooke's characters. Young Michael in the story above hurries his mother and aunt home so that he can get back to the bar before the girl he has spotted leaves. Unaware of his hopes, his mother plans a long list of errands for Michael to run. In 'A Family Occasion', Beattie, the daughter of the Protestant family who has married a Catholic and who produces children year after year to the annoyance of her own family, also misreads her family's real irritation. True, they insensitively and often remark on 'all the chick-a-beatties', who, the grandmother notes, disapprovingly, are as 'wild as goats'. But the sister who gives Beattie *Planned Parenthood*, wrapped in brown paper, and who places a cardigan 'gently' around her shoulders shows concern for her sister. (22)

Humour spices Cooke's work: as Beattie passes a church, impressions flash through her head. The children 'always wanted to stop and look at the tombstones. Organ music pealed inside. A funeral march. Mr Watson practising. Someone must be sick.' (21) The twelve-year-old home from her first year at boarding school is questioned by her aunt: 'How do you like Dublin?' Polly inquired. 'She loves it,' replies the child's mother, replaying a pattern mothers and daughters have played for generations. (21)

In the title story, Cooke invades the consciousness of a male protagonist who sees women only as forms, 'cute or lumpy'. Wife, lovers, and 'daily woman' appear to him as slivers, shapes, photographs; emotions, ideas, feelings he neither knows nor wishes to know. The hot spicy curry which his present lover, a warm-hearted easy-going girl, cooks proves indigestible to the thin-blooded Talbot and prompts his feelings of irritation and resolution to dismiss the cook! Unable or unwilling to connect with the pulse of humanity, Talbot is finally left alone to his icy coffin-like bed, as even his 'daily' leaves him.

Works:
Female Forms. Dublin: Poolbeg, 1981. Stories.
A Single Sensation. Dublin: Poolbeg, 1982. Novel.
Eve's Apple. Belfast: Blackstaff Press, 1985. Novel.

Notes
1. Personal communication.
2. In *Female Forms*, 9-10.

Cowman, Roz (Róisín)
Born: Ireland, 1942
Educated: Ireland.

Roz Cowman was born in Cork, attended school in Clonmel, Co. Tipperary, and Cork, and took her BA and Diploma of Higher Education at University College, Cork. She has taught French in Ireland and Nigeria. She lives in Cork, and includes in her family of four, her daughter Sophie, who died at three months, one son and two daughters. Like so many of her generation who were compelled not only to learn Irish, but also to pass exams in it to qualify for entrance to university, she turned against her native language. Again like so many, she realises this loss now and is attempting to compensate.

'Every circumstance of my life affects my writing sooner or later,' she notes. For example, 'Catskin's Song' 'springs from ocelot lapels on a coat my mother wore in the 1940s — no other fur would suit the poem, as this was how I visualised Catskin in the Grimm Fairy Tale!' 'The more I read,' she concludes, 'the more I realise how deeply grounded all writing is in personal experience, usually from childhood.'[1]

Her poems and reviews have appeared in many literary magazines and anthologies; her first volume of poetry, *The Goose Herd*, appeared in 1989. In 1985 she won the Patrick Kavanagh Award for poetry.

As she notes, her poems grow out of her experience, and they certainly grow out of a girl's and woman's life. Both elusive and allusive, they conflate history, religion, or fairy-tale with the ordinary events of a woman's life, and in so doing they invest the ordinary with mystery which leads to deeper understanding. The volume opens appropriately with 'Annunciation', a poem which economically and vividly evokes Gothic and Renaissance pictures to conclude with the mystery of the unspoken: 'the frail tympani of her ears/snap like furze-pods,/and with everything still/unsaid between them,/the word is made flesh.'[2]

In 'Shopping', the mother figure attempts to escape the mirror's rebuke, absorbed by young girls from tales such as 'Snow White' and from society at large. 'I'm too wise to question you,/whose faraway eyes are green and greedy/for forbidden food', she notes. But still the mirror 'bad-mouth[s]' her turned back, miming 'the hag, shouldering faggots'. The old wisdom appears fresh. 'I have seen how light first/ripens, then rots. My child in her apple flesh/walks separate from me; she/once lived only/through my lungs, my heart.'[3] Other poems bristle with the sharp insights of a sort of twilight zone, the woman with influenza, for example, who sees her house 'as a machine-for-/dying in,' or the woman admitted to Bon Secours Maternity Hospital, who questions, 'Who'll succour/me, Mary and no-man's bastard/on the wall.'[4]

Humour abounds, sometimes tinged with bitter insight. The persona of 'Lot's Wife' sympathises with the woman's irritation at 'God's loudspeaker' (Lot), and understands her preference for 'her oily kitchen' over Lot's 'back/to Nature' plan.[5] The 'Matriarch' is compared to the 'ancient cat' who plays with the foolish before mangling them.[6] 'Full Moon In Menopause' may be the most fey poem, short, so it can be quoted in full.

She lures me, plum bitch
with her blooms; my lady
lecherous leaches me
in her lustres. Her white
wash flenses my skin.

I'll not shoal to her trawl.
I'll watch while her monofilament
dissolves; her funnel, diminished,
will falter and slacken
its gastropod suction.[7]

Wider aspects of Irish society are explored in poems such as 'In The Promontory Fort' and 'Medea Ireland'. The volume concludes as appropriately as it opened, with the poet/witch in 'The Old Witch Sings Of Lost Children' mourning the escape of her poem/children, who leave her 'to clinker by the fire/I made to warm them.'[8]

Works:
The Goose Herd. Galway: Salmon Publishing, 1989. Poetry.

Notes
1. Personal communication.
2. In *The Goose Herd*, 1.
3. In *The Goose Herd*, 4.
4. In *The Goose Herd*, 7, 18.
5. In *The Goose Herd*, 36.
6. In *The Goose Herd*, 29.
7. In *The Goose Herd*, 34.
8. In *The Goose Herd*, 49.

Crommelin, May (Maria Henrietta de la Cherois)

Born: Ireland, 1850; Died: 1930
Educated: Ireland.

May Crommelin spent her early life in Ireland and travelled widely. John Sutherland notes that travel was listed as her only occupation in *Who's Who*.[1] She wrote travel books, many novels, and poetry. Her novels are set in Ireland, South Africa and the East. She was the daughter of Louis Crommelin, the Huguenot founder of the Ulster linen industry.

Cromellin's accounts of the places and the practices of the people she visits on her travels are interspersed with anecdotes and local tales. The guide in *Over the Andes* directs her to the embalmed body of the conquistador, Francis Pizarro:

> striking a match, he held it close to the pane, displaying a dark, grinning skull laid on a red cushion, and a shrunken, coffee-coloured thing − a horrible caricature of the human shape, not unlike a blackened doll, with cotton-wool protruding from its interior. Against one thigh-bone was propped a vulgar spirits bottle, in which some shapeless horrors could be dimly seen. That is all that remains of the cruel conqueror's heart and brain.[2]

Another guide remarks the twelve apostles in a dim painting:

> 'Quite so; only there are surely fourteen!' was my polite comment, after a momentary puzzle over the unusual crowd. 'Ah, si! They have with them St Joseph and another for company,' replied the verger in a jovial tone, as who should say, 'Would you deny them a guest now and again?' (336)

Selected Works:
Orange Lily and Other Tales. London: Routledge, 1889. Short Stories.
Poets in the Garden. London: Fisher Unwin, 1886. Poetry.
Cross-Roads. 3 vol. London: Hurst & Blackett, 1890. Novel.

Over the Andes. London: Bentley, 1896. Travel Book.
Divil-May-Care. 8 vol. London: White, 1899. Novel.

Notes
1. *Longman Companion to Victorian Fiction* (Harlow, Essex: Longman, 1988), 162.
2. *Over the Andes*, 335.

Crone, Anne
Born: Ireland, 1915; Died: 1972
Educated: Ireland, England.

Anne Crone was born in Dublin and educated in Belfast and Oxford. She has written three novels which are all set in Co. Fermanagh. Lord Dunsany, introducing the first, *Bridie Steen* (1948), proclaims that 'this unforgettable novel' preserves Fermanagh in the way Hardy preserved Dorset. Full of bigotry, as you would expect of one that tells of an Irish border county; but what seems to me to place the author on a higher plane than even a famous playwright like Galsworthy, is that there is no clear indication in the book as to whether Miss Anne Crone is a Protestant or a Catholic.'[1]

Bridie Steen is a memorable character and the bog country she delights in also delights the reader. Brought up by her miserable, bigoted aunt and her tolerant, sympathetic uncle, Bridie feels in her own history the scald of Catholic-Protestant relations in Ireland: 'There were two kinds of people, Catholics and Protestants. They were people who lived close to one another, worked together, whose children learned and played together. Yet, naturally, there flowed between them a river of darkness of which the current could bear neither bridge nor boat. ... And Bridie's mother had committed the unthinkable sin of marrying one of them!'[2]

Crone illustrates the religious bigotry clearly and humorously. Aunt Rose Anne instills and nurtures a sense of shame for her dead mother in Bridie. Born nine years after Rose Anne, Bridie's mother was a burden to her sister from the start. Prettier and less devout than Rose Anne, her marriage to a Protestant was just what Rose Anne would expect of her. And then to escape in death, 'leaving the rearing of Bridie with its attendant inconveniences to the already long-suffering Rose Anne.' (5) Bridie sees Rose Anne's religion 'as an immense greed for every form of pious observance. The systematic adoration of the saints, even the most obscure, was a rigid law unto her. She was continually attributing trivial happenings in her daily life to their beneficence or displeasure. Saint Anthony guided her to find the lost crook for the kettle. If the frost blighted the potatoes in the patch behind the house, Saint Teresa was angry with the three in the house because they had neglected her so long.' (7) Bridie is saved from despair by her kind uncle, who changes the world when he confides that her mother 'was a tremendous nice girl, gentle and good-looking. ... As nice a girl as you'd see in a day's walking was Bridget Fitz,' warning Bridie not to mention this, however, to her aunt. (12)

In *Bridie Steen*, as in her other novels, Crone examines young women's emotional and intellectual development as both evolving with and different from the realistic, complicated background of Ulster.

Works:
Bridie Steen. New York: Scribner's, 1948; London: Heinemann, 1949. Novel.
This Pleasant Lea. New York: Scribner's, 1951; London: Heinemann, 1952. Novel.
My Heart and I. London: Heinemann, 1955. Novel.

Notes
1. 'Introduction', *Bridie Steen*, v, vi.
2. *Bridie Steen*, 5.

Crowley, Elaine
Born: Ireland, c 20th century
Educated: Ireland.

Elaine Crowley was born in Dublin and left school at fourteen to become an apprentice tailor. At eighteen, she went to England and joined the ATS (Auxillary Territorial Services). In 1949 she married a regular soldier and lived for a time in Egypt and Germany. After her six children grew up, she worked at several occupations before turning to writing, articles first, then novels. She now lives in Wales.

Works:
Dreams of Other Days. London: Penguin, 1984. Novel.
A Man Made to Measure. London: Penguin, 1986. Novel.
Waves Upon the Shore. London: Penguin, 1989. Novel.
The Pentunia-Coloured Coat. London: Penguin, 1991. Short Stories.

Crowley, Vicki
Born: Malta, 1940
Educated: Ethiopia, Malta, Libya, England.

Vicki Crowley was born in Malta and attended schools in the many countries to which the family moved: Ethiopia, Malta, Libya, and England. At times she attended two schools concurrently, one in the morning and one in the afternoons, with homework in different languages. She speaks five languages fluently. She trained in Architectural drawing in Valletta, Malta, and worked in the Architectural Office in Benghazi, Libya, and in the Audio Visual Department of the Libyan American Joint Services. She is well known as a painter; her paintings and silk wallhangings hang in many public and private collections. She travelled extensively in Europe and Africa before settling in Galway, where she now lives and works as a professional artist. She has six children. She illustrated her first volume of verse, *Oasis in a Sea of Dust* (1992).

Crowley paints and describes the exotic — from Africa to Aran — in this volume. The first poem suggests the voyage to come:

Paint me a picture
Let it be blue:
The sea where I once swam
Had boats with painted eyes
That watched as phosphorescence
Studded my hair and fingertips
With diamonds.[1]

The final poem confronts the empty, new canvas, rich with potential:

I succumb at last
And with deliberate strokes,
I lay the single colour
That feels so right
For now I know
With white on white,
That I shall always see
Into its emptiness.[2]

In the interval, we are exposed to 'The palette of wild expression', the glorious colours of African, Mediterranean, and Irish life.[3]

Works:
Oasis in a Sea of Dust. Galway: Salmon Publishing, 1992. Poetry.

Notes
1. 'Song of an Exile', *Oasis in a Sea of Dust*, 9.
2. 'The New Canvas', *Oasis in a Sea of Dust*, 54.
3. 'Desert Love', *Oasis in a Sea of Dust*, 45.

Cullen, Linda
Born: Ireland, 1963
Educated: Ireland.

Linda Cullen was born in Dublin and attended school in the Sacred Heart Convent in Monkstown and later in the Dominican Convent, Sion Hill. She works as a TV/video director and thus necessarily moved into writing scripts.[1]

The tragic death of her brother turned her to writing, writing for herself at that stage, not for publication. School left her with negative impressions about the effect of the Catholic church on Irish society, impressions which are reflected in her writing. Although her favourite writers are Jennifer Johnston and John Fowles, the writers who have influenced her most are those she has met, Rita Mae Brown and the native American, Beth Brant, both of whom gave her the courage to write her own first novel, *The Kiss* (1990). She also credits Terry Prone, with whose video company she worked for six years, with encouraging her writing.[2]

The Kiss tells of two childhood friends who unexpectedly discover their friendship has turned to love. The love scenes between Joanna and Helen are sensitively presented, the tenderness of the two women emphasised. The love between the two women is the central concern, a love that is threatened by Helen's prior and still existing relationship with a male lover. The problems of a lesbian relationship in Ireland are also explored: the need to conceal their love from friends and relatives strains the relationship but at the same time makes it more intimate, a delicate secret which while isolating also bonds the women. 'When did you know?' Helen asks Joanna, as they make love. 'About this?' Joanna questions in reply, 'I didn't. ... I didn't know at all.' Not until the night they kissed.[3] As the relationship progresses, Joanna wonders why 'she hadn't told anyone. Hadn't told anyone about the happiest thing that had ever happened her. She wondered was she afraid to admit she had fallen in love with a woman, with her best friend. Or was it that she felt it too ...

fragile, too new? She didn't know. One part of her wanted to scream it aloud to everyone she met. Another part was afraid of mentioning it at all.' (100) Cullen makes a good choice in telling the story from Joanna's perspective, the reader endures and sympathizes with her agony as she anxiously waits for Helen's decision.

Works:
The Kiss. Dublin: Attic Press, 1990. Novel.

Notes
1. Personal communication.
2. Personal communication.
3. *The Kiss*, 85.

Cummins, Geraldine Dorothy
Born: Ireland, 1890; Died: 1969
Educated: Ireland.

Geraldine Cummins (G D Cummins) was born in Cork in 1890. She was active in the woman's suffrage movement, and with Suzanne R Day wrote two plays produced by the Abbey Theatre, *Broken Faith* (1913) and *Fox and Geese* (1917). She also wrote two novels, a book of short stories, a biography of Edith Somerville, and books on psychical research.

'The Tragedy of Eight Pence' — one of Cummins' best short stories — was republished recently. The tale of a perfectly matched couple, content only in and of themselves, Cummins saves it from sentimentalism by a nice balance of comedy and tragedy. The reclusive Patrick Moore encourages his wife, Kate, to accept the visit proposed by his sister: '"My dear, to please me." Patrick stretched out the hand from which four fingers were missing; they had been amputated after the battle of the Somme. It now rested caressingly on Kate's bare arm. He was taking advantage of a weakness of hers. She could never resist the pathos of that hand.'[1] The miserly sister is also a snob who talks 'with great gusto' of the aristocratic members of the Oxford Group Movement. 'You talk as if there were no good people anywhere else, but in Oxford,' Kate remarks, trying to divert the 'devouring' Angelina from Patrick. '"Oh, I suppose there are some holy people in Ireland," the oracle responded, "but those in England are so well connected."' (213-14) Kate, a sympathetic and caring Anglo-Irishwoman, is, as Janet Madden-Simpson notes, an infrequent character in Anglo-Irish fiction.[2]

Selected Works:
Fox and Geese, with Suzanne R Day. Dublin & London: Maunsel, 1917. Play.
The Land They Loved. London: Macmillan, 1919. Novel.
Fires of Beltane. London: Michael Joseph, 1936. Novel.
Unseen Adventures. London: Rider, 1951. Autobiography.
Dr E O E Somerville. London: Dakers, 1952. Biography.
Variety Show. London: Barrie & Rockliff, 1959. Short Stories.

Notes
1. In *Woman's Part, An anthology of short fiction by and about Irishwomen 1890-1960*, Janet Madden-Simpson, ed. (Dublin: Arlen House, 1984), 211.
2. Introduction, 'The Tragedy of Eight Pence,' *Woman's Part*, 209.

Cussen, Clíodna
Born: Ireland, 1932
Educated: Ireland, Italy.

Clíodna Cussen was born and went to school in Co. Limerick. She attended University College, Dublin, and took her BA in history and French, her MA in history; she also qualified as an attorney-at-law. She attended art college in Dublin and Florence and has worked as a free-lance sculptor since 1959. She writes in Irish, but prefers sculpture to anything else.

Her early stories were unsuccessful, written in what she calls 'Kiltartanesque, Hiberno-English'. When she married the poet, publisher, and historian, Pádraigh O Snodaigh, they spoke Irish with their six sons, and she turned to writing in Irish. She had always wanted to write children's stories, and she found the rhythms right in Irish, with 'no self-conscious de-Hibernising' needed. She has written children's stories, collected and illustrated folklore, stories, and verse, and contributed to many Irish magazines.[1]

Works:

Stair na hÉireann. Baile Atha Cliath: Chapman, 1969. Edited. History.

Máirín. Corca Dhuibhne, Co. Chiarraí: Cló Dhún Chaoin, 1970.

Trupall, Trapall. Baile Atha Cliath: An Gúm, 1970. Children's Book.

Tomhais. Baile Atha Cliath: An Gúm, 1972. Children's Book.

Síle Bhuí. Baile Atha Cliath: An Gúm, 1974. Stories.

Ealó ón gCaisleán. Baile Atha Cliath: An Gúm, 1975. History.

Colm agus a Chairde. Baile Atha Cliath: Clodhanna Teo, 1976. Children's Book.

Gearóid Iarla Baile Atha Cliath: Clodhanna Teo, 1978. History.

Báile Shuibhne. Baile Atha Cliath: Clodhanna Teo, 1978.

Bainne agus Bánbhianna. Baile Atha Cliath: An Gúm, 1980.

An Droch-Shaol. Baile Atha Cliath: Clodhanna Teo, 1984.

Inniu an Luan. Baile Atha Cliath: Coisceim, 1987. Drama.

An Bhean Ud Thall. Baile Atha Cliath: Bord na Gaeilge. 1988. Novel.

Torfin. Baile Atha Cliath: Coiscéim, 1988.

Notes
1. Personal communication.

— *D* —

Dáibhís, Bríd
Born: Ireland, 1930
Educated: Ireland.

Bríd Dáibhís was born in old Ballybrittas, Laois, and educated in Killenard National School and the Presentation College in Mountmellick, Co. Laois. She trained as a primary teacher in Carysfort Training College, Dublin, and took her Diploma in Irish Literature from Dáimh an Léinn Cheiltigh, Máigh Nuad. She entered the Presentation Novitiate in Killenard in 1947, was professed in 1950 and assigned to Kilcock Presentation Convent where she has taught primary classes. Very active in Irish language activities, she was chairperson of the local Glór na nGael committee, a body that promotes Irish outside the classroom, provides scholarships to the Gaeltacht, and sponsors Irish Christmas cards and Irish Week.

Dáibhís writes in both Irish and English, of nature, spiritual matters, people – often students – who impress her, and conflicts involved in living in a community. Her poem, 'An Gineadh', won the 1916 Commemoration Prize for an Irish poem in 1966; she has also won prizes in the Oireachtas competition, was short-listed for the Hennessy Award, and won a prize for a short story in the Maxwell House Women's Writing Competition. She enjoys writing plays in Irish and English for her school classes, and would like to spend more time on drama. A founder member of Comhaltas Ceoltóirí Éireann, an association for the promotion of traditional Irish music, dance, and song, she would like to see more native hymns in the Irish liturgy.[1]

Spiritual themes are expressed through natural images in poems such as 'Braon Meala'.

Aoine an Chéasta a bhí ann;
Mé brúite tar éis achasáin,
M'ionracas m'aon bhraon meala,
Agus gur thuig tusa mo chás,
A Chaomhnóir an Ghíolcaigh.[2]

'Eibhlín' catches the lighter side of a teacher's unwilling amusement at her student's exuberance for living and doubts about maths, while the persona in 'Ar na Gréine' imagines the white window frame becoming her means of escape from darkness, just as the white horse became Oisín's means of escape.[3]

Bríd Dáibhís has published two volumes of poetry to date and one book of rhymes to popular airs, as well as several poems and short stories for newspapers and anthologies.

Works:
Ceol a Pháid. Baile Atha Cliath: Fallons, 1960. Songs.
Corrán Gealaí. Baile Atha Cliath: Clóchomhar, 1978. Poetry.
Cosán na Gréine. Baile Atha Cliath: Coiscéim, 1989. Poetry.

Notes
1. Personal communication.
2. In *Cosán na Gréine*, 35.
3. In *Cosán na Gréine*, 21, 6.

Daly, Ita
Born: Ireland, 1945
Educated: Ireland.

Ita Daly was born in Co. Leitrim in 1945, attended St Louis High School in Rathmines, Dublin, and received her BA, MA, and Diploma of Education from University College,

Dublin. She lives in Dublin with her husband, David Marcus, and daughter Sarah.

She has written short stories, novels, and a children's book. Two of her stories, 'The Lady with the Red Shoes' and 'Virginibus Puerisque', received the Hennessy Literary Award, and 'Compassion' won *The Irish Times* Short Story competition. Her work has been translated into German, Swedish, and Danish.

Many of Daly's short stories are first person narratives, often from the perspective of an unusual, unsympathetic character. The narrator of the much-anthologised, 'Aimez-vous Colette?' for example, is a snobbish, provincial school-mistress, satisfied to abandon 'an Ireland that continues to rot in obscurantism and neurosis' for the company of French writers, especially Colette.[1] But Daly arouses her readers' sympathy also, as she reveals the slights that prompted the plain, self-conscious girl to turn from a world that seemed to reject her. Reflecting on the narrowness of the townspeople, the narrator/teacher notes early on her 'irritation at their absurd attempts at liberalism. Such as collections and fasts outside church doors for the Biafrans, when every mother within twenty miles would lock up her daughter if a black man came to town. And would be encouraged by their priests to do so.' (80) The narrator's own racism is revealed at the end of the story, not in any melodramatic way, but in the petty and superior fashion that seems to characterise both the narrator and her society.

Time after time, Daly enters the consciousness of solitary characters; their names are often undisclosed, perhaps a metaphor for their condition. Each narration allows us uncomfortable glimpses of lives, glimpses that shatter facile character generalisations.

Works:
The Lady with the Red Shoes. Dublin: Poolbeg, 1980. Short Stories.
Ellen. London: Cape, 1986. Novel.
A Singular Attraction. London: Cape, 1987. Novel.
Dangerous Fictions. London; Bloomsbury, 1989. Novel.

Candy on the Dart. Dublin: Poolbeg, 1989. Children's Book.

Notes
1. In *The Lady with the Red Shoes*, 80.

Davys, Mary
Born: Ireland, 1674; Died: 1732
Educated: Ireland.

Mary Davys was born in Dublin. She and her husband, the Reverend Peter Davys, headmaster of the school attached to St Patrick's Cathedral, were friends to Swift. When her husband died in 1698, she moved to York, then to Cambridge. She opened a coffee house in Cambridge, and her patrons approved of, and subscribed to, her printed works. Her novels were well received, and she also wrote plays and her memoirs. Her complete works were published in two volumes in 1725.[1]

Familiar Letters Betwixt a Gentleman and a Lady (1725) is a series of twenty-two letters between Berina and Artander, two good friends who initially denounce the follies of love. A Tory and a Whig, they debate politics, exchange news, and draw moral lessons from events and tales. The letters move — reluctantly and predictably — towards love, concluding with Artander's declaration: 'how much I dread to meet Berina's Eyes, lest one indifferent Look from them shoul'd, with a Basilisk Force, strike poor Artander dead: The very Dread of losing you, has seiz'd my vital Spirits, and all I am able to add, is, that you will call up that Good-nature (of which you have so great a Share) to help you to pity your dying Artander.'[2] Berina answers with more spirit: 'I'll swear, Artander, I was never so merry in my Life, as at the reading of your last Letter; ... The next time you put on the Lover, do it with an easier Air; 'tis quite out of fashion to talk of Dying, and Sighing, and Killing Eyes, and such Stuff; you should say, Damn it, Madam, you are a tolerable sort of a Woman, and, if you are willing, I don't much care if I do you the Honour to marry you.' (306)

Josephine Grieder believes that Mary Davys' success was based on her understanding of and interest in the psychology of ordinary men and women.[3]

Works:

The Works of Mrs Mary Davys: Consisting of Plays, Novels, Poems, and Familiar Letters. London: H Woodfall, 1725.

Notes

1. See 'Introduction' by Josephine Grieder in *The Reform'd Coquet, Familiar Letters Betwixt a Gentleman and a Lady* by Mary Davys, and *The Mercenary Lover* by Eliza Haywood (New York & London: Garland Publishing, 1973).
2. *Familiar Letters*, 305-306.
3. Introduction to *The Reform'd Coquet, Familiar Letters Betwixt a Gentleman and a Lady*, 9.

de Valera, Sinéad

Born: Ireland 1878; Died: 1975
Educated: Ireland.

Sinéad Ní Fhlannagáin trained as a primary school teacher. An active member of the Gaelic League, she met her future husband and the future president of Ireland, Eamon de Valera, at Coláiste Chonnacht, where she taught Irish. Many of her books are translations or retellings of fairy and folk tales.

Works:

Plays for children:
Buaidhirt agus Bród. Baile Atha Cliath: Mac an Ghioll, 1934.
Na Buidéil Draoidheachta. Baile Atha Cliath: Mac an Ghioll, 1935.
Teach in Airde. Baile Atha Cliath: Mac an Ghioll, 1936.
Lá Bealtaine. Baile Atha Cliath: Mac an Ghioll, 1936.
Cluichí Gaedhilge don aos óg. Baile Atha Cliath: Mac an Ghioll, 1936.
Niall agus Gormfhlaith. Baile Atha Cliath: Mac an Ghioll, 1940.

Forbhas Chluain Meala. Baile Atha Cliath: Mac an Ghioll, 1940.

Bronntanas Nollag. Baile Atha Cliath: Mac an Ghioll, 1940.

Morann an Ceart Bhreitheamh. Baile Atha Cliath: Mac an Ghioll, 1940.

An tSeanbhean a bhí ina comhnuidhe i mBróig. Baile Atha Cliath: Mac an Ghioll, 1940.

An Choróinn ar Iarraidh. Baile Atha Cliath: Mac an Ghioll, 1940.

Máighistir no Máighistreas. Baile Atha Cliath: Mac an Ghioll, 1943.

Cathal Crobhdearg. Baile Atha Cliath: Mac an Ghioll, 1943.

Oilibhéar Beannaithe Ploingcéad. Baile Atha Cliath: Mac an Ghioll, 1948.

A House to Let. Dublin: Gill, 1954.

May Day. Dublin: Gill, 1954.

Luaithrín agus prionsa. Baile Atha Cliath: Mac an Ghioll, 1961.

Poetry for children:
Dánta do Leanbhaí. Baile Atha Cliath: Mac an Ghioll, 1961. Trans (Fontaine).

Stories:
Fairytales, retold by Sinéad de Valera. Dublin: Fallons, 1958.

An Spéir Bhean ina suan. Baile Atha Cliath: Mac an Ghioll, 1958.

The Emerald Ring and other Irish fairytales. Baile Atha Cliath: Mac an Ghioll, 1960.

The Stolen Child and other stories. Baile Atha Cliath: Mac an Ghioll, 1961.

Cochaillín Dearg agus an mactíre. Baile Atha Cliath: Mac an Ghioll, 1961.

The Fourleaved Shamrock and other stories. Dublin: Fallons, 1964.

Fairytales of Ireland. London: Four Square, 1967.

Fairytales of Ireland (New edition). New English Library, 1970.

The Misers' Gold and Other Stories. Dublin: Fallons, 1970.

An tUll Orga. Indreabhan: Cló Cois Fharriage, 1977.

More Irish Fairytales. London: Pimlico, 1979.

Deevy, Teresa
Born: Ireland, 1894; Died: 1963
Educated: Ireland.

Teresa Deevy was born in Waterford and attended the Ursuline convent there. She began her university education at University College, Dublin, developed a disease which would result in permanent deafness and transferred to University College, Cork, from which she received her degree. Her father died when she was three; her mother encouraged her writing. In London, after her graduation, she learnt lip-reading and became passionately interested in the theatre, particularly admiring the work of Chekhov and Shaw.

When she returned to Ireland, she began writing plays. Her first two were rejected by the Abbey, but the author was encouraged and advised to continue writing. *Reapers*, a three-act play, was accepted and received positive reviews when it was produced in March 1930. In all, she wrote twenty-five plays, six of which were produced at the Abbey.[1]

Deevy's plays are distinguished by their dialogue and often by their heroines. The dialogue is unaffected and appropriate, and the heroines are brave, independent girls. Confined, restricted by their class and gender, Annie Kinsella in *The King of Spain's Daughter*, produced in 1935, and Katie Roche in the play of this name, produced in 1936, yearn for something more than what is available. Annie Kinsella may be the most honestly realised: Deevy refuses melodrama or contrivance and simply focuses on the awful restrictions, the limitations forced on the young, imaginative girl. Imagination — or courage — wins out, and Deevy's heroines create adventure and excitement from the meagre materials available.

Works:
Three Plays. Katie Roche, The King of Spain's Daughter, and The Wild Goose. London: Macmillan, 1939. Plays.

Notes
1. Eileen Kearney, 'Teresa Deevy: Ireland's Forgotten Second Lady of the Abbey Theatre', in *The Theatre Annual*, Special Issue: Women in Theatre, Vol xxxx, 1985.

Devas, Nicolette
Born: Ireland, 1912
Educated: Ireland, England.

Nicolette Devas was born in Co. Clare, the daughter of Francis MacNamara, and sister of Caitlín, who married Dylan Thomas. Her father was a cousin to Brindsley MacNamara, the novelist. She lived in England as a child with Augustus John's family and knew many of the 'great' figures of the art and literary worlds. She wrote one novel, *Bonfire* (1958), and her memoirs, *Two Flamboyant Fathers* (1966) and *Susannah's Nightingales* (1978), which give an account of the life of her father and of Augustus John.

Bonfire captures children's perspectives very well, especially their vague and undefined fears and fantasies. Robert and Constance Ollier lead a happy life with their three children until Vera Montrasina comes to help Robert write a book. Vera enchants both Robert and Constance and becomes Robert's mistress. The children see Vera as a witch, dislike − though they do not understand − her presence in their father's bedroom, and troubled, attempt to break her spell.

Works:
Bonfire. London: Chatto and Windus, 1958. Novel.
Two Flamboyant Fathers: Reminiscences of Francis MacNamara and Augustine John. London: Collins, 1966. Memoir.
Susannah's Nightingales. A Companion to Two Flamboyant Fathers. London: Collins and Harvill Press, 1978. Memoir.

Devlin, Anne
Born: Ireland, 1951
Educated: Ireland.

Anne Devlin was born in Belfast, and now lives in Birmingham with her son. She writes fiction and plays about the women of northern Ireland. She won the Hennessy Literary Award in 1982 for her short story,

'Passages', adapted for television as *A Woman Calling*. Her first collection of plays, *Ourselves Alone*, which includes *A Woman Calling* and *The Long March*, was published in 1986 and reprinted in 1988. She received the Samuel Beckett Award in 1984 and the Susan Smith Blackburn Prize in 1986.

Ourselves Alone is the story of women committed to political struggle in Belfast: daughters, sisters, and lovers who deliver explosives, shelter fugitives, interrogate new recruits, and try to achieve some measure of emotional fulfillment. But the women are brutally used, abused, and thrown aside. At the end of the play, Donna, Josie, and Frieda discuss their situations. Josie announces that she's pregnant, by the new English recruit, not by her long-time lover Cathal, whose wife has had ten children, 'A child for every year that I knew him,' Josie says.[1] The men, Malachy, father of Josie and Frieda, and Liam, brother of Josie and Frieda and lover of Donna and father of her child, burst in on the women and announce that the English recruit has betrayed them, but Josie refuses to believe this. The dialogue illustrates the attitude toward women:

Josie:	No. No. No!
Liam:	How many months pregnant are you?
Josie:	Three.
Liam:	Kill it. I want you to kill the child!
Josie:	Why?
Liam:	The father is a traitor He did not love you; he used you. It's better that his child should not be born at all.
Josie:	But it's my baby — it doesn't matter about anything else.
Liam:	It's his child!
Donna:	No. It's not, Liam. It's what you never understood. A child doesn't belong to anyone. It's itself. (Liam grabs Josie's arms.)
Liam:	Do it. Don't force us! (87-88)

Devlin's short stories are equally powerful and uncompromising, combining the ordinary events of everyday life with the dramatic and terrible events of war. In a city torn apart, women still wait for men to call, mothers still keep the secrets of childbirth from their adult daughters. 'Naming the Names' is a haunting story about a young woman's involvement in an 'illegal organisation', and her refusal to name the names, to betray her associates. In a few short pages, Devlin implies the whole complex, tortured situation of northern Ireland, and the personal story of Finnula. The killings and activities of the illegals and the soldiers are recounted with admirable brevity, the horror emphasised – in retrospect – by the brief and detached accounts. Confined to jail for her part in the death of her lover, Finnula watches a spider and reflects on the web of Belfast life.

'The gradual and deliberate processes weave their way in the dark corners of all our rooms, and when the finger is pointed, the hand turned, the face at the end of the finger is my face, the hand at the end of the arm that points is my hand, and the only account I can give is this: that if I lived for ever I could not tell: I could only glimpse what fatal visions stir that web's dark pattern. I do not know their names. I only know for certain what my part was, that even on the eve, on such a day, I took him there.'[2]

Works:
Ourselves Alone with *A Woman Calling* and *The Long March*. London: Faber and Faber, 1986; rpt. 1988. Plays.
The Way-Paver. London: Faber and Faber, 1986; rpt. 1987, 1988. Stories.

Notes
1. *Ourselves Alone*, 85.
2. In *The Way-Paver*, 118-119.

Devlin, Polly
Born: Ireland, 1941
Educated: Ireland.

Polly Devlin was born in Ardboe, Co. Tyrone. Her old family home is situated between the very large Lough Neagh and an aerodrome. 'Lough Neagh played such an enormous role in our childhood,' she notes, 'that we never analysed it. It was like our parents, being there all the time. ... Wherever you went you could hear the sough and hiss of the lough – without hearing it, as it were.'[1] She believes her childhood was unusual in that 'my brother and sisters were people of great quality and I was lucky to grow up among them.' The lives of the six sisters and one brother 'were so much enmeshed in each other, so netted together, that there was, it seemed to me, no way to extricate myself'. (38)

In the memoir, *All of Us There* (1983), she describes her childhood as both golden and bleak. The scene of harvesting on her father's farm is Hardyesque: the men resting and discussing the weather, the maid gathering up the cups and plates from the meal, the children playing in the grain. 'We thrust our hands into the golden spill and turn them round and round as though washing them in a golden downpour, as if summer could solidify its liquid essence as winter can in snow and hail.' (Quoted in *Portrait*, 40)

Polly Devlin has had a varied and adventurous career. In 1964 she won the *Vogue* Talent Competition, and left Ireland to work in London and New York for *Vogue* magazine. She did the first interview in England with Bob Dylan, the first profile of Seamus Heaney in the English press, a controversial portrait of Barbra Streisand, and a long interview with the Empress Farah Dibah in Tehran. She was with John Lennon and Yoko Ono when they were setting up their Art Show in New York State and travelled through the Trucial Oman States when the city of Abu Dhabi did not yet exist, when the Bedu still lived their nomadic life. Married, she has three daughters, and divides her time between Somerset, London, and Ireland. She was awarded the OBE for her writing in 1992.[2]

Dora, or the *Shifts of the Heart* (1990), explores a woman's attempt to come to terms with her memories of her mother and of her mother's unhappiness. A writer, Dora attempts re-creation by re-naming herself and leaving Ireland for England. In the process, she moves from an abusive lover who shows her an Ireland she had denied, the elegant Ireland of ascendancy houses, to an English husband secure in his sense of himself and of his history, and finally to a completely passionate affair. Dora turns to the lives of writers, often Yeats and Joyce, as guides for her own actions, but as she moves from dreams to their interpretations, Freud's Dora seems a more appropriate and ironic foil.

When Jacqueline Kennedy's name comes up at dinner, for example, Dora recalls the pictures from Dallas. 'The legend was that she was either gathering up the shards of skull and hair that had been her husband's head a moment before or was crawling towards the secret service man flinging himself across the divide that nothing mortal could span. Dora knew better. Dora knew when she saw instinct at work, and in Dora's scenario Mrs K was crawling away from the scene, escaping as fast as she could. She found that more heroic than the given interpretations. The woman was a mother. She had children at home. She was going to live.' Later that evening, Dora tells her theory to her lover, Theodore, who listens impatiently, and finally explodes. 'The bile in his voice simmered, etching his words with acid. "I don't want to hear these stories which tell me what you're afraid to tell me directly. I am too grown-up, too valuable, to spend my life waiting for someone who wants the best of both worlds. I won't love a woman who is divided between two men. You must choose. I will not be a stepping stone to your future without me."'[3]

Full of rage and anger at her history, national and personal, Dora recognises — but rarely controls — the onset of the tides of fury which threaten to engulf herself, husband, and children. Tenderness for her children, however, ultimately prevails and in doing so heals Dora's past wounds.

Besides the novel and memoir, Devlin has written a book of short stories, one of which, 'The China Doll', is frequently anthologised and broadcast, and a history of photography.

Works:
The Vogue History of Photography. London: Thames and Hudson, 1979; New York: Simon and Schuster, 1979. History.
All of Us There. London: Weidenfeld and Nicholson, 1983; London: Pan, 1984; London: Pavanne, 1988. Memoir.
The Far Side of the Lough. London: Gollancz, 1983; London; Magnet, 1985. Chidren's Stories.
Dora, or the Shifts of the Heart. London: Chatto and Windus, 1990; London: Arrow, 1992. Novel.

Notes
1. In *A Portrait of the Artist as a Young Girl*, John Quinn ed. (London: Methuen, 1986), 36. Following references noted in parenthesis in text.
2. Personal communication.
3. *Dora*, 210.

Dillon, Eilís
Born: Ireland, 1920
Educated: Ireland.

Eilís Dillon was born in Galway in 1920. Her father, Thomas Dillon, professor of chemistry at University College, Galway and her mother, Geraldine Plunkett, were members of distinguished Irish families. Her life, she writes, was shaped by 'association with people who took part in the Irish war of independence. As a child I knew scarcely anyone who had not been in that struggle.' Her parents insisted that 'we ... should attempt to understand the people who lived on the periphery of society under the old regime, and that we should work towards giving them a sense of belonging to the new Ireland.' To this end the children all learned Irish and attended the local schools with the least-privileged children. The 'whole Gaelic tradition was opened to me and I had no difficulty in recognising it for the precious gift it was.' The combination of childhood exposure to the great classics of English literature, along with awareness of 'the existence of another, quite different language was what turned me into a writer'. Being of Ireland, she concludes, is 'a great privilege, and one that I've always appreciated."[1]

Eilís Dillon's personal and professional life is rich and varied. She studied music intensively and plays chamber music with amateurs. In 1940, she married Cormac O Cuilleanáin; the couple had three children, one of them the poet Eiléan Ní Chuilleanáin. Widowed in 1970, she married Vivian Mercier in 1974. She toured American universities several times, lecturing on Irish literature. She has also lectured at the Gorky Institute in Moscow. She taught creative writing and acted as writer-in-residence at several institutions in Ireland and the United States of America.

Distinctions have come to Eilís Dillon personally and to her work. In 1971 she was appointed member of the Advisory Committee of the International Commission on English in the Liturgy; in 1972 she was appointed by the Irish government member of the newly-constituted Arts Council of Ireland; in 1979 she was elected a Fellow of the Royal Society of Literature; in 1981 she received a Rockefeller Foundation Fellowship at Bellagio, Italy, and was also created a member of Aosdána, the newly-formed Irish register of distinguished artists; in 1990 she was elected Chair of the Irish Writers' Union, and also Chair of the Irish Children's Book Trust; in 1992 she was awarded a D Lit Honoris Causa, by the National University of Ireland. Her 1973 novel, *Across the Bitter Sea*, was a Book-of-the-Month Club alternate choice in the USA and the choice of several English and German book clubs; her books for children have garnered many awards: *The Island of Horses* (1956), was listed in a London *Sunday Times* survey as one of the hundred best books for children in English; *The Shadow of Vesuvius* (1976), and *The Island of Ghosts* (1989) were Junior Literary Guild choices, and the latter was Irish Best Children's Book of the Year in 1991.

Besides youth and adult fiction, she writes plays, several of which have been presented in Dublin, short stories, poetry, book reviews, and scholarly articles. She has translated 'The Lament for Arthur O'Leary'; her translations, poems, and stories have appeared in many anthologies. Her adult novels are often set in the 'troubles'. *The Bitter Glass* (1958), for example, shows both the frightening and disturbing effects of Irish Civil War on those caught in its tentacles, and the confusion and uncertainty of the young, untrained revolutionaries themselves. Dillon's work preserves a record of life in Connemara in the 1920s: the people, the work, the songs, including a delightful version of 'The Twelve Days of Christmas'. Character sketches contain sharp insights into the motives and habits of common 'types'. Her novels have been published widely and repeatedly.

Selected Works:

Adult Novels:
Sent to His Account. London; Faber and Faber, 1954; New York: Walker, 1966; New York: Harper and Row, 1986.
Death in the Quadrangle. London: Faber and Faber, 1956; New York: Walker, 1965; New York: Harper and Row, 1986.
The Bitter Glass. London: Faber and Faber, 1968; New York: Appleton Century Crofts, 1969; Dublin: Ward River, 1981; Dublin: Poolbeg, 1987.
The Head of the Family. London: Faber and Faber, 1965; Dublin: Ward River, 1982; Dublin: Poolbeg, 1987.
Bold John Henebry. London: Faber and Faber, 1965. Freiburg: Herder, 1967.
Across the Bitter Sea. London: Hodder and Stoughton, 1973; New York: Simon and Schuster, 1973; Tubingen: Wunderlich, 1974.

Blood Relations. London; Hodder, 1977; New York: Simon and Schuster, 1977; Tubingen: Wunderlich, 1978.

Wild Geese. New York: Simon and Schuster, 1981; London: Hodder and Stoughton, 1981; Tubingen: Wunderlich, 1982.

Citizen Burke. London; Hodder and Stoughton, 1984; London: Coronet, 1987.

The Interloper. London: Hodder and Stoughton, 1987; London: Coronet, 1989.

Children's Books:

The Island of Horses: London: Faber and Faber, 1956; New York: Funk and Wagnalls, 1956. Many Translations.

The Singing Cave. London: Faber and Faber, 1969; New York: Funk and Wagnalls, 1969; Freiburg: Herder, 1960; Dublin: Poolbeg, 1991. Many Translations.

A Family of Foxes. London: Faber and Faber, 1965; New York: Funk and Wagnalls, 1964. Many Translations.

The Sea Wall. London: Faber and Faber, 1965; New York: Funk and Wagnalls, 1965; Freiburg: Herder, 1966.

The Seals. London: Faber and Faber, 1968; New York: Funk and Wagnalls, 1968; Freiburg: Herder, 1970. Many Translations.

A Herd of Deer. London: Faber and Faber, 1969; New York: Funk and Wagnalls, 1969; Freiburg: Herder, 1969.

Living in Imperial Rome. London: Faber and Faber, 1974; New York: Nelson, 1976; Dublin: O'Brien Press, 1991.

The Shadow of Vesuvius. London: Faber and Faber, 1976; New York: Nelson, 1976.

Down in the World. London: Hodder and Stoughton, 1983.

The Seekers. New York: Charles Scribner's Sons, 1986; New York: Viking/Puffin, 1988; Dublin: Poolbeg, 1991.

The Island of Ghosts. New York: Charles Scribner's Sons, 1989; London: Faber and Faber, 1990.

Notes
1. Personal communication.

Donohoe, M J
Born: Ireland, 1932
Educated: Ireland.

M J Donohoe was born in Navan in 1932. She took her BA
and MA in English literature in Ireland. She joined a
convent and served as a missionary in Rawalpindi,
Peshawar, and Kashmir. In 1959, when the Indo-Pakistan
war broke out, Sister Donohoe's school was burnt to the
ground. She moved to Delhi and taught for three years.
The stories in her volume of short stories were inspired by
events she witnessed in Pakistan, India, Europe, and the
USA. The tension and horror in the stories belie the title, *So
So Stories* (1989).[1]

Works:
So So Stories. New York: Vantage Press, 1989. Stories.

Notes
1. Author Introduction in *So So Stories.*

Dorcey, Mary
Born: Ireland, 1950
Educated: Ireland, England.

Mary Dorcey was born and attended school in Dublin, and
was the first Irish student to enroll in British Open
University. She has travelled a great deal and turned her
hand to many jobs. In 1972 she joined the Irish Women's
Movement and was a founder member of Irishwomen
United, a coalition of women spanning a wide variety of
political and social viewpoints. Her first volume of poetry
was published in 1982. Her first collection of short stories,
A Noise from the Woodshed, 1989, was awarded the Rooney
Prize for Irish Literature.[1]

Open about her lesbianism, Dorcey writes of love
between women and of the anger of men toward lesbians;
although she presents a woman's perspective, the difficult

situations she explores, such as ageing, are universal. In the title story, 'A Noise from the Woodshed', a woman muses repeatedly and poetically on her first meeting with her lover and on the wonder and freedom of women striding out fearlessly to claim a new kind of life. 'Like a warrior in white armour, did she come,' she wonders,

> gallant and fearless though double-breasted, come like an answer to prayer; a maiden's prayer – yours – though no maiden, ... Or did she come like a woman; unheralded, unassuming, a woman struggling to keep a footing, to make a living, to make a loving? [2]

She remembers the movement toward love:

> two grown women getting serious, looking into each other's eyes seriously; seeing one another entire, absolute and not as some stop-gap, mediator, sympathiser, counsellor in the doings of men, that look; that long, tasting, touching look is one of the most serious and the best things going. And who can keep it going without laughing? (2-3)

And the persona concludes her reflections, as almost a hymn of delight:

> And it was another of those days. And more and more women are having them – days that is – snatched from drought and the torrents of life. More and more women riding about footloose, tongue loose and fancy free, crossing the river when they come to it: the deep, rushing tide, keeping their heads ... well above water and gaining the bank; they lie down where the grass lies green and growing in wait all round, lie down where the yellow iris waves in wait, the wild poppies blow and, a cuckoo – yes, it was unmistakably from over the heather – a cuckoo, calls. (21-22)

Dorcey's stories and poems touch many aspects of women's lives. The stories feature strong, uncompromising description and accurate insight. The poems are sensitive, often narrative, and deeply moving. 'When You're Asleep' describes the emotional burden of a daughter's visit to her ageing mother. 'I'm worn out with you' the poem opens, and the persona continues with a list of complaints against her mother. The mother tries to keep her daughter in the room by repeated questioning and recalling memories. Despite her exhaustion, the daughter knows these are 'festival days' for her:

days you can talk
all day long
out loud for a change
morning to night,
banqueting
because I'm here
to listen.

The daughter becomes the mother, repeating the 'old litany' of warnings, until, finally, looking in on her sleeping mother, she is returned to her own childhood:

when I would call out
at night
as you closed the door
to hold you there
one moment longer
Do you love me still? [3]

Works:

Kindling. London: Onlywomen Press, 1982. Poetry.

A Noise from the Woodshed. London: Onlywomen Press, 1989. Stories.

Moving into the Space Cleared by Our Mothers. Galway: Salmon Publishing, 1991. Poetry.

Notes

1. 'The spaces between the words: Mary Dorcey talks to Nuala Archer', *Woman's Review of Books*. 8, 3 (December 1990) 21.
2. In *A Noise from the Woodshed*, 1.
3. In *Moving into the Space Cleared by Our Mothers*, 79-82.

Dufferin, Lady (Helen Selina Sheridan Blackwood)
Born: England, 1807; Died: 1867
Educated: England.

Helen Selina Sheridan was born in England. She married Captain Price Blackwood, heir to the marquess of Dufferin and Ava in 1825, and the couple lived in Italy where their son was born. She was the grand-daughter of Richard Brinsley Sheridan, the ancestor of Caroline Blackwood.

Her husband died in 1841, and in 1862 she married the Earl of Gifford. She wrote poems and ballads, some of which were set to music, including the very popular 'The Irish Emigrant', from which the following lines are taken.

I'm sitting on the stile, Mary,
Where we sat, side by side,
That bright May morning long ago
When first you were my bride.
The corn was springing fresh and green,
The lark sang loud and high,
The red was on your lip, Mary,
The love-light in your eye.[1]

Works:
Lispings from Low Latitudes. London: J Murray, 1863. Poetry.

Notes
1. In *Pillars of the House*, edited by A A Kelly (Dublin: Wolfhound, 1988), 38.

— E —

Edgeworth, Maria
Born: England, 1767; Died: 1849
Educated: England.

There is some confusion as to whether Maria Edgeworth was born in 1767 or 1768; she was born to Richard Lovell Edgeworth and Anna Maria Elers Edgeworth at Black Bourton, her mother's family home. She spent her first five years at Black Bourton with her mother and her mother's family, while her father absented himself from his unhappy marriage, the education of his young son his object and excuse. When her mother, whom Maria remembers as 'always crying', died, Richard Lovell married Honora Sneyd and brought his family to live at his family home, Edgeworthstown, in Ireland. Maria was both unhappy and difficult here — perhaps the one state led to the other — and after two years was sent to boarding-school in England. Letters from the school years suggest the child's eagerness and anxiety to remain in her distant family's good graces and affections, while the rather chilly responses from the parents frequently note the child's inadequacies.[1]

In 1782, however, when Honora died and Richard Lovell married her sister Elizabeth, Maria returned home to be her father's assistant and book-keeper, and teacher to her younger siblings. In her journeys with her father to his tenants and through the countryside, she absorbed the experiences and opinions that would be reflected in her fictions about Ireland. But these were in the future. For the moment, the practical Richard Lovell Edgeworth was intent on turning his daughter into a useful and knowledgeable member of the community. The first task he assigned her was to research the Irish economy and constitution and to write a report on 'the causes of poverty in Ireland'. Thus began the teacher/apprentice relationship that Maria Edgeworth prized so highly, and the career as prolific author of stories for children and novels.

In her fiction, Maria Edgeworth is a keen observer in two areas: the comedy of manners and Irish life. *Ennui* (1809) and *The Absentee* (1812) draw somewhat exaggerated pictures of ideal landlords and thieving agents. The problems created by absentee landlords are dramatised, the same problems Richard Lovell faced on his return to Ireland and which Maria recounts in her *Memoirs of Richard Lovell Edgeworth, Esq.*(1820). Trips to London and Paris gave Maria Edgeworth the opportunity to become a close observer of the manners and characters of society. *Belinda* (1801) and *Patronage* (1814) rely on these observations. Cross-dressing plays an important part in *Belinda*, a daring innovation for Edgeworth

Another work written with her father, *Essays on Irish Bulls* (1802), a collection of the unique, humorous, and contradictory expressions in the English language of Irish people, reveals her keen ear for the colourful phrase. The accurate rendering of this language enriches much of her fiction, particularly her masterpiece, *Castle Rackrent* (1800). This brings up a critical problem: commentators have long debated the nature of Richard Lovell Edgeworth's influence on his daughter. Many, citing the excellence of *Castle Rackrent*, the novel written without his assistance, have blamed him for the didacticism that mars some of her work. Certainly she prized her father's good opinion — her letters show her anxiety that he consider her a 'worthy' partner — and her fiction was usually designed to illustrate themes he suggested. But evidence also suggests, as Marilyn Butler demonstrates in her biography, that Maria herself was the source of the didacticism. In addition, the anxiety born in the child by her mother's death and nourished through years of exile in English schools may have caused her excessive desire to please her father. What we can say with certainty is that *Castle Rackrent*, the novel written without the father's advice or assistance, is the one instance where Maria Edgeworth's material seems to take on a life of its own, a life than soars above confining morals.

Castle Rackrent was rehearsed and written in the company of her closest intimates, her Ruxton relatives, particularly her Aunt Ruxton to whom she was particularly close and her cousin Sophy. It was written, the author notes, 'for mere amusement without any ideas of publishing'. As a result, Maria Edgeworth felt free to explore delicate areas she might not have entered otherwise. The work examines four generations of Irish landlords who exemplify horrors of landlordism that no system of contracts, even that proposed by Richard Lovell Edgeworth, could mitigate. Further, in this one work, Edgeworth, who usually wrote comedy concluding in marriage, 'frees' all the Rackrent wives from their miserly, tyrannous, or parasitical husbands. This aspect, arguably the most revolutionary in all of Edgeworth's work, has been ignored, as critics focus on the traditional area of interest, the Rackrent men as landlords. Maria was herself a spinster, who refused a proposal of marriage.

Unfortunately Maria Edgeworth never risked such freedom again, and after her father's death in 1817 she wrote little. Ireland, she said, had become too dark, the situation – land struggles – too terrible for her to depict. She died in 1849.

Selected Works:
The Parent's Assistant: or Stories for Children. 1796; 1800; rpt. New York: Garland, 1976. Children's Stories.
Essays on Practical Education. 1798; rpt. New York: Garland, 1974. Children's Stories.
Castle Rackrent. 1800; rpt. London: Oxford, 1964, 1982. Novel.
Belinda. London: Johnson, 1801. Novel.

Moral Tales for Young People. London: Johnson, 1801. Childen's
Stories.
Essays on Irish Bulls. London: Johnson, 1802. Essays.
Popular Tales. London: Johnson, 1804. Stories.
The Modern Griselda. London: Johnson, 1805. Novel.
Leonora. London: Johnson, 1806. Novel.
Ennui. 1809; rpt. New York: Garland, 1978. Novel.
The Absentee. 1812; rpt. London: Oxford University Press, 1988.
Novel.
Patronage. London: Johnson, 1814. Novel.
Ormond. 1817; rpt. New York: Garland, 1978. Novel.
*Memoirs of Richard Lovell Edgeworth, Esq. Begun by himself and
completed by his daughter*. London: Hunter, 1820. Memoirs.
Helen: A Tale. London: Bentley, 1834. Novel.

Notes
1. For information on Maria Edgeworth's life, see Marilyn
   Butler, *Maria Edgeworth: A Literary Biography* (Oxford:
   Clarendon Press, 1972).

Edwards, Ruth Dudley
Born: Ireland, 1944
Educated: Ireland, England.

Ruth Dudley Edwards was born in Dublin, took her BA
and MA in History at University College, Dublin, in 1964,
and 1968, and her D Lit in 1990. She received the Diploma
in Business Studies from the City of London Polytechnic in
1973. She has held many positions, including lecturer in
History and English, marketing executive, civil servant,
and company historian to *The Economist*. Currently living
in England, she is chairwoman of the British Association
for Irish Studies, a member of the Executive Committee of
the British-Irish Association, and a reviewer in Irish and
English newspapers and journals.

Ruth Dudley Edwards has published history,
biography, and crime fiction. She received the Irish
Historical Research Prize in 1978 for her work on Patrick

Pearse, a leader of the 1916 Rising. She also received the James Tait Black Memorial Prize for Biography in 1988 for her biography of the publisher Victor Gollancz. At first glance, historical biography and crime fiction may seem distant relatives, but she notes her prime interest in both is 'the human personality'. Her mother introduced her in childhood to the classic English crime novelists, Dorothy Sayers, Margery Allingham, Cyril Hare and Ngaio Marsh, and she has retained this interest since.[1]

Edwards' biographies have certainly succeeded in revealing the 'human personality' so often buried beneath the facts and events of history. Her detailed examination and analysis of the life of Patrick Pearse, and the resultant picture of an often tortured character, sparked fresh interest in both the Rising and in Pearse. Similarly, the picture of Victor Gollancz holds the reader, whether or not she is interested in the history of publishing.

The four thrillers are set in England. *Corridors of Death* (1981), the first, presents a picture of British civil servants as viciously involved in petty schemes for their own recognition and their peers' downfalls. The wonder is not that two murders are committed, but that at least one was not committed long before. Edwards knows British institutions well; fond of them, she views them with the 'natural irreverence' of the Irish.[2] Her thrillers are well-worked-out; despite the clues, most readers will be surprised at the denouement.

Works:

An Atlas of Irish History. London: Methuen, 1973,1981. History.

Patrick Pearse: The Triumph of Failure. London: Gollancz; New York: Taplinger, 1977; London: Faber & Faber, 1979; Dublin: Poolbeg, 1990. Biography.

James Connolly. Dublin: Gill and Macmillan: 1981. Biography.

Harold Macmillan: A Life in Pictures. London: Macmillan, 1983. Biography.

Victor Gollancz: A Biography. London: Gollancz, 1987. Biography.

Corridors of Death. London: Quartet; New York: St Martin's Press, 1981; Italy: Mondadori, as *Tutti E Nessuno*, 1985; London: Gollancz, 1991. Novel.

The Saint Valentine's Day Murders. London: Quartet; New York: St Martin's Press, 1984; London: Gollancz, 1992. Novel.

The School of English Murder. London: Gollancz; New York: St Martin's Press, as *The English School of Murder*, 1990. Novel.

Clubbed to Death. London: Gollancz; New York: St Martin's Press, 1992. Novel.

Notes

1. Personal communication.
2. Personal communication.

Egerton, George

Born: Australia, 1859; Died: 1945
Educated: Australia, Ireland.

Mary Chavelita Dunne Bright, who wrote under the name George Egerton, was born to Irish parents in Australia; her father's improvidence caused the family great hardship. She was brought up in Ireland, became travelling companion to Mr and Mrs Higginson, and eloped with Higginson to Norway, where she was very impressed with the Norwegian literary revolution. In 1891, after Higginson's death, she married George Egerton Clairmonte, lived in Co. Cork, and wrote a collection of short stories, *Keynotes* (1893), which introduced the Ibsen women to Ireland.[1] She wrote several other volumes of stories or tales, as well as translations and biographies of her contemporaries.

Egerton focuses on women's sexuality as desirable and condemns those, mothers or husbands, who fail to see it so. 'Virgin Soil', from *Keynotes*, illustrates the high cost of Victorian modesty and ignorance.

The bridegroom is waiting in the hall; with a trifle of impatience he is tracing the pattern of the linoleum with the point of his umbrella. He curbs it and laughs, showing his strong white teeth at a remark of his best man; then compares the time by his hunter with the

118

clock on the stairs. He is florid, bright-eyed, loose-lipped, inclined to stoutness, but kept in good condition; his hair is crisp, curly, slightly grey; his ears peculiar, pointed at their tops like a faun's. He looks very big and well-dressed, and, when he smiles, affable enough.

Upstairs a young girl, with the suns of seventeen summers on her brown head, is lying with her face hidden on her mother's shoulder; she is sobbing with great childish sobs, regardless of reddened eyes and the tears that have splashed on the silk of her grey going-away gown.[2]

Five years later, the young woman returns to blame her mother for condemning her to a life of revulsion with a man she could not love: "'I say it is your fault, because you reared me a fool, an idiot, ignorant of everything I ought to have known, everything that concerned me and the life I was bound to lead as a wife; my physical needs, my coming passion, the very meaning of my sex, my wifehood and motherhood to follow. You gave me not one weapon in my hand to defend myself against the possible attacks of man at his worst. You sent me out to fight the biggest battle of a woman's life, the one in which she ought to know every turn of the game, with a white gauze" — she laughs derisively — "of maiden purity as a shield.'" (29)

Works:

Keynotes. London: Matthews & Lane; Boston: Roberts Brothers, 1893. Stories.

Discords. London: Lane, 1894. Stories.

Symphonies. London: Lane, 1897. Stories.

The Wheel of God. London: Richards, 1898. Novel.

Fantasias. London/New York: The Bodley Head, 1898. Stories.

Rosa Amorosa: The Love Letters of a Woman. London: Richards, 1901. Novel.

Flies in Amber. London: Hutchinson, 1905. Novel.

Notes

1. *A Biographical Dictionary of Irish Writers*, Anne M Brady and Brian Cleeve, eds. (Mullingar: The Lilliput Press, 1985), 71-72.

2. In *Woman's Part, An Anthology of Short Fiction By and About Irish Women 1890-1960*, Janet Madden-Simpson, ed. (Dublin: Arlen House, 1984), 21.

Enright, Anne

Born: Ireland, 1962
Educated: Ireland, Canada, England.

Anne Enright was born in Dublin and went to school there and in Vancouver, Canada. She attended Trinity College, Dublin, and the University of East Anglia, worked as an actress and writer, and is currently employed at RTE (Irish Radio and Television).[1] Her first volume of short stories to date, *The Portable Virgin* (1991), won the Rooney Prize.

Enright's style is unconventional: the narrative generally moves through a series of very short, paragraph-long sections, precisely focused shots into a character's consciousness. Her characters are sharply intelligent, keen and ironic observers of themselves and those around them. Betrayals, or perceived betrayals, abound. Mary, the narrator of the title story, thinks her husband has betrayed her with a woman also called Mary: 'She was one of those women who hold their skin like a smile, as if she was afraid her face might fall off if the tension went out of her eyes. I knew that when Ben made love to her, the thought that she might break pushed him harder. I, by comparison, am like an old sofa, welcoming, familiar, well-designed.'[2]

This is a conventional story, the narrator warns, so, as Ben, her husband, drinks his gin and tonic in placid contentment, she interrupts: '"Thoroughly fucked?" I asked and he spilt his drink.' (82) Three short sections follow; Ben answers in the affirmative, and the narrator imagines possible resolutions. A fourth short section suggests a more definite resolution: 'Mrs Rochester punched a hole in the ceiling and looked at Ben where he sat at the end of the bed, maimed and blind. She whispered a long and very sensible monologue with an urgency that made the mattress smoulder, and we both had a good laugh about that.'(83)

Enright often uses literary and historical references to reveal personality and shed light on situations. Her intelligent narrators humour with their wit, but they also demand that the reader exercise her intelligence and put the pieces together.

Works:
The Portable Virgin. 1991; rpt. London: Minerva, 1992. Stories.

Notes
1. Introductory Note in *The Portable Virgin.*
2. *The Portable Virgin,* 81.

— *F* —

Finlay, Lilian Roberts
Born: Malta, 1915
Educated: Ireland.

Lilian Roberts Finlay tells her story eloquently: 'My father, a professional soldier in a Welsh Regiment, and my mother were honeymooning in Malta when the 1914 War was declared. In December 1914 my father's regiment was ordered to the Front. Seven weeks later I was born. In great wartime difficulty, my mother managed to get home to Dublin with her infant. When my father had furlough, the pair met in London. He never saw his daughter. In November 1918, released and on the way home, he (and many thousands) contracted Spanish Flu. He died and was buried in Holland. Four years later, the tragic (and very lovely) war-widow married again – a handsome libertine, a man beloved of many women, and irresistible to a lonely child. The festering memories of a child set aside, had to find a catalyst in *Always In My Mind*'.[1]

The child, Lilian Roberts Finlay, was educated by the French nuns at Mount Sackville, 'the very best and most expensive that my beautiful mother aspired to, and to pay for which she toiled to death'. She studied acting at the Abbey Theatre School from 1936-38, and submitted many plays to the theatre, all of which were rejected. The play themes were taken from the life she saw: 'too many children, too little money, the need for contraception, the pleas for divorce, the grinding subjugation of women,' and greatly agitated the manager of the Abbey, Ernest Blythe,

122

who finally bawled her out. 'Stop sending in plays about adultery, divorce, birth-control. If I were to stage any of your efforts (and I have no intention of so doing) the Archbishop of Dublin, Dr John Charles McQuaid, would close down this Theatre, and I would get the sack. ... Moreover, your plays have no basis in truth or fact. There will never be divorce in Ireland, nor prostitutes. And as for your sexual-congress out of the marriage-bed, that may happen in England, but never here, and certainly not on the stage of this National Theatre.'[2] The dispirited author went home and built bonfires with her manuscripts.

During the busy days of bringing up ten children and losing two to diphtheria, 'a never forgotten heartbreak', she wrote and published short stories in magazines. Now widowed and a full-time writer, she has published *Always In My Mind* (1988), the fictionalised story of her mother and father, and is working on the sequel and on a TV script for this very popular novel. *A Bona Fide Husband*, a collection of short stories, was published in 1991, and another novel, *Stella*, in 1992. Indefatigable, however, she has also completed a volume of verse, *The Distaff of Despair*, and is attempting to find time and resources for the project she most wants to write: the life of Susanna Centlivre, a seventeenth-century romantic Irish dramatist in the London theatre. Her work is inspired not by single events, but by all events. 'Sometimes I think writing is the bad wish given by the bad fairy at birth. Ideas swarm and demand words to hold them.'[3]

Always In My Mind is a story of love remembered, of moral courage and integrity in the most brutal of times. Living in Dublin during the years after World War I, the young Catholic Lia is spoiled and neglected until she meets and loves a Jewish boy. Although their ways part, Lia remembers, loves, and defends Tadek through her years of schooling and acting in the Abbey, and during the awful days of World War II.

In contrast, *A Bona Fide Husband* explores the small moments of clarity amidst the disillusionments and disappointments that make up most lives. Full of variety, this collection runs from the defining – though ordinary – moments of life, to the strange romance of 'Sea Horses', and the mysteries underlying apparently mundane surfaces. Misinterpretation and the inability to communicate are often problems, as in the dryly humorous 'A Bona Fide Husband', 'A Kind of Comfort', and 'Letter from the Past'. Ironically, the failure of communication becomes the text of the richest communications, 'The Love-Gift', for example, and 'Framed in Silver'. The reader returns to these stories, drawn by the many and various meanings in Finlay's suggestive prose.

Works:
Always In My Mind. London: Collins, 1988; New York: St Martin's Press, 1988. Novel.
A Bona Fide Husband. Dublin: Poolbeg, 1991. Stories.
Stella. Dublin: Poolbeg, 1992. Novel.
Forever In The Past. Sequel to *Always In My Mind*. Publication scheduled Spring 1993. Novel.

Notes
1. Personal communication.
2. Personal communication.
3. Personal communication.

Finney, Patricia
Born: England, 1958
Educated: England.

Patricia Finney was born in London in 1959 and educated in England. She is the daughter of barrister parents, of Irish descent on her father's side, Hungarian on her mother's. Her father's mother was a Gallagher from Cork and her uncle was Frank Gallagher, an Irish writer and friend of Lady Gregory. Her father's father was a Liberal MP and worked in the Council of Action for Peace and

Reconstruction. Her mother's father was leader of the last opposition in the Hungarian parliament, and her grandmother was a novelist in Hungary.[1] Politics and literature loom large in Patricia Finney's background, so it is not surprising that this writer's two novels would investigate and intermingle the politics of myth, Irish, with the myths of history, Roman.

Finney was only seventeen when she wrote the first novel, *A Shadow of Gulls* (1977), a story by and of Lugh Mac Romain, the Harper, which continues in the second novel, *The Crow Goddess* (1978). Lugh's adventures take place in Ireland and Britain in the second century AD. Lugh is the son of Roman and Irish parents, and the stories he tells his friend, the Emperor Hadrian, are the stories of the Ulster Cycle, of the Great Cattle Raid of Cooley, of Maeve, Cuchulain, and Deirdre of the Sorrows.

Works:
A Shadow of Gulls. London: Collins, 1977. Novel.
The Crow Goddess. London: Collins, 1978. Novel.
The Firedrake's Eye. New York: St Martin's, 1992. Novel.

Notes
1. Author's Introduction, *A Shadow of Gulls*.

Fitzgerald, (née Gregg) Barbara
Born: 1911; Died: 1982
Educated: England, Ireland.

Barbara Fitzgerald Gregg went to school in London and later graduated from Trinity College, Dublin with high honours in French and Italian. She was the youngest daughter of Dr J A F Gregg, who was Bishop of Ossory, Archbishop of Dublin, and Primate of the Church of Ireland (1939-59).

After she married Michael Fitzgerald Somerville from Co. Cork, they spent most of their lives in West Africa.

Barbara's first novel *We are Besieged* (1946) was published with a Book Society recommendation. Her second novel *Footprints Upon Waters* although completed in 1955, was not published until 1983. It concerns an Anglo-Irish family struggling to come to terms with 'a frightening new Ireland.'[1]

Works:
We are Besieged. London: Davies, 1946. Novel.
Footprints upon Water. Belfast: Blackstaff, 1983. Novel.

Notes:
1. Publicity material from Blackstaff Press.

Fitzgibbon, Theodora Rosling
Born: England, 1916; Died: 1991
Educated: England, Belgium, France.

Theodora Rosling was born to Irish parents in London. She was brought up in Tipperary and Clare and is best-known as a writer of excellent cookbooks. She contributed a weekly column to *The Irish Times*, and also wrote her memoirs and one novel. *A Taste of Ireland* (1968), which features nostalgic photographs of Ireland in the nineteenth and early twentieth centuries, alongside traditional recipes, rhymes, and friendly words of wisdom, was extremely popular and introduced Irish food to international audiences.

Selected Works:
A Taste of Ireland. New York: Avenel Books, 1968. Cookery.
Flight of the Kingfisher. London: Dent, 1967. Novel.

FitzSimon, Ellen O'Connell

Born: Ireland, 1805; Died: 1883
Educated: Ireland.

Ellen O'Connell wrote romantic, sentimental, and nostalgic poetry. 'To the Queen', written in 1837 opens with broad flattery:

Fair Queen! We greet thee
With blessings and smiles
Thou art the hope
And the pride of these Isles.
May thy deeds still be
What good men approve;
May each day increase
Thy people's love!

The flattery paves the way for the request:

For reform made complete
England looks up to thee,
And Scotland expects
A like blessing to see;
While Ireland, long wronged,
In the dawn of thy reign
Sees the day star of hope
Rise triumphant again![1]

Other poems are lighter, 'To a little niece, on Valentine's Day', for example, or more nostalgic, such as, 'The Song of the Irish Emigrant in America'. Ellen O'Connell was the eldest daughter of Daniel O'Connell, the statesman credited with achieving Catholic Emancipation.

Works:
Derrynane in 1832 and Other Poems. Dublin: W B Kelly; London: Burns and Lambert, 1863. Poetry.

Notes
1. In *Derrynane in 1832 and Other Poems*, 68, 69.

Flitton, Sheila

Born: Ireland, 1937
Educated: Ireland, England.

Sheila Flitton was born in Cork where she attended Saint Mary's of the Isle Convent from the age of five to thirteen. She did various jobs until she was sixteen and then left for England. There, like the heroine in her first novel, *Notions* (1991), she bluffed her way into nursing college, pursued the acting career she had begun in Cork, married and began her family of four children. The family returned to Ireland, and while bringing up her children, Sheila 'had time to observe human behaviour,' and began writing three minute talks for radio. 'I wrote about thirty-two in a year,' she notes, 'while sitting at rivers fishing with my kids. I have never stopped writing since.'[1] The challenge of The Irish Life Competition in a national newspaper prompted her to try her hand at a play; the result was *Harbour Nights*. Although criticised by the competition adjudicator, the play — starring the author — received excellent reviews in 1979. She has received awards in the Listowel Writers' Week for her first full-length play, *For Better or for Worse* (1984), and for an essay.

Notions, the novel published in 1991, is set in the 1940s, and the heroines move from Cork to England. The girls, Julia and Lil, reflect much of the young Sheila Flitton's originality and independence: bored with work in the shoe factory in Cork, they refuse to take the dullness of life seriously. Even when their boss, Mr O'Sullivan, fires them, warning, 'We'll see how far your notions get you when you find yourselves on the dole queue,' the girls take refuge in the toilet to collapse in laughter.[2] When the local paper carries an ad for a maid in England, the girls both apply rather than split up, 'Two for the price of one.' Although England is a strange place, Julia and Lil laugh and charm their way through domestic service, nursing, and romance. Nothing gets these girls down, and this tale of their loyalty to each other sparkles with their humour.

Works:
Notions. Cork: Glencree Publications, 1991. Novel.
Whispers. Cork: Glencree Publications, 1992. Novel.

Notes
1. Personal communication.
2. *Notions*.

Flood-Ladd, Doris
Born: Ireland, c̲ 20th century
Educated: Ireland.

Doris Flood-Ladd's popular novel, *The Irish* (1982), tells the story of Nora and Seán O'Sullivan, emigrants in the USA in the early 1900s.

Works:
The Irish. London: Star, 1982. Novel.

Frances, Mary E
Born: Ireland, 1859; Died: 1930
Educated: Ireland.

Born of an Anglo-Irish family at Killiney Park, near Dublin, Mary E Frances grew up in Co. Laois (then known as Queen's County). As a child Mary and her sisters (two of whom also became writers) wrote fiction and founded their own family magazine. Mary's own first short story appeared in the *Irish Monthly*. Throughout her long career many of her stories had a religious influence. *Daughters of the Soil* (1895) was the first novel to be published serially in the weekly edition of *The Times*. Besides writing many novels and shorts stories she also wrote her reminiscences. Her fiction takes up themes which are distinctly, resoundingly feminist. Mary Frances' ability to appeal to her readers' emotions explains her great popularity during her writing career. Several of her novels, particularly *Miss Erin* (1898) are serious examinations of the evils of Irish society, especially as they affect the lives of women. She published her work as Mrs Frances Blundel.

Selected Works:
Miss Erin. Methuen, London: 1905. Novel.

Furlong, Alice
Born: Ireland, 1875; Died: 1946
Educated: Ireland.

Alice Furlong was born in Co. Dublin. Her poetry and stories of Ireland were published in many journals and papers, and collected into two volumes. She is listed as vice-president of the *ad-hoc* committee of women, 'The Patriotic Children's Treat Committee', founded to establish a treat for Irish children who were not invited, or did not choose to attend, the treat put on to welcome Queen Victoria to Dublin in 1900. She was also present at the inaugural meeting of Inghinidhe na hÉireann, the Daughters of Ireland, in October 1900, and was elected one of the vice-presidents.[1]

Works:
Roses and Rue. London: Mathews, 1899. Poetry.
Tales of Fairy Folks, Queens and Heroes. Dublin; Browne & Nolan, 1907. Stories.

Notes
1. Margaret Ward, *Unmanageable Revolutionaries* (London: Pluto Press, 1983), 48, 50.

— G —

Gallagher, Miriam
Born: Ireland, 1940
Educated: Ireland.

Born in Co. Waterford, Miriam Gallagher has had plays professionally produced in Dublin for over ten years.

She completed a very successful speaking tour of North America in 1992 and has directed many workshops in venues as diverse as community areas to prisons.

Her plays draw on real-life events; *Labels* is set in a hospital where an investigation into over-prescribing of drugs is about to take place. She has won many awards at amateur drama festivals, and recently finished a commissioned screenplay.[1]

Works
Let's Help Our Children Talk. Dublin: O'Brien Press. 1977. Prose.
Fancy Footwork. Dublin: Society of Irish Playwrights. 1991. 12 plays.

Notes
1. *Evening Press*, 8 August 1992.

Gore-Booth, Eva
Born: Ireland, 1870; Died: 1926
Educated: Ireland.

Eva Gore-Booth was born in Lissadell, Co. Sligo, the daughter of Anglo-Irish landlords and sister of Constance, Countess Markievicz. Unlike her militant sister, Constance, she did not believe in armed struggle, and worked instead in organisations to improve industrial conditions and to educate women politically. She lived in England from 1914-16, was secretary to the Women's Textile and Other Workers' Representation Committee, edited *The Women's Labour News*, and was an enthusiastic member of the Women's Peace Crusade. During this time, she wrote poems and plays and spent many years in partnership with Esther Roper.

Returning to see her imprisoned sister in 1916, she was horrified to arrive in Dublin on the day of James Connolly's execution. Like her sister she was beautiful, fearless, and admired by Yeats.[1]

Gore-Booth's poetry is beautifully crafted and sophisticated; subjects include separatist and woman-loving themes. Though many are conventional in subject and pattern. 'Roses,' which follows, is a good example:

When her twigs are bare
In the grim air,
And her leaves are shed,
Is the rose dead?

Does she dream, does she sleep,
In her roots buried deep?
Does she lie at rest
With the earth on her breast?

Ah no, the Rose goes —
The spirit of the Rose
Blooms, and is fair
Elsewhere.

Behold, there is no birth
From the earth to the earth,
But the Roses, wise and dear,
Live in heaven half the year.[2]

Selected Works:
Poems of Eva Gore Booth. Introduced by Esther Roper. London: Longmans, Green and Co. 1929. (Complete Works)

Notes
1. Esther Roper, 'Introduction', *Poems of Eva Gore-Booth*.
2. 'Roses' from *The Egyptian Pillar* in *Poems of Eva Gore-Booth*.

Greene, Angela
Born: Ireland, c 20th century
Educated: Ireland.

Angela Greene was born in Dublin and now lives in Drogheda, Co. Louth. Her poetry has been published in newspapers, poetry journals, anthologies, and textbooks; selections appear in *Trio Poetry 6* and *New Women Poets*. Her poems have been broadcast on BBC Radio Ulster and RTE radio. Her poem, 'The Path', was performed in 'Sunny Side Plucked', in association with Dublin 1991 – European City of Culture and RTE. She won the Patrick Kavanagh Award in 1988 and was shortlisted for the *Sunday Tribune*/Hennessy Literary Award in 1989. She has one volume of poetry, *Silence and the Blue Night* (1992).[1]

Greene's poetry focuses on human and plant life. 'Destiny', the first poem in the *Trio* collection, is an imaginative recreation of the persona's mother, young and beautiful, 'her eyelids were the damson's bloom/and her cheeks were ripe.' Then married, pregnant, and pregnant again as the child watches through the window:

I saw her thighs
heaped like bruised poppies onto the white sheet.

I shush by that April window
till, in its searchings, her voice finds me out.
Its thin cries pierce me.

They sift down my blood like blown seed
from somewhere
far off.[2]

In 'For This Day', the very sick woman tries 'to forget the unriddable — the quick/cold hands, cold words/dropped in those textbook rooms,' as life throbs all around her, 'a fragile thing,/ or unmeant gift, which might be snatched away.' (11) 'Wasteland' and 'A Life' celebrate a woman's busy life, even unto death:

Were you the tissue paper on flapper's finery,
the outraged at Hollywood's latest;
the lamp's-glow mothing children,
the ceaseless care of the aged?

Were you the art of living
clinched in that brittle diminishing round ...

You are a sprig of rosemary at a wake,
You are a handful of clay on a coffin lid. (13)

Works:
Silence and the Blue Night. Galway: Salmon Publishing, 1992.
    Poetry.

Notes
1. Personal communication.
2. *Trio Poetry 6*, 4; All poetry quoted is from *Trio Poetry 6*.

Gregory, Lady Isabella Augusta Persse
Born: Ireland, 1852; Died: 1932.
Educated: Ireland.

Isabella Augusta Persse was born at Roxborough House, Co. Galway. She met Sir William Gregory on a visit to Italy in 1879 and married him in 1880. She was twenty-eight; he sixty-three. Robert, the only child of the Gregorys, was killed during World War I. William Gregory was a scholar, a supporter of liberal causes, and owner of the Coole estate, one of the great joys of Lady Gregory's life. Lady Gregory attributed her sympathetic response to Irish causes to her nurse Mary Sheridan, who probably also developed her interest in mythology long before the famous meeting with Yeats in 1897 or 1898.

After her first biographical work, Lady Gregory turned to Irish myth and poetry; *Cuchulain of Muirthemne* (1902), *Poets and Dreamers* (1903), *Gods and Fighting Men* (1904). Her interest turned to the theatre when she met Yeats, and she, Yeats, and Synge became the directors of the theatre they founded, the Abbey. Lady Gregory's *Spreading the News* in *Seven Short Plays* (1909) was produced at the opening of the Abbey in 1904, along with Yeats's *Hour Glass*. She became an ardent defender of the Abbey's right, indeed duty, to stage plays which she deemed educational but not didactic, nationalistic but not simplistic. She condemned the *Playboy* riots in 1907, although she did not like the play, and she even took on Dublin Castle over the Abbey's right to produce Shaw's *The Showing Up of Blanco Posnet*.

Lady Gregory gathered Irish stories with Yeats and on her own. She spoke Irish and engaged in active research on the eighteenth-century blind poet Raftery, rediscovered by her friend Douglas Hyde. She translated several of Hyde's plays and collected Irish poetry and history. Besides the collection and research work, and work on behalf of the theatre and playwrights, she also wrote and fought for the preservation of Coole and for the establishment of a gallery to house the art bequest of her nephew Hugh Lane. Despite all this activity, she also wrote many plays. Several of these, *Grania* (1912), for instance, present Irish myths from a woman's perspective – a change indeed on the originals.[1]

Selected Works:

Cuchulain of Muirthemne. London: J Murray, 1902. Myth.

Poets and Dreamers. London: J Murray, 1903. Essay and Translations from Irish.

Gods and Fighting Men. London: Murray, 1904. Myth.

A Book of Saints and Wonders. London: Murray, 1906. Folktales.

The Kiltartan History Book. Dublin: Maunsel, 1909. Folk History.

Seven Short Plays. Dublin: Maunsel, 1909. Plays.

The Kiltartan Wonder Book. Dublin: Maunsel, 1910. Folktales.

The Kiltartan Moliere. Dublin: Maunsel, 1910. Translations.

Irish Folk-History Plays. First Series. London: Putnam, 1912. Plays.

Irish Folk-History Plays. Second Series. London: Putnam, 1912. Plays.

New Comedies. London: Putnam, 1913. Plays.

Our Irish Theatre. London: Putnam, 1913. Memoir.

The Kiltartan Poetry Book. London: Putnam, 1918. Poetry.

Visions and Beliefs in the West of Ireland. London: Putnam, 1920. Folktales.

Hugh Lane's Life and Achievement. London: Murray, 1921. Biography.

The Image and Other Plays. London: Putnam, 1922. Plays.

Three Wonder Plays. London: Putnam, 1923. Plays.

A Case for the Return of Sir Hugh Lane's Pictures to Dublin. Dublin: Talbot, 1926. Argument.

Three Last Plays. London: Putnam, 1928. Plays.

My First Play: Colman and Guaire. London: Elkin Mathews and Marrot, 1930. Play.

Coole. Dublin: Cuala, 1931. Memoir.

Lady Gregory's Journals 1916-1930. Edited by Lennox Robinson. London: Putnam, 1946. Journals.

Notes

1. See *Lady Gregory's Journals*, or any biography, for details of her life. For an account of both her life and her work, see Hazard Adams, *Lady Gregory* (Lewisburg: Bucknell, 1973).

Grierson, Constantia
Born: Ireland, 1706; Died: 1733
Self-taught.

Constantia Grierson is recognised as an entirely self-taught poet and scholar. She lived in Kilkenny in the eighteenth century and enjoyed the patronage of Lord Cartenet, who helped to have her work published in 1755. [1]

Works:
Poems by Eminent Ladies Vol. 1. London, 1755. Poetry.

Notes
1. *Pillars of the House.* A A Kelly. Dublin: Wolfhound, 1988.

Grimshaw, Beatrice
Born: Ireland, 1871; Died: 1953
Educated: England, France.

Beatrice Grimshaw was born in Cloona, Co. Antrim, and educated in Belfast, London, and Normandy. In her twenties, she moved to Dublin to work as a journalist, where her record-breaking bicycling achievements earned her the sub-editorship of a sporting paper She was also editor of the *Social Review.*

Tired of life in Dublin, she moved to London, where she offered press coverage to shipping companies in exchange for her passage to exotic places. She journeyed to Tahiti in 1906, and this six-month round-the-world trip so delighted her that she devoted the rest of her life to seeing the world. An expert on the Pacific islands, she ran a coffee plantation in Papua, New Guinea, and was the first white woman to go up the Sepik and Fly rivers. She earned her living by writing over thirty novels, several travel books, articles for *Wide World Magazine* and *The National Geographic,* and material for the in-house journals of shipping companies. Often set in the exotic spots she visited, the novels were very popular.[1]

Selected Works:
Brokenaway. London & New York: Lane, 1897. Novel.
The Little Red Speck, and Other South Seas Stories. London: Hurst & Blackett, 1921. Stories.
My South Sea Sweetheart. New York: Macmillan, 1921. Novel.
Conn of the Coral Seas. New York: Macmillan, 1922. Novel.
Black Sheep's Gold. New York: Holt, 1927. Novel.

Notes
1. A A Kelly: Paper presented at International Association for the Study of Anglo-Irish Literature, Trinity College, Dublin, July 1992.

Gubbens, Charlotte

Born: c 1825; Died: nd
Educated: Ireland.

Little is known about Charlotte Gubbins. She published a long narrative poem relating how poteen-makers get caught. This is contained in *One Day's Journal: a story of the revenue police and other poems*.[1]

Works
One Day's Journal; a story of the revenue police and other poems. Independant and General Printing Office, Sligo. 1862. Poetry.

Notes
1. From A A Kelly's *Pillars of the House*, 47.

— H —

Hall, Anna Maria Fielding
Born: Ireland, 1800; Died: 1881
Educated: Ireland.

Born in Dublin, Anna Maria Fielding was taken as a baby to Bannow, Co. Wexford, the home of her mother's second husband. She lived there until the family moved to London, where she met and married Samuel Carter Hall, a young man interested in a literary career. From 1824 on, the Halls worked together, writing, editing, travelling, and conducting philanthropic work.

She wrote nine novels, many books for children, and books of travel and religious tracts. Like many of her contemporaries, Maria Edgeworth for instance, she examines Irish peasants from outside, but her work receives less attention than Edgeworth's, today. Her early Irish novels, *Sketches of Irish Character* (1829), for example, are idyllic, but *Lights and Shadows of Irish Life, Vol 2,* (1838), written after she revisited Ireland in 1834, is a grimmer work, one, as she said herself, that contains more 'shadows' than 'lights'.[1]

Selected Works:
Sketches of Irish Character. London: F Westley & AH Davis, 1829. Sketches.
The Buccaneer. London: R Bentley, 1840. Novel.
The Outlaw. London: R Bentley, 1847. Novel.
Tales of Women's Trials. London: Houlston, 1835. Stories.
The Groves of Blarney. London: Chapman & Hall, 1838. Plays.

Lights and Shadows of Irish Life. London: H Colburn, 1838.
Sketches.

The Whiteboy. London: Chapman & Hall, 1845. Novel.

Stories of the Irish Peasantry. Edinburgh: W & R Chambers, 1850.
Stories.

The Fight of Faith. London: Chapman & Hall, 1869. Novel.

Notes

1. Quoted in Robert Lee Wolff, 'The Irish Fiction of Anna Maria
Hall,' *The Whiteboy*, 1845; rpt. (New York & London: Garland,
1979), x.

Hartigan, Anne Le Marquand
Born: England, c 20th century
Educated: England.

Poet, painter, playwright, performer, farmer, wife, mother
— it's hard to keep up with Anne Le Marquand Hartigan's
many occupations. Born in England to a mother from
Ireland, a father from Jersey, Channel Islands, she was
nurtured by three cultures. Her mother brought her 'back
home' to Ireland each year, fed her Irish folk tales and
encouraged her love of music and art. Her father brought
her to Jersey and 'shared his love of Shakespeare, Milton,
Spenser, Horace, and poetry in general'. She attended St
Joseph's Convent in Reading and the Convent of the
Sacred Heart in Tunbridge Wells. An only child, her
'consuming passion from the age of about five was to act',
but she also loved learning poetry by heart at school. She
writes plays, poetry, and scholarly essays.

Two of her plays, *Beds* and *La Corbiere*, were produced
in the Dublin Theatre Festival in 1982 and 1989. She wrote
her first poem at the age of eight 'and continued writing
poetry (secretly) through school'. 'I was never encouraged,'
she notes, 'just to do spelling corrections.' At the University
of Reading, she studied Fine Art, specialising in painting.
When she married Tim Hartigan, they farmed her mother's
farm in Co. Louth, Ireland, and reared their six children

(five of whom were born in six and a half years) there. She turned to poetry in Ireland, she thinks, because she was severed from her painting roots in England and had no place to paint.

Educated in England, she never learnt Irish, but loves Irish poetry and believes the 'rhythms and word patterns' Irish brings to Irish/English have influenced her own work. Ancient English verse was very important to her, as was the work of the moderns. She believes her painting complements her poetry and did the drawings herself for *Now is a Moveable Feast* (1991). Her poetry and short stories have been published in many papers and magazines; her poetry has been translated into Russian and German, and she has received many bursaries and prizes.

The experiences of birth and death touched her deeply at a young age: her mother died a month before the birth of her own first child, her father before she was thirty. She writes of what moves her 'passionately. From the desire to express the unsayable, the sub-text in life, what lies behind the mind.'[1] *Now is a Moveable Feast* wells up from universal depths. 'It is a poem that celebrates women, but, over and through, under and in everything is the ever-enduring land,' Hartigan notes in the introduction. 'The land links us with prehistory, history and myth; with the sea, sky, birds, animals and the continuous flow of the great River Boyne itself.'[2] The speakers identified only as the Woman, the Man, and God suggest a timelessness, continuity, and universality of function, ironically underlined by the Auctioneer, whose advertising gambits suggest – in contrast to the timelessness – the house's conformity to a 'person of taste', a rich executive. The spare and allusive quality of the poetry reminds one of the Psalms, of J M Synge, and indeed of native American poetry – the simplicity that transcends the mundane and reaches religion or myth.

Besides the many voices of her poetry, Hartigan has written four plays and a mime. The experimental *Beds* – almost a series of mini plays linked by themes of life and death and using song, dance, and mime — was a theatrical innovation in the Irish theatre in 1982. *La Corbiere* continues to develop this exploration. A new collection of poetry is due from Salmon Publishing in 1993.

Works:
Long Tongue. Dublin: Beaver Row, 1982. Poetry.
Return Single. Dublin: Beaver Row, 1986. Poetry.
Now is a Moveable Feast. Galway: Salmon Publishing, 1991. Poetry.
Clearing the Space: The Why of Writing. Galway: Salmon Publishing, 1992. Essay.

Notes
1. Personal communication.
2. Introduction to *Now is a Moveable Feast*.

Hickey, Emily Henrietta
Born: 1845; Died: 1924
Educated: England.

Emily Hickey was born in Wexford and educated in Cambridge. She wrote narrative poetry, stories, and criticism. She converted to Roman Catholicism, was involved with the Catholic Truth Society, and wrote criticism in Catholic journals. A religious sentiment pervades many of her poems.

Thou new-annealed, who in thy love dost ache
To pour out suffering nard-like on His feet,
'Tis great things thou art fain to do; His wheat
Sow, reap, and thresh, nor any wages take;
The stones upon His roadway sit and break;
Panting and thirsty, for the desperate heat,
Or shivering in the heavy wind and sleet;
Only to suffer, suffer for His sake.

And what if thus the Lover of lovers said;
'Not thine the way of brake and tearing brier;

Not thine the torment of the frost and fire;
I give thee gladness, or My passion bred;
I give thee joy; and this is My desire
Thou keep its morning-dew upon my head.'[1]

Selected Works:
Later Poems. London: Grant Richards, 1913. Poetry.
Verse-Tales, Lyrics and Translations. Liverpool: Arnold, 1889.
    Poetry.

Notes
1. 'The Master's Will,' in *Pillars of the House*, edited by A A Kelly
    (Dublin: Wolfhound, 1988), 54.

Higgins, Rita Ann
Born: Ireland, 1955
Educated: Ireland.

Rita Ann Higgins was born in Galway and has lived there
all her life. She left school early, but fortunately discovered
reading at twenty-two when tuberculosis confined her to a
sanatorium. The first book she read was Orwell's *Animal
Farm*, 'because it was a small book ... Then I went on to
Wuthering Heights. These two books got me started. It was
such a revelation.' And Rita has kept on going, reading
what she can on her own. She counts herself lucky to have
'woken up'; she joined a Galway Writers' Workshop in
1982, and learned to put words to her feelings.[1]

Rita Ann Higgins has published three collections of
poetry, two of which have been reissued in one volume.
She was awarded Arts Council writing bursaries in 1986
and 1989, was writer-in-residence in Galway Library in
1987, and received a Peadar O'Donnell award in 1989. Her
poetry is very popular, as are her readings. She has read
her work on RTE, at universities, and in prisons, at
festivals in Ireland and England, and at conferences in
Germany and Hungary. Her play, *Face-Licker Come Home*,
played to full houses at the Galway Arts Festival in 1991.

Her subjects are mostly 'character sketches', she notes. She writes to release the angry voice in her head, but not only that.[2] Some of her poems, 'Middle-Aged Irish Mothers', for example, lovingly sketch and celebrate her subjects. Like many of Higgins's poems, this poem is dramatic and narrative, the commentary on the mothers interrupted by lines from Catholic prayers.

Germinating sopranos in conservative head squares
are the middle-aged Irish mothers in heavy plaid
coats, who loiter after Mass in churches.

> *Lord make me an instrument of your peace;*
> *Where there is hatred, let me sow love;*

The poem echoes the prayers for all the needy family members and friends, acquaintances and the 'Pope's intentions,' to conclude,

I like these middle-aged Irish mothers, in heavy plaid
coats,
one of them birthed me on the eve of a saint's feast day,
with a little help from Jesus and his Sacred Heart.

> *I tell you most solemnly, anything you ask for*
> *from the father he will grant in my name.*[3]

'Witch in the Bushes' is a humorous parable/poem about an angry man 'who tried/to eat a rock/a big rock/grey and hard,/unfriendly too'. The man becomes isolated over the years, until one day 'an old woman' comes out of the bushes to ask him 'if all that anger/for all those years/was worth it'. 'He concluded,/"Anger is ok/if you spill it,/but chewing/is assuredly/murder on the teeth."' He tries to reform, but occasionally the militant rock voice breaks through, also an 'uncle' of that voice, who warns, 'About/the witch in the bushes,' 'Watch her,/she never sleeps.'[4]

'Woman's Inhumanity to Woman' and 'Poetry Doesn't Pay' are two of the angry poems. The first lists all the arbitrary, unearned powers women use to belittle other women. The sub-title 'Galway Labour Exchange' may suggest that these powers are exercised by the employees of the Labour Exchange against the women who apply for assistance. 'Poetry Doesn't Pay' — while depicting the very real plight of the poet who can't pay the rent — has more humour 'People keep telling me/ "Your poems, you know,/you've really got something there,/I mean really."'

When the rent man calls, I go
down on my knees, and through
the conscience box I tell him.

This is somebody speaking,
short distance, did you know
I have something here with my poems?

After several threats, one more severe than the other, the rent man concludes,

If you don't have fourteen pounds
and ten pence, you have nothing
but the light of the penurious moon.[5]

A poem which itself transcends anger, while accepting and foretelling the anger of the future is 'Daughter of the Falls Road', 'In memory of Mairéad Farrell, murdered in Gibraltar, by SAS.'

And from the eyes of her brothers
tumbled acid tears,
passing the place of their heart
seeping into closed fists,
and there was an acid tear ocean there
doing nothing. Waiting.[6]

Works:
Goddess on the Mervue Bus. Galway: Salmon Publishing, 1986. Poetry.
Witch in the Bushes. Galway: Salmon Publishing, 1988. Poetry.
Goddess & Witch. Galway: Salmon Publishing, 1988. Poetry.
Face-Licker Come Home. Galway: Salmon Publishing, 1991. Play.
Philomena's Revenge. Galway: Salmon Publishing, 1992. Poetry.

Notes

1. In *Sleeping with Monsters*, Gillean Somerville-Arjat and Rebecca E Wilson, eds. (Dublin: Wolfhound Press, 1990), 44-45.
2. In *Sleeping with Monsters*, 45.
3. In *Goddess & Witch*, 38, 39.
4. In *Goddess & Witch*, 76, 78, 79.
5. In *Goddess & Witch*, 20, 21.
6. In *Goddess & Witch*, 115.

Hill, Niki

Born: Ireland c̲ 20th century
Educated: Ireland.

Niki Hill was born and educated in northern Ireland. A journalist, she is editor of *Women's News* in Belfast. Her first novel is a story of terror in northern Ireland.[1]

Works:
Death Grows on You. London: Paladin, 1992. Novel.

Notes
1. Author Introduction in *Death Grows on You*.

Hinkson, Pamela

Born: England, 1900; Died: 1982
Educated: Ireland, Germany, France.

Pamela Hinkson was born in London, the daughter of Kathleen Tynan. When her father was appointed resident magistrate in Mayo, the family moved to the Ireland her parents had left. She was educated privately in Ireland, Germany, and France, and after her father's death in 1919, the family moved to England. She accompanied her mother as a journalist to many parts of Europe, and also travelled in America and India. She collaborated with

Lady Fingall on her autobiography, *Seventy Years Young* (1937), and also wrote many successful novels, several of which feature scenes in India, and stories for school children.

Selected Works:
The End of All Dreams. London: [First Novel Library], 1923. Novel.
The Girls of Redlands. London: Partridge, 1923. School Story.
Patsy at School. London: Nelson, 1925. School Story.
St Mary's. London: Longmans, 1927. School Story.
Schooldays at Meadowfield. London and Glasgow: Collins, 1930. School Story.
The Ladies Road. London: Gollancz, 1932; New York: Penguin, 1946. Novel.
The Deeply Rooted. London: Gollancz, 1935. Novel.
The Light on Ireland. London: Muller, 1935. Novel.
Irish Gold. London: Collins, 1939. Sketches.
Indian Harvest. London: Collins, 1941. Novel.
Golden Rose. London: Collins, 1944. Novel.
The Lonely Bride. London: Collins, 1951. Novel.

Hobhouse, Violet
Born: Ireland, 1864; Died: 1902
Educated: Ireland.

Violet Hobhouse was born in Co. Antrim. A Unionist, she campaigned against Home Rule, but was also very interested in Irish folklore and traditions. She wrote poetry and fiction.[1]

Selected Works:
An Unknown Quantity: A Tale. London: Donney, 1898. Novel.
Warp and Weft: A Story of the North of Ireland. London: Skeffington, 1899. Novel.

Notes
1. *A Biographical Dictionary of Irish Writers*, Anne M Brady and Brian Cleeve, eds. (Mullingar: Lilliput Press, 1985), 107.

Hoey, Frances Sarah Johnston Cashel
Born: Ireland, 1830; Died: 1908
Self-taught.

Frances Sarah Johnston was born in Dublin and self-educated. She married A M Stewart at sixteen and was widowed at twenty-five. She had contributed to *The Freeman's Journal* and *The Nation* before her husband's death and went to London after his death with a letter of introduction from William Carleton to Thackeray. There she married John Cashel Hoey, who had edited *The Nation*, and she became a Catholic. There also she began her busy and fruitful career, as translator from French, journalist, and novelist. She is believed to have contributed to several novels published under Edmund Yates's name.[1]

Works:
A House of Cards. 3 vol. London: Tinsley, 1868. Novel.
Falsely True. 3 vol. London: Tinsley, 1870/revised, London: Ward & Downey, 1890. Novels.
A Golden Sorrow. 3 vol. London: Hurst & Blackett/New York: Harper, 1872. Novel.
Out of Court. 3 vol. London np, 1874. Novel.
The Blossoming of an Aloe, and the Queen's Token. 3 vol. London np 1875/New York: Harper, 1975. Novel.
Griffith's Double. 3 vol. London np 1876. Novel.
Kate Cronin's Dowry. New York; Harper, 1877. Novel.
Ralph Craven's Silver Whistle. London np 1877. Novel.
All or Nothing. 3 vol. London np 1879. Novel.
The Question of Cain. 3 vol. New York: Harper, 1881/London: Hurst & Blackett, 1882/revised, London: Ward & Downey, 1890. Novel.
The Lover's Creed. 3 vol. London: Chatto & Windus/New York: Munro, 1884. Novel.
A Stern Chase. 3 vol. London: Sampson Low/New York: Harper, 1886. Novel.
The Queen's Token. London np 1888. Novel.

Notes
1. *Dictionary of Irish Literature*, Robert Hogan, ed. (Westport, Conn.: Greenwood Press, 1979), 297.

Holmes, Máire C

Born: Ireland, 1952
Educated: Ireland.

Máire Holmes was born in Dublin. After the sorrow of her mother's early death in 1965, she went as a boarder to the Dominican Convent in Eccles Street, Dublin. Her mother wrote under the name Brídín Bheasach, and their home, though close to Dublin centre, was filled with music, poetry, and the Irish language. Máire Holmes was a child actress on the bi-lingual programme 'Siopa an Bhreathnaigh', in the early days of RTE, and later on several other programmes. She lives with her husband and son in Spiddal, Co. Galway.[1]

She works as poet, playwright, writer, and broadcaster in English and Irish. Her short story, 'Smile for Mammy' won a Hennessy Literary Award in 1988; her play, *The Butterfly who couldn't Dance*, won a National Drama Award in 1989 and was staged at the Peacock Theatre in Dublin; *An Fáinne* was staged at Taibhdhearc na Gaillimhe, and *Hollydaze* toured Irish colleges with Taibhdhearc na Gaillimhe. Her plays have also been produced on Raidió Éireann. She is a regular broadcaster on Raidió na Gaeltachta and has presented popular radio programmes for children. Telefís Éireann screened a thirty minute programme on Máire Holmes, interviewed by the late Brendán O hEithir.

Works:
Dúrún. Baile Atha Cliath: Coiscéim, 1988. Poetry.

Notes
1. Personal communication.

Hopkin, Alannah

Born: Singapore, 1949
Educated: England.

Alannah Hopkin was born in Singapore in 1949; her father is English and her late mother Irish; thus she describes herself as half-English and half-Irish. The Hopkin family returned to Cork, Ireland, from Singapore when Alannah was six months, and moved to London when she was four years old. Educated in England she stayed with an aunt in Carrigaline, Co. Cork, when her parents travelled, and the family spent most Easter and summer holidays in her grandmother's house in Kinsale. She always felt more at home in Ireland than in London, she notes, and lives in Kinsale now. In the 1970s she exchanged her British passport for an Irish one: 'I did not want to be a citizen of a country that was inflicting such grief on Ireland.'[1] She has been area editor for *Fodor's Guide to Ireland* since 1986, is arts correspondent and drama critic (Ireland) for the *Financial Times*, reviewer for *The Irish Times* and the *Financial Times*, and occasional contributor to Aer Lingus magazine, *Cara*, *Sunday Independent*, and RTE radio.

In her first two novels, *A Joke Goes a Long Way in the Country* (1982) and *The Out-Haul* (1985), her interest is in 'contemporary rural Ireland'. Recently obsessed by an eighteenth-century novel project that she began before *The Out-Haul*, she notes that this may not signal a change of interest. 'Even though I've lived here nearly ten years now, I'm still absolutely stunned by the beauty and the drama of the countryside and the sea which seem to give a quite different perspective to very mundane events in daily life; it's the interplay of the two that I like to catch — whether in the eighteenth-century or the present day, so there is a kind of link.'[2]

The Out-Haul demonstrates this interest in country and sea. Set in Bally C in West Cork, this is the story of adventures the sophisticated Celia never expected to find in such a remote and apparently quiet spot. Tragedy and comedy rub shoulders here, and the romance is that of the ocean itself; the out-haul, the noise of the tide going out. The earlier novel, and even *The Living Legend of Saint Patrick* (1990), also chart Irish rural life.

Works:
A Joke Goes a Long Way in the Country. London: Hamish Hamilton, 1982; New York: Atheneum, 1983; London: Sphere Books, 1983. Novel.
The Out-Haul. London: Hamish Hamilton, 1985; London: Sphere Books, 1986. Novel.
The Living Legend of Saint Patrick. London: Grafton Books, 1989; New York: St Martin's Press, 1990. Legend.

Notes
1. Personal communication.
2. Personal communication.

Hoult, Norah
Born: Ireland, 1898; Died: 1984
Educated: England.

Norah Hoult was born in Ireland of Anglo-Irish parents. Orphaned very young, she was sent to English boarding schools. She was delighted to find her Irish Aunt Anna an amusing narrator, but saddened to discover that her Irish Catholic family disowned her mother because she married a Protestant. This and much of the bigotry she found in early twentieth-century Ireland became the material for *Holy Ireland* (1935), one of her best-known novels, reprinted in 1985 by Arlen House, Dublin. Her first published work was a collection of short stories, *Poor Women* (1928), which was also very popular and reprinted many times.

Holy Ireland is the story of a Catholic family, the O'Neills, in the Ireland of 1898-1903. Patrick O'Neill is a narrow Catholic who sees Protestants as damned. To his horror, his eldest daughter, Margaret, marries an English Protestant. The tragedy of Patrick's bigotry is the central drama, but Hoult introduces a wide cast of characters and enriches the text with incidents of sibling rivalry, neighbourly gossip, and cold Anglo-Irish divisions. Hoult wrote a second novel about Ireland, *Coming from the Fair* (1937), a sequel to *Holy Ireland*.

Works:
Poor Women! London: Scholartis, 1928. Stories.
Time Gentlemen! Time! London: Heinemann, 1930. Novel.
Violet Ryder. London: E Mathews & Marot, 1930. Novel.
Apartment to Let. London: Heinemann, 1931. Novel.
Youth Can't Be Served. London: Heinemann, 1933. Novel.
Holy Ireland. London: Heinemann, 1935; Dublin: Arlen House, 1985. Novel.
Coming from the Fair. London: Heinemann, 1937. Novel.
Nine Years is a Long Time. London: Heinemann, 1938. Stories.
Four Women Grow Up. London: Heinemann, 1940. Novel.
Smilin' on the Vine. London: Heinemann, 1941. Novel.
Augusta Steps Out. London: Heinemann, 1942. Novel.
Scene for Death. London: Heinemann, 1943. Novel.
There Were no Windows. London: Heinemann, 1944. Novel.
House Under Mars. London: Heinemann, 1946. Novel.
Selected Stories. London/Dublin: Maurice Fridberg, 1946. Stories.
Farewell Happy Fields. London: Heinemann, 1948. Novel.
Cocktail Bar London: Heinemann, 1950. Stories.
Frozen Ground. London: Heinemann, 1952. Novel.
Sister Mavis. London: Heinemann, 1953. Novel.
A Death Occurred. London: Hutchinson, 1954. Novel.
Journey into Print. London: Hutchinson, 1954. Novel.
Father Hone and the Television Set. London: Hutchinson, 1956. Novel.
Father and Daughter. London: Hutchinson, 1957. Novel.
Husband and Wife. London: Hutchinson, 1959. Novel.
The Last Days of Miss Jenkinson. London: Hutchinson, 1962. Novel.
A Poet's Pilgrimage. London: Hutchinson, 1966. Novel.
Not for our Sins Alone. London: Hutchinson, 1972. Novel.

— J —

Jacob, Rosamund

Born: 1888; Died: 1960
Educated: Ireland.
Rosamund Jacob, born in Waterford, was the child of a Quaker family. She absorbed and adopted all their beliefs and opinions — which differed in almost every respect from those of her class and contemporaries, most notably in relation women's rights, Irish independence, religious freedom and animal rights.

She lived in Dublin from 1920 and became an accomplished author. A suffragette and member of Sinn Féin, her intense love of Ireland, its countryside, mythology and culture informs everything she wrote. Two of her published books include *The Rebel's Wife* (1957), *The Raven's Glen* (1960). She continued to write throughout her life.

Selected Works:
The Rebel's Wife. Tralee: The Kerryman 1957. Novel.
The Raven's Glen. Dublin: Figgis, 1960. Novel.

Jenkinson, Biddy

Born: Ireland c 20th century
Educated: Ireland.

Biddy Jenkinson is the pen name of a woman who prizes her privacy, so I focus at once on the written words of the poet. 'A Letter to an Editor' in the *Irish University Review*, eloquently describes the work of the poet as intimately connected with the reason she will not permit her poetry to be translated into English, 'I prefer not to be translated into English in Ireland. It is a small rude gesture to those who think that everything can be harvested and stored without loss in an English-speaking Ireland. If I were a corncrake I would feel no obligation to have my skin cured, my tarsi injected with formalin so that I could fill a museum shelf in a world that saw no need for my kind.'[1]

Recognition has nothing to do with the writing of poetry. 'Writing poetry, ... is a way of loving whatever there may be by exploring to the driven limits of capacity and opportunity everything that can be reached.'(30) She explains, 'I have emphasised the effort to transcend because I think that it is in the effort to see, know and understand that the poet loves. She loves both in arrogance and in humility. With the arrogance of her calling she will not adopt any ready-made system of belief – who is she, in all humility, to decide, which, if any, creed has got it right? Instead she will hunker down on the most recent high water mark of her own understanding and handle the shells and weeds and theories and fossils and facts, squeeze the hand, or it may be the toe, of the beloved, confident that if there is a God she can come closest to Its influence among these particulars and peculiars.'(31)

Awake to the improbability of existence, the poet delights in the miracle. Her love is 'vigorous and unsentimental'. She loves the lamb, the parasites, the flukes, all, but this does not mean that she will not kill. 'She will slit each chicken's neck with an apology and live all the more intensively in reparation. ... I am talking of love that is aware of what it is taking and translates its obligation into poetry.' (32) Life itself in all its marvellous transmutations is Divinity: 'The world is so full of wonders that the glory of it all is enough to make me glad to be aware even for a little while and it is in this gladness that poems grow.' (33) 'The writing is a matter of love, the kind I have been describing, a sustaining through my veins and verbs of something infinitely precious, a stretching back along the road we have come, a stand here in the present among the outnumbered and beleaguered but determined survivors of Gaelic Ireland.' (33-34)

As we might expect from the above, Jenkinson's poetry is filled with natural images. Three poems are translated into French in *Wildish Things*.[3] The following lines are from 'Uisce Beatha'.

Bhí tart ar an sliabh inniu
an bogach scarbháilte, an móinteán doíte
is dusta an fhraoigh ag eírí mar cheo bóthair
Is tá tart orm arís, seantart, an íota,
an triomach a dheighlfeadh ón saol táite mé im
              chaithnín snaoise

is nach bhfuil múchadh air go bá
san fheacht a ritheann faoi choim na cruinne
tríd na dúile, timpeall
in úscadh ceo, i dtuilte geimhridh, i sruthlam taoide
i mún spideoige, uisce na bhfiacla, deora caointe.[2]

Many of Jenkinson's poems have been anthologised. She has published three volumes of poetry and received an Arts Council Award for the second in 1992. She has also written radio plays, three of which have been broadcast on RTE, produced by Seán O Briain. Her stage plays received prizes from the Peacock Theatre and Taibhdhearc na Gaillimhe, but unfortunately have not been staged. Yet.

Works:
Báisteadh Gintlí. Baile Atha Cliath: Coiscéim, 1987. Poetry.
Uiscí Beatha. Baile Atha Cliath: Coiscéim, 1988. Poetry.
Dán na hUidhre. Baile Atha Cliath: Coiscéim, 1991. Poetry.

Notes
1. 'Letter to an Editor', in *Irish University Review* (Spring/Summer 1991) 34.
2. In *Uiscí Beatha*, 16.
3. In *Wildish Things*, Ed. Ailbhe Smyth, Dublin: Attic Press, 1989.

Johnston, Jennifer
Born: Ireland, 1930
Educated: Ireland.

Jennifer Johnston was born in Dublin in 1930, the daughter of Denis Johnston, novelist, playwright and war correspondent, and Shelah Richards, a well-known actress. Jennifer and her brother had good relationships with their parents because, she suggests, a wonderful nanny 'looked after all our wants and wishes and kept us safe from our parents and our parents safe from us.'[1] At three years of age, she went to Park House School and remained there twelve years. At seventeen, she thought she might be an actress, but decided to attend Trinity College, Dublin instead because that seemed to be her parents' wish. She brought up her four children in London, where she lived with her first husband. She is now remarried and living in Derry.

Jennifer Johnston remembers being a 'lonely child', and, like so many other lonely children who became writers, an avid reader. (61) She wrote plays at school and frequented her mother's rehearsals in the Olympia and Gaiety. 'Almost from the moment' she started thinking, she 'would have preferred to have been a man'. She thought of her mother, a well-known actress, as 'an extraordinary person', because the opportunities for women seemed very limited. (57) Ireland of the 1940s and 1950s was also a very insular society, and it was a rare treat for the young woman to meet 'intelligent people – painters, writers and actors – from outside Ireland ... talking about the world.' (54) She herself was about thirty before she decided what she wanted to do with her life.

Although she has written several plays since the early school attempts, Jennifer Johnston is best known for her novels. She is not proud of the first, *The Gates* (1973), though most writers might be happy with this maiden performance. Many of her novels are set in a Big House. Although two of her early protagonists are male, the centre of consciousness in the majority of her novels is female. The novels stage encounters between Anglo- and Gaelic-Irish characters and often end in disappointment or death. Her novels have been reprinted many times, in Britain, the USA, and Europe. All have been translated into French, several into German, Dutch, Russian, Polish, and Hungarian, and two into Lithuanian. They have been adapted for television and film, and awarded many prizes, including the Whitbread.

The heart of a Johnston novel is the conflict between personal and public − or group − loyalties. Johnston's prose is poetic, allusive and suggestive rather than definitive and confined. Much is left unsaid, and the reader must speculate, assess motives, and balance positions. Clues abound, of course, but as in all complex situations, these clues are often divergent or contradictory. Plot is not so important as the mysteries of human character. The dialogue in *Fool's Sanctuary* (1987) reveals Johnston's typical, delicate nuances. The time is 1920, and Andrew Martin returns to his home in Donegal after a long absence serving in the British army during and since the war. Andrew, accompanied by another British officer, Harry Harrington — finds his now grown-up sister Miranda on the beach. With Miranda is Andrew's childhood friend, Charlie Dillon, now known as Cathal Dillon, the son of a Martin employee. Andrew does not recognise Cathal Dillon as Miranda calls him to welcome Andrew home. Andrew speaks first:

'Cathal? I don't know anyone ... Don't tease, Miranda ...?'

'Cathal,' she repeated as Cathal arrived beside them. 'Look at your shoes.'

'I'm sorry,' said Andrew. 'I've been away such a long time, I'm afraid ... '

Cathal held out his hand.

'I wouldn't have recognised you either Charlie Dillon. We've all changed a bit, not just Miranda ... It's good to see you home again. Welcome back.'

He stood with his hand outstretched.

'Good Lord, old Charlie Dillon. So it is.'

Andrew looked from Cathal to Miranda, than took Cathal's hand briefly.

'Yes. This brings me back a few years all right. Still shooting, old man?'

Cathal shifted his wet feet and turned to look out to sea. Andrew addressed Harry in an explicatory way.

'Charlie and I used to play together when we were children. Mess around, you know. His father taught us both to shoot. Yes. This is my friend Captain Harrington, by the way, Charlie.'

'How do you do, Ch-charlie?'

Harry took a step towards him and held out his hand.

Cathal smiled briefly and continued to look out to sea.

'How do you do ... sir?'[2]

Briefly – in less than 200 pages – Johnston's novels deal with many sensitive, difficult issues: the fate of the Anglo-Irish in contemporary Ireland, of women victimised by a violence and order they had no part in creating. Misunderstandings and tragedies are seen to result from the difficulties of human communication: ironically, the language that Johnston uses so well, she represents as a poor, imprecise instrument to sound the intricacies of the human soul.

Works:

The Captains and the Kings. London: Hamish Hamilton, 1972. Novel.

The Gates. London: Hamish Hamilton, 1973. Novel.

How Many Miles to Babylon? London: Hamish Hamilton, 1974. Novel.

Shadows on our Skin. London: Hamish Hamilton, 1977. Novel.

The Old Jest. London: Hamish Hamilton, 1979. Novel.

The Christmas Tree. London: Hamish Hamilton, 1981. Novel.

The Railway Station Man. London: Hamish Hamilton, 1984. Novel.

Fool's Sanctuary. London: Hamish Hamilton, 1987. Novel.

The Nightingale and Not The Lark. Dublin: Raven Arts Press, 1988. Plays.

The Invisible Worm. London: Hamish Hamilton, 1991. Novel.

Notes

1. *Portrait of the Artist as a Young Girl*, John Quinn, ed. (London: Methuen, 1986), 51. Following references in parenthesis from same text.
2. *Fool's Sanctuary*, 23-24.

Johnston, Myrtle

Born: 1909
Educated: Ireland, England.

Myrtle Johnston's work was popular in the 1930s. She published several books of stories and novels. One of the richest and most ironic is *Hanging Johnny* (1927). This is the story of an executioner who took this particularly grim job because he needed money. His first victim, however, Tim Derrybawn, is known to him, and both the executioner and the attending priest are faced with the dilemma of Tim's innocence.

Works:

Hanging Johnny. London: Murray, 1927. Novel.

Relentless. London: Murray, 1930. Novel.

The Maiden. London: Murray, 1932. Novel.

Laleen and Other Stories. London: Murray, 1937. Short Stories.

The Rising. London: John Murray, 1939. Novel.
A Robin Redbreast in a Cage. London: Heinemann, 1950. Novel.

Jones, Mary
Born: Wales, 1942
Educated: Wales.

Mary Jones was born in Aberystwyth, Wales, and educated at St Padarn's Convent School in Aberystwyth and the University of Sheffield. Although one of her parents spoke Welsh and the family lived in a Welsh-speaking area, she did not speak the language and 'was conscious,' she notes, 'of hardly belonging in Wales, where I'm English, or in England, where I'm Welsh'. Consequently, she enjoys living in northern Ireland, where she has lectured in English at the University of Ulster since 1969, 'and where,' she adds, 'it is quite clear that I do not belong.'[1] She publishes critical articles as well as fiction.

Set in a crumbling hotel in Wales, Jones's first novel, *Resistance* (1985), may remind readers of Irish characters and places. The lurking Welsh nationalists and the witty drunks, as well as the remote setting and intermittent use of the Welsh language, are reminiscent of contemporary novels of northern Ireland. The novel bristles with tension as the irritable, troubled heroine encounters the strange, insolent hotel staff, and the reader must attempt to distinguish between her illusion and the reality of danger.

Works:
Resistance. Belfast: Blackstaff Press, 1985. Novel.

Notes
1. Personal communication.

— K —

Kavanagh, Julia
Born: Ireland, 1824; Died: 1877
Educated: Ireland France.

Julia Kavanagh was born in Thurles, Co. Tipperary, the only child of Morgan Peter Kavanagh, a philologist and novelist. Her childhood was spent in France, in Paris and Normandy. In 1844 she and her mother returned without her father to England, where she supported her invalid mother by writing many novels for adults and stories for children. John Sutherland notes the 'extraordinary literary quarrel' with her father in 1857, which obliged her to disown any connection with a novel, *The Hobbies*, which he wrote and tried to pass off as partly hers.[1]

Her work features French settings and resourceful, independent heroines. It reflects her strong Catholic faith and was very popular in her lifetime.

Selected Works:
Madeleine: A Tale of Auvergne. London: np, 1848. Novel.
Daisy Burns. 3 vol. London: np, 1853. Novel.
Grace Lee. 3 vol. London: np, 1855. Novel.
Adele. 3 vol. London: np, 1858. Novel.
Beatrice. 2 vol. London: np, 1864. Novel.
Dora. 3 vol. London: np, 1868. Novel.
Two Lilies. 3 vol. London: np, 1877. Novel.

Notes
1. John Sutherland, *Longman Companion to Victorian Fiction* (Harlow, Essex: Longman, 1988), 343-44.

Kavanagh, Rose
Born: Ireland, 1859; Died: 1891
Educated: Ireland.

Rose Kavanagh wrote poetry for journals and newspapers. Her work was very popular during her lifetime and was collected and published in a volume after her death. The following lines are from 'Knockmaney' celebrating her beloved homeplace.

Knockmaney, my darling, I see you again,
As the sunrise has made you a King;
And your proud face looks tenderly down on the plain
Where my young larks are learning to sing.[1]

Works:
R *Kavanagh and Her Verses.* Dublin & Waterford: Gill, 1909. Poetry.

Notes
1. 'Knockmaney,' in *Pillars of the House*, edited by A A Kelly (Dublin: Wolfhound, 1988), 61.

Keane (née Boylan), Katherine
Born: Ireland, 1904; Died: 1987
Educated: Ireland.

Katherine Keane *(née* Boylan), was born and educated in Drogheda, Co. Louth. She wrote radio plays and two novels, *Who Goes Home?* (1947) and *So Ends My Dream* (1950).

Who Goes Home? is the story of an Irish member of Parliament, a friend of Charles Stuart Parnell, during the eventful years of 1880-91. A man of principle, Hugh Donnellan is loyal to Parnell, but his own career is clouded by his brothers' various and questionable activities, activities which allow Keane to set the historical events amidst the snobbery of middle-class Ireland. Jane Freeman, Keane's heroine, is more than a stereotype: Jane opens a school to support herself and her mother, and her relationship with her mother is often sharply drawn. *Who Goes Home?* – the cry after every parliament session – attains new significance for Hugh as he returns to his hometown at the end of the novel.

Works:
Who Goes Home? 1947; rpt. Dublin: Arlen House, 1987. Novel.
So Ends My Dream. Dublin: Talbot, 1950. Novel.

Keane, Molly
Born: Ireland, 1904
Educated: Ireland.

Molly Keane was born in Co. Kildare in 1904. One of five children, she was born into an Anglo-Irish, Big House family similar in some respects to the families in her novels. Her mother, the poet Moira O'Neill, was reclusive and absorbed in her writing, her father cared most for the hunt, and the children were left to the care of governesses, in cold, dirty nurseries, where they were fed 'disgusting' food. Although life at home was often boring, she was not happy either when sent to the French School in Bray, Co. Wicklow, when she was fourteen: 'Education had no practical end in my case', she notes. 'It would never have been considered that I should get a *job*'.[1]

The Great War seemed remote, but not the 1916 rebellion. 'I remember hearing about the occupation of the GPO in Dublin and then everybody thinking that we were all going to be murdered.'[2] No one in the immediate family was hurt, however, though the family home was burned down as a reprisal for Black and Tan atrocities. Molly remembers her father's brandishing a shotgun, and the 'boys' admonishing him that unless he behaved 'they would have to shoot him.'[3] She began writing from sheer boredom, Keane notes, when confined to bed as a teenager; elsewhere she suggests that she wrote for pin money to supplement her tiny dress allowance.[4] She used the pen-name M J Farrell because, she says, writing was unacceptable in the hunting society she enjoyed: 'For a woman to read a book, let alone write one was viewed with alarm. I would have been banned from every respectable house in County Carlow.'[5]

Her writing career was extremely successful, and she wrote several plays and eleven novels between 1928 and 1956. When her young and beloved husband died suddenly, leaving her to mother two young children, she stopped writing. The world had changed, and her novels of a vanished society no longer seemed popular. When she returned to writing in the 1970s, publishers initially rejected the black comedy, *Good Behaviour*, because the characters were so unsympathetic. Luckily, however, Peggy Ashcroft read the manuscript, recognised with delight its originality, and guided it to Andre Deutsch; the rest is history. *Good Behaviour* (1981) was an instant success, translated into several languages, and on to television, and Molly Keane was again a celebrity, whose work, new and old, was in demand. Two more novels, *Time After Time* (1983) and *Loving and Giving* (1988) have followed, and a beautiful cookbook, *Molly Keane's Nursery Cooking* (1985).

Children are neglected in Keane's novels to the point of cruelty, and in their turn they become cruel, malicious adults. The world she describes is vicious, a world in which idle people condemn the unfortunate, governesses and children, to hours of tedious boredom, while enlivening their own existences with illicit love affairs and petty thievery. Keane's novels reveal the lack of any moral or ethical centre under the beautiful veneer of gracious living. They never descend to polemic or class reproach, however, for the author dwells lovingly – but clear-sightedly – on the beauty of the houses, gardens, dinners, and the leisurely quality of life. Keane's fine sense of humour, her detached vision, her limited narrators, also turn potentially wrenching scenes into hilarious comedy.

Aroon, the narrator of *Good Behaviour*, tells of coming in to see her father (who lost a leg in World War I) one evening after he's had a stroke. Rose, the maid who has been upsettingly close to the major, keeps him company.

> He was asleep. He was leaning back, hollowing his wall of pillows. His eyelids were loosely downwards on his cheeks, and in his entire expression there was a grave concentration of pleasure. Rose sat beside him, her head bent low as if she were whispering; her hand was under the bedclothes warming his foot — his phantom foot that felt the cold as much as his real foot. Rose snatched her hand from under the sheets, and Papa opened his eyes to look up and towards her in a surprised, questioning way. He didn't see me standing in the doorway. Only Rose saw me, and her eyes blazed, raging, across the bed. "His feet are perishing,"

Rose excuses herself! (212)

Good Behaviour is the most sophisticated and most risque of Keane's novels, but the earlier work was also ahead of its time in treating sex and class; she deals with a lesbian relationship, for example, in *Devoted Ladies* (1934) typical of the era, the attitude is negative. *Good Behaviour* goes beyond exposure and humour, however, to reveal how the same social forces responsible for the elegance, beauty, and graciousness of Anglo-Irish ascendancy life are also responsible for the shrivelled and distorted lives of many Anglo-Irish women.

Works:
Young Entry. 1929; rpt. London: Virago, 1989. Novel.
Taking Chances. 1929; rpt. Middlesex: Penguin, 1987. Novel.
Mad Puppetstown. 1931; rpt, London: Virago, 1986. Novel.
Conversation Pieces. 1932; rpt. London: Virago, 1991. Novel.
Red Letter Days. London: Collins, 1933. Novel.
Devoted Ladies. 1934; rpt. London: Virago, 1984. Novel.
Full House. 1935; rpt. London: Virago, 1986. Novel.
The Rising Tide. 1937; rpt. London: Virago, 1984. Novel.

Spring Meeting: A Play in 3 Acts. With John Perry. London: Collins, 1938. Play.

Two Days in Aragon. 1941; rpt. London: Virago, 1985. Novel.

Loving Without Tears. 1951; rpt. London: Virago, 1988; In USA, *The Enchanting Witch*. New York: Crowell, 1951. Novel.

Treasure Hunt: Comedy in 3 Acts. London; French, 1951. Play.

Treasure Hunt. 1952; rpt. London; Virago, 1990. Novel.

Good Behaviour. London: Deutsch, 1981; New York: Dutton, 1981. Novel.

Time After Time. London: Deutsch, 1983; New York: Knopf, 1984. Novel.

Molly Keane's Nursery Cooking. London: Macdonald, 1985. Cook Book.

Loving and Giving. London: Deutsch, 1988; Published in USA as *Queen Lear*. New York: Dutton, 1989. Novel.

Notes

1. In *A Portrait of the Artist as a Young Girl*. John Quinn, ed. (London: Methuen, 1986), 70.
2. In *A Portrait*, 74.
3. Personal Interview, June 1985.
4. Polly Devlin, 'Introduction,' in *Two Days in Aragon*, viii.
5. Polly Devlin, 'Introduction,' in *The Rising Tide*, v.
6. *Good Behaviour*, 15-16 Dutton edition.

Kelly, Maeve
Born: Ireland, 1930
Educated: Ireland, England.

Maeve Kelly was born in Co. Clare, grew up and was educated in Dundalk, Co. Louth She was a student nurse in London, and did post-graduate theatre nursing in Oxford. She is a founding member of the Limerick Federation of Women's Organisations, and a founder of Adapt, the Limerick Centre for Abused Women and their children, of which she is Administrator. She lived and farmed with her husband and two children for many years in Clare, and now lives in Limerick. Her beloved daughter died in March 1991.

She has written and published poetry for many years. In 1971, she published her first short story in the *Irish Press*; she received a Hennessy Literary Award for a short story in 1972. Her work has appeared in many poetry and fiction anthologies, and a collection of poetry, *Resolution*, was published in 1986, a collection of her short stories, *A Life of Her Own*, in 1976. She has also published two novels.

Her work reflects the life she knows well, the life of the farm, of hospitals, and of women's issues in Limerick. Details of farm life, the feeding of the hens and calves, the smells of the farmyard and the kitchen where animal feedings are prepared, and the heartbreak of loss of animals are sensitively and unsentimentally presented. The short stories often concentrate on the isolated lives of the women and men who live remote from city or even from the mainland.

'Amnesty', the beautiful first story in *A Life of Her Own*, takes us into the mind of an island woman, whose grim silence repels the mainlanders, but who, along with her deaf-mute brother, is attuned to the beauty and loveliness of nature. She never speaks as she sets out on her journey to town to sell the fish she and her brother catch, but she talks non-stop on the way home. Haggling over the price with the greedy fish-merchant on one trip, she is filled 'with an old and terrible humiliation', when he turns his back, seeming to reject her fish. Memories of a young girl sent to the mainland in the hungry year of 1939 to sell the new potatoes fill her mind: memories of squandering the potato money on a pretty dress patterned with flowers and butterflies, of her brother's delight in the dress, and of her mother's slapping her across the face and calling her a terrible name. The bitter pictures stir her into fight, and the fish-merchant finally gives her a fair price. Now, instead of banking the money, she buys a dress as near to the pretty one of memory as possible, and once again delights her brother with the patterns and colours. 'The pink dress', the story concludes, 'was not now a rent flag thrown on a burial mound. It was a song of triumph, a declaration of peace. "I'll wear it to Mass on Sunday", she said. "And I'll pray for Ma's soul."' [1]

'Love' allows us to see both the joy and the worry of the mother who gives birth to a son late in life. Maeve Kelly catches the rhythm and gentleness of rural speech exactly: 'He's just finding his feet, the creature. But he'll come,' the mother of the slow boy placates and attempts to reassure herself at the same time. Loving him greatly, she praises him fulsomely and makes little of his mistakes. Broken dishes and uprooted seedlings are dismissed, 'If you looked at that old thing it would break,' and 'Ah, they were too crowded anyway. A thinning will do them no harm.'[2] 'The Last Campaign' reveals the unexpected senses of humour and of sorrow in a taciturn farmer; 'A Life of Her Own', the grimness that overtakes a comfortable farmer when, to his annoyance, his good-housekeeping-sister marries and leaves him.

Necessary Treasons (1985), the first novel, is the story of a young woman's growing awareness of the plight of Irish women. The heroine's involvement in the Limerick women's movement allows Kelly to include without polemic several of the situations and social assumptions women object to. The blindness of many men to women's humiliations, their belief that women 'bring it on themselves' – whatever the 'it' may be, their boredom with women's issues, all make this the ideal novel both for women who, like the sisters in the story, collaborate with the patriarchal order, and for the men who think the 'it' is again all in women's minds.

Works:
A Life of Her Own. Dublin: Poolbeg Press, 1976. Short Stories.
Necessary Treasons. London: Michael Joseph, 1985; London: Methuen, 1986. Novel.
Resolution. Belfast: Blackstaff Press, 1986. Poems.
Florrie's Girls. Belfast: Blackstaff Press, 1991. Novel.

Notes
1. In *A Life of Her Own*, 17.
2. In *A Life of Her Own*, 38, 40.

Kelly, Rita

Born: Ireland, 1953
Educated: Ireland.

Rita Kelly was born in Galway and educated at St Mary's Secondary School, Convent of Mercy, Ballinasloe, Co. Galway. She is currently living in New York. Her childhood landscapes were rural: the houses peopled by the ghosts of the Persse family including Lady Gregory, and the O'Kelly clan, famous both for their fourteenth-century hospitality to poets and musicians and their seventeenth-century betrayal of the town of Aughrim. Her mother was born on the Castle Ellen estate near Athenry, home to Edward Carson's mother, and Edward and Oscar Wilde spent their holidays there. Her education began in Ballinasloe, where she was taught by Thomas Fenton from the Kerry Gaeltacht, cousin of the poets Pádraig O Fiannachta and Nuala Ní Dómhnaill. She writes in both Irish and English, the union of the two languages enriching her work.

Rita Kelly writes fiction, poetry, drama, and criticism. She has won several literary awards and an Arts Council bursary, and has participated in the National Writers' Workshops. Her work is translated into German, Dutch, and Italian, published in numerous journals, and aired on radio and television.[1] Her first book *Dialann sa Díseart* (1981) was written with her husband Eoghan O Tuairisc and records her life with him.

Poems and stories are filled with concrete nouns, active verbs, descriptive adjectives, a rich texture that derives from English infused with Gaelic linguistic perception. Brutality is rendered very vividly, as is the persona's sympathy and identification with the victims. The female persona in a narrative poem, 'The Patriarch', remembers her father's butchering of sheep and heifers. The sheep were easy: not strong enough to endanger him, 'he beat them/about the head/with the sticking-knife,/held clenched in his fist.' He roped the stronger heifers, however, brought them to their knees, 'And then I should wrap that rope/ about my childish waist/and keep all that vibrating flesh on its knees.' Brutal with the animals, 'the patriarch' is also brutal with his daughter, whom he slaps if she fails to keep her footing. Noting the stress of rope on waist, the speaker identifies with the animals,

> but I could step toward her
> and ease my pain, seeing the neat hole which never bled
> above the dead open eyes.

> The entrails of the dead beasts
> warmed me in that place of terror
> and their blood ran down my legs,
> long before I woke to find
> my own blood hot and sticky
> between my legs.

The father's actions seem predetermined, he 'kicked me down the stairs/before going to the slaughter-house/because he had no choice.' The same man shares his daughter's delight in the opera. Confined – in the present of the poem – to a mental home, 'his head wired/and his limbs kicking with electric shock,' the father wishes his daughter to remember only the delight, not the bitterness. Unable to strike any more with his fist, he strikes his daughter with his tongue, until she reponds by striking him: 'and suddenly I am no longer/tethered by a thick rope/to a dead animal.'[2]

Kelly's most recent work, *Fare Well: Beir Beannacht* (1990), is a dual-language selection of poetry, which moves from expressing terrible losses to evoking the most subtle perceptions. 'Your loss is without a corpse./There is no burying an emptiness,' or 'Tá do chailleadh gan chorp./Ní féidir an fhoilmhe a chur faoin bhfód,' the persona notes at the end of the title poem. 'In the car with you,' reaches for the 'faint aside', the 'held breath', which, with 'no word', causes 'another wording' of hands finding each other.[3]

Works:
Dialann sa Díseart. (with Eoghan O Tuairisc) Baile Atha Cliath: Coiscéim, 1981. Poetry.

An Bealach Eadóigh. Baile Atha Cliath: Coiscéim, 1984. Poetry.
The Whispering Arch and Other Stories. Dublin: Arlen House, 1986.
   Stories.
Fare Well: Beir Beannacht. Dublin: Attic Press, 1990. Poetry.

Notes
1. Private communication.
2. In *Wildish Things*, Ailbhe Smyth, ed. (Dublin: Attic Press,
   1989), 17-20.
3. In *Fare Well: Beir Beannacht*, 57, 56, 73.

Kennedy, Anne
Born: USA, 1935
Educated: USA.

Anne Kennedy was born in Los Angeles, grew up in
Beverly Hills, and was taught English at the Marlborough
School for Girls by a woman who brought 'literature
vibrantly alive'. 'There was an unforced, semi-reverential
clarity to her readings of Amy Lowell, H D, etc. that
completely answered some early need of my own,' she
writes.[1] Attending Stanford and the University of
California at Berkeley in the 1950s, she was again fortunate
in her teachers, Yvor Winters and Mark Schorer, the latter
now better known for his criticism than for his fiction. This
was an era of mental expansion: the 'Beat' poets, Oriental
mysticism, the return from Korea of the veterans, 'bringing
a world awareness and disillusion that counterbalanced to
a small degree the ruthless reign of terror known as
"McCarthyism"'[2].

   During the 1960s, she lived in Laurel Canyon and is
currently working on a memoir of her life there, among
artists, musicians, and writers. In the early 1970s, she
moved to Orcas Island in the San Juans, north of Seattle,
and this is the experience she records in *Buck Mountain
Poems* (1989). After seven wonderful years, she and the two
youngest of her five children moved to Galway. Here she

began her career in photography, joined the Galway Writers' Workshop, wrote her first poems, originally a radio documentary for RTE, and here, too, she now gives writing workshops herself.

Kennedy introduces her reader to the Chinese hermit Han Shan in her 'Introduction' to *Buck Mountain Poems* — appropriately, because her own poems catch something of the serenity and minute attention to nature of both Chinese and Japanese poetry. A few brief lines quietly convey each experience, sometimes the grandeur of nature:

> Last night my road sliced the sky
> all the way to the Arctic;
> my neighbour called it the Northern Lights.[3]

Or the odd harmony of human beings and nature: 'the glittering caps from beer bottles; ... companions of pebbles and shells and spouting ferns, / machined symmetry / amidst the crazy chaos of the ordinary.'(6) Or the juxtapositions of observed life:

> Branches breaking at midnight
> too loud to be rabbit or racoon
> or the surefooted deer
> moving with ease
> on the steep slopes of Buck Mountain.
> After drinking so much beer
> has my neighbour lost his footing
> and fallen among the crackling ferns? (19)

Allison Judd, Anne Kennedy's daughter, illustrated *Buck Mountain Poems*.

Works:
Buck Mountain Poems. Galway: Salmon Publishing, 1989. Poetry.

Notes
1. Personal communication.
2. Personal communication.
3. *Buck Mountain Poems*, 1.

Kenny, Mary

Born: 1944
Educated: Ireland.

Born in Dublin, Mary Kenny was very involved in the formation of the Irish Women's liberation movement in the seventies. She wrote for the *Irish Press*, before becoming a Fleet Street journalist. She now lives in London.

Most of Mary's writing is serious non-fiction, on subjects ranging from abortion and motherhood to Christianity, but she has published a collection of short stories, *A Mood for Love* (1989). This is a sharp witty collection of stories which move from the 1960s to the 1980s. The backdrops range from Dublin to Budapest and Brussels, though many are based in London.

Selected Works:
Woman X Two: how to cope with a double life. London, Sidgewick & Jackson, 1978. Non-fiction.
Why Christianity Works. London: Joseph, 1981. Non-fiction.
Abortion:the whole story. London: Quartet, 1986. Non-fiction.
A Mood for Love. New York/London: Quartet Books, 1989. Stories.

Kinahan, Coralie

Born: England, 1924
Educated: England.

Born in Surrey in 1924, Coralie Kinahan was 'un-educated by three nurses, fourteen governesses, and four schools, the last of which the Germans mercifully dropped a bomb on, ensuring my release, aged fourteen'. Thereupon her mother essayed, unsuccessfully, to teach her Roman and Greek History, and she took a correspondence course in art. She worked as under-matron in a boys' school, and reports being sacked for swopping her chocolate ration for boys' oranges. When she became an under-matron in a girls' school, she finally educated herself: the geography and history mistress fell, breaking five ribs; Coralie was roped in, spent nights learning the next day's lessons, and – along with her class of fifteen-year-olds – became educated.

After the war, she returned to art, studied book illustration for two years at Chelsea Polytechnic and took private lessons in portrait painting. To pay her expenses she took in sewing, making fine lingerie from silk parachutes; clothes and fabrics were still rationed. She was immediately successful as an artist: her portraits hung in the Royal Academy, London, and in the Royal Society of Portrait Painters. She won a bronze medal for her portrait of 'The Huntsman' at the British Olympic Exhibition in 1948 in London. Her painting career was temporarily halted by her marriage to Sir Robin Kinahan in 1950 and the birth and care of her five children. She returned to painting when the youngest child went away to school and has had a One Woman Exhibition every year since 1964 in an Irish or English town. She opened her own gallery in 1981 in the old brewery of the once-tumbling-down castle she and her husband bought in Castle Upton, Co. Antrim.

'Pitchforked into political, urban, and business life,' in 1956, when she became Lady Mayoress of Belfast, her own inclinations were toward solitude, nature, and fox-hunting. She has always enjoyed writing and became very interested in Ulster/Irish history: she 'felt Ulster was very much mis-represented ... nothing but bigotry and graffiti, whereas it is a most beautiful, peaceful and friendly place ... victimised by politicians, press, and terrorists, so I decided to write absolutely accurate, easy to understand, happy novels telling its story.' Because her father was from a Norman-Irish family in Kildare, her mother from a Scottish ancestor who escaped to Ulster before the massacre at Glencoe, and because she was not herself brought up in Ulster, she believes she has an objective view of the Irish situation.

She writes about what she knows: 'Country gentry ... who worked hard for their country, served it and frequently suffered and died for it, but had a great rapport with their workers.' 'I think Ireland does itself untold damage by playing to the American misconception of it. I feel that being married to a leading Irish businessman, who is a shrewd natural politician, and was honoured by being made HMS Lord Lieutenant, I have met all the pieces on the Irish chessboard and have a rather particular insight.' Although she loves writing about her beloved country, she regrets that Irish Ulster political novels are not popular with English publishers, who associate them 'with Salman Rushdie-like repercussions'. Her two historical novels are set in Ulster from 1912-20. She has also written a biography of George A Birmingham, and is completing a 'hilarious' dual-autobiography of herself and her husband. She is working on two more novels.[1]

Works:
You can't shoot the English! Belfast: Pretani, 1982. Novel.
After the War came ... Peace? Belfast: Pretani, 1988. Novel.

Notes
1. All information is personal communication.

— L —

Lane, Temple (Mary Isabel Leslie/Jane Herbert)

Born: Irelnad, 1899; Died: 1982
Educated: England, Ireland.

Temple Lane's real name was Mary Isabel Leslie, though she also wrote under the name Jane Herbert. She was born in Dublin and attended Trinity College, Dublin, where she won a gold medal and later became a doctor of philosophy. Her poetry was collected in two volumes and her work enjoyed popularity in the 1940s.[1]

Selected Works

Burnt Bridges. London: Long, 1925. Novel.
No Just Cause. London: Long, 1925. Novel.
Defiance. London: Long, 1926. Novel.
Second Sight. London: Long, 1926. Novel.
Watch the Wall. London: Long, 1927. Novel.
The Bands of Orion. London: Jarrolds, 1928. Novel.
The Little Wood. London: Jarrolds, 1930. Novel.
Blind Wedding. London: Jarrolds, 1931. Novel.
Sinner Anthony. London: Jarrolds, 1933. Novel.
The Trains Go South. London: Jarrolds, 1938. Novel.
Battle of the Warrior. London; Jarrolds, 1940. Novel.
Fisherman's Wake. London: Longmans, 1940. Poetry.
Curlews. The Talbot Press, Dublin, 1946. Poetry.
Fisherman's Wake. Longmans, London, 1940. Poetry.

Notes

1. from A A Kelly's Pillars of the House, 99.
House of My Pilgrimage. Dublin: Talbot, 1941; London: Muller, 1941. Novel.

Friday's Well. Dublin: Talbot, 1943. Novel.
Come Back! Dublin: Talbot, 1945. Novel.
Curlews. Dublin: Talbot, 1946. Poetry.
My Bonny's Away. Dublin: Talbot, 1947. Novel.

Notes
1. *Dictionary of Irish Literature, Robert Hogan,* ed. (Westport, Conn.: Greenwood Press, 1979), 360-61; and *A Biographical Dictionary of Irish Writers,* Anne M Brady and Brian Cleeve, eds. (Mullingar: Lilliput Press, 1985), 126.

Laverty, Maura (Kelly)
Born: Ireland, 1907; Died: 1966
Educated: Ireland.

Maura Kelly was born and raised in Rathangan, Co. Kildare, and trained as a teacher in Carlow. She spent three years in Spain, working as a governess and journalist. She continued journalism when she returned to Ireland, where she also became a broadcaster, expert in cooking, and novelist.

She was very well-known in Ireland during the 1950s and 1960s; her programmes were popular and her cookbooks were in many homes. Her first novel, *Never No More* (1942), introduced a gentle, nurturing grandmother (surely modelled on her own grandmother), the young heroine's comfort in a harsh, insensitive world. Laverty wrote of what she knew well: her own life, convent schools, rural Ireland in the 1930s, and the friction between family members. Ordinary events are remarked with common sense wisdom, but not exaggerated. Although Delia, the heroine of *Never No More,* identifies with and adores her lazy, easy-going father, she also understands that this very personality contributes to her mother's sharpness, and to her mother's criticism of herself as too like him. In her grandmother's house, however, Delia can do no wrong and notes, 'I was as tractable and obedient and willing as I had been impudent and difficult at home. It was just that Gran and I reacted on each other in such a way that we always gave, one to the other, our very best. With my mother it was the opposite, although with others of her children she enjoyed the relationship that Gran enjoyed with me. I have found that it is the same with people everywhere. Kinship has nothing to do with it, nor virtue, nor lack of virtue. Human nature is like bread, I think. Soda-bread calls for buttermilk, and baking powder bread for new milk. Use the wrong kind of milk, and the bread is sodden. Gran was the right kind of milk for me.'[1]

No More than Human (1944) focuses on an Irish governess in Spain, while *Lift Up Your Gates* (1946) explores the life of Dublin slums and middle-class homes. The latter was the source of the popular Telefís Éireann series, *Tolka Row. Alone We Embark* (1943), was banned in Ireland, but received an Irish Women Writers' Award.[2] Besides novels, Maura Laverty wrote cookbooks and children's stories. Maeve Binchy writes a warm, affectionate introduction to the Virago edition of *Never No More.*

Selected Works:
Never No More. 1942; rpt. London: Virago, 1985, 1992. Novel.
Alone We Embark. London: Longmans, 1943; in USA as *Touched by the Thorn.* New York: Longmans, Green, 1943. Novel.
No More than Human. 1944; rpt. London: Virago, 1986. Novel.
The Cottage in the Bog. 1945; rpt. Dublin: Town House, 1992. Young Adult.
Lift Up Your Gates. London: Longmans, Green, 1946; in USA as *Liffey Lane.* New York: Longmans, Green, 1947. Novel.

Notes
1. *Never No More,* 24. (1942 edition)
2. *Dictionary of Irish Literature,* Robert Hogan, ed. (Westport, Conn: Greenwood Press, 1979), 363.

Lavin, Mary
Born: USA, 1912
Educated: Ireland.

Mary Lavin was born in 1912, to Irish parents living in Massachusetts. Her mother hated the USA and wanted to go back to Ireland immediately after her marriage; pregnancy delayed her, but she eventually got her way and returned with her nine-year-old daughter to her home town, Athenry, Co. Galway. Her husband eventually joined them and managed a farm in Bective, Co. Meath. Mary visited him regularly in Meath, while living with her mother in Dublin and attending the Loreto Convent, Stephen's Green. When she married her first husband, William Walsh, she continued this pattern, buying a farm in Meath and keeping a small home in Dublin, from which her three daughters attended school.

She writes of a happy, privileged childhood. She was an only child, much loved by both parents, and treated as a special person in the Athenry of her mother's large family. She loved her father very much and believes that he was a person 'well worth loving'. 'I always assume that any gifts I have inherited came from my father because of the real depth and power of his emotion ... and yet, looking back on it, I think that I may be unjust to my mother, because I thought of her as a rather giddy little person, full of stories. She was always telling me stories of her own childhood. Unlike me she had a great memory. There was simply nothing she forgot about her childhood and later, when I came to write, I think I drew on *her* memories. Her memories seemed to become more real than my own.'[1]

Mary Lavin's stories have won many awards, and she has earned an international reputation as a gifted short story writer. She excels in revealing the many strange twists love takes, and as we read we are struck by a sense of familiarity, as someone at last untangles and verbalises the tangled threads of emotions we have ourselves experienced. Tensions threaten to spill over in 'A Family Likeness,' for example, as the elderly Ada, her tired daughter Laura, and Laura's small child Daff search for primroses. On the rather long walk to the woods, Ada suggests that primroses grow on banks, not in woods, and points to a bank close by.

'Oh. Do you not want to go any farther, Mother? Is that it?' Laura asked. 'You could go back from here, if you wish, and I could take Daff to the edge of the woods and let her get a glimpse of ...'

'Of what? The primroses are on the bank.'

'That's right.' Laura ceded graciously enough. 'Well, suppose you and Daff go over there and you sit down, while she picks a little bunch, and I go on to the woods. It's ages since I've been over there and it's important I keep fit.'

Fine as the prick of the smallest needle ever made, one with an eye so narrow it was quite impossible to thread, Ada's heart was pierced with sadness. Had her daughter seen that she was failing? She, who up to such a short time ago had been indefatigable, possessed indeed of far more energy than Laura herself had ever enjoyed.

'I don't want to sit down, Laura,' she said. With a pang she remembered the way her own mother had laid a querulous emphasis on some words. 'The grass may be damp,' she added meekly.

'Damp? That bank, with the sun pouring down on it since dawn?' Laura laughed, but glancing at her mother, she seemed to suffer a change of heart. 'I suppose it wouldn't be any harm for us all to take a short rest,' she said. 'Come on, Daff. This way.'

Why did she have to speak so peremptorily to the child, Ada wondered. 'The primroses are over there, dear,' she explained. When Daff didn't budge, she appealed to Laura. 'The child really is tired,' she said.

'All to the good. Maybe after this she might sleep through the night for a change.' Laura swung around savagely. 'Last night, she woke me at least three times.'

'I didn't hear a sound. Why didn't you call me?'
Ada tried to keep her voice down.

'And if I did?'[2]

Later Ada tries to make up to Laura, noting that her own
mother used to upset her when she offered advice on
mothering. Laura rejects the palm, however, and rejoins
with her own memories of the good times she and her
grandmother shared, insisting that Ada never understood
her own mother. All the old frustration wells up as Ada
recalls the hours her mother kept her waiting as a child,
'while she attended to some fiddle-faddle.' 'Such as?' Laura
asks.

'Oh' Ada sighed wearily. Those memories of her
mother were becoming too painful to contemplate.
'In those days, I think it was letter-writing,' she said
apathetically. 'She'd sit for hours at the dining-room
table dashing off page after page and then she'd go
out to the pillar box before she'd pay any attention to
us.'

'Letters to whom?'

'How do I know?' Ada was exasperated by this
inquisition, but just then it was as if a shaft of light
fell on the hand of that long-dead writer and she was
confounded by what it revealed. 'Wait, Laura. I *do*
know. She was writing to her own mother. To my
grandmother. How could I have forgotten? She
wrote to her every other day, long interminable
letters.' (16)

Lavin's short stories have been collected in several
volumes in the USA and Britain; the original titles only are
listed below.

Selected Works:
Tales from Bective Bridge. 1942; Dublin: Poolbeg Press, 1978. Short
Stories.
The Long Ago and Other Stories. London: Michael Joseph, 1944.
Short Stories.
The House in Clewe Street. London: Michael Joseph, 1945. Novel.

The Becker Wives. 1946; New York: New American Library, 1971. Short Stories.

At Sallygap. Boston: Little, Brown, 1947. Short Stories.

Mary O'Grady. London: Michael Joseph, 1950. Novel.

A Single Lady and Other Stories. London: Michael Joseph, 1951. Short Stories.

The Patriot Son and Other Stories. London: Michael Joseph, 1956. Short Stories.

The Great Wave and Other Stories. London: Macmillan, 1961. Short Stories.

In the Middle of the Fields and Other Stories. London: Constable, 1967. Short Stories.

Happiness and Other Stories. London: Constable, 1969. Short Stories.

A Memory and Other Stories. London: Constable, 1972. Short Stories.

The Shrine and Other Stories. London: Constable, 1977. Short Stories.

A Family Likeness and Other Stories. London: Constable, 1985. Short Stories.

Notes

1. In *A Portrait of the Artist as a Young Girl*, John Quinn, ed. (London: Methuen, 1986), 85-86.
2. 'A Family Likeness', *A Family Likeness*, 10.

Lawless, Emily
Born: Ireland, 1845; Died: 1913
Educated: Ireland, England.

Emily Lawless was the second child of Lord Cloncurry, the son of Valentine Lawless, a sympathiser with the United Irishmen of 1798 and opponent of the 1800 Union with England. Her great-grandfather left the Catholic church, was elected to parliament and created a baronet. One of the best-known novelists and poets of her day, her most interesting work focuses sympathetically on Anglo-Irish relations; she can be seen as a forerunner of the Irish literary renaissance, but she herself remained a unionist.

Gladstone admired her work, believing it shed light on the Irish question, and Yeats listed two of her novels, *With Essex in Ireland* (1890) and *Maelcho* (1894) among the sixteen best Irish works of fiction.[1]

The first Irish novel, *Hurrish* (1886), explores the relationship of Irish tenant farmers and English rule, or misrule. Set in the beautiful and strange landscape of the Burren, Co. Clare, this is one of the earliest Irish novels to introduce this beauty. 'Most small hills', she writes, 'are rich in grass,

> But these Burren hills are literally not clothed at all.
> They are startlingly, I may say scandalously, naked.
> From their base up to the battered turret of rock which
> serves as a summit, not a patch, not a streak, not an
> indication even, of green is often to be found in the
> whole extent. On others a thin sprinkling of grass
> struggles upward for a few hundred feet, and in
> valleys and hollows, where the washings of the rocks
> have accumulated, a grass grows, famous all over
> cattle-feeding Ireland for its powers of fattening. So,
> too, in the long vertical rifts or fissures which
> everywhere cross and recross its surface, maiden-hair
> ferns and small tender – petalled flowers unfurl, out of
> reach of the cruel blasts. These do not, however, affect
> the general impression, which is that of nakedness
> personified — not comparative, but absolute. The rocks
> are not scattered over the surface, as in other stony
> tracts, but the whole surface is rock. They are not hills,
> in fact, but skeletons – rain-worn, time-worn, wind-
> worn, – starvation made visible, and embodied in a
> landscape.[2]

With Essex in Ireland (1890), written in Elizabethan English, purports to be Henry Harvey's account of Essex's march through much of Ireland – again a record of tragic misconceptions. *Grania: The Story of an Island* (1892) is a tragic love story set on Inishmaan, Aran Islands. In this pre-Synge account, Lawless attempts to translate the Gaelic of the islanders into English, while suggesting the differences between the languages. *Maelcho* (1894) goes back to the sixteenth century and the atrocities of the competing armies on Irish soil. *Traits and Confidences* (1898), her last completed work of adult fiction, includes several stories and an autobiographical essay. A spinster, she spent her last years living with her devoted friend Lady Sarah Spencer in Surrey, England.

Works:
A Chelsea Householder. 3 vol. London: Sampson Low, 1882. Novel.
Ireland, with additions by Mrs A Browson. London: Unwin, 1885; revised, with two new chapters, London; Unwin, 1912. History.
A Millionaire's Cousin. London: Macmillan, 1885. Novel.
Hurrish. Edinburgh: Blackwood, 1886. Novel.
Major Lawrence, F L S. 3 vol. London: J Murray, 1887. Novel.
Plain Frances Mowbray and Other Tales. London: J Murray, 1889. Stories.
With Essex in Ireland. London: Smith, Elder, 1890. Historical Novel.
Grania: The Story of an Island. 2 vol. London: Smith, Elder, 1892. Novel.
Maelcho. 2 vols. London: Smith, Elder, 1894. Historical Novel.
Traits and Confidences. London: Methuen, 1898. Stories.
A Garden Diary. September 1899 - September 1900. London: Methuen, 1901.
With the Wild Geese. London: Isbister, 1902. Poetry.
Maria Edgeworth. London: Macmillan, 1904. Literary Biography.
The Book of Gilly: Four Months Out of a Life. London: Smith, Elder, 1906.
The Race of Castlebar. Finished by Shan F Bullock. London: J Murray, 1913. Novel.

Notes
1. Robert Lee Wolff, 'The Irish Fiction of the Honourable Emily Lawless', *Traits and Confidences* (1897; rpt. New York and London: Garland, 1979).

Leadbeater, Mary
Born: Ireland, 1758; Died: 1826
Educated: Ireland.

Mary Leadbeater was born into a Quaker family, the Shackletons of Ballitore, Co. Kildare. She wrote sketches of cottage life and tales for cottagers, as well as poetry. Her account of the life of her village in the *Leadbeater Papers* (1862) includes an account of the 1798 Rebellion. She was a friend to Maria Edgeworth, who helped circulate the *Cottage Dialogues Among the Irish Peasantry* (1811).

The quality of her poetry is not remarkable, but the poems – like the papers – often shed light on interesting aspects of life in an early nineteenth-century Irish village. 'On a Visit Paid to Ballitore', for example, celebrates the visit of the great Edmund Burke to Ballitore, while a note on the poem confirms his kindness and sensitivity. Burke, Leadbeater notes, presented his son to the steward who knew Burke as a boy: "You have many friends in Ireland, Sir," – "I am happy, Mr Gill, you are one of them – You look very well. – Am I much changed since you saw me?" The old man, whose eyes were dimmed by age, and perhaps by grateful tears, answered that he could not see. Then Edmund Burke, with all that kindness and affability for which he was so remarkable, took up a candle, and holding it to his own face, gave poor Gill a full view of it, and afforded a scene which those who were present cannot easily forget.'[1]

Selected Works:
Poems. Dublin: Martin Keene/London: Longman, Hurst, Rees & Orme, 1808. Poetry.
Cottage Dialogues among the Irish Peasantry. London: Johnson, 1811. Sketches.
Tales for Cottagers, Accommodated to the Present Condition of the Irish Peasantry. Dublin: Cumming, 1814. Short Stories.
Cottage Biography. Dublin: C Bentham, 1822. Biography.
Memoirs and Letters of Richard and Elizabeth Shackleton. London: Harvey & Darton, 1822. Memoir.

Biographical Notices of Members of the Society of Friends, Who Were Resident in Ireland. London: Harvey & Darton, 1823. Brief Biographical Notes.

The Pedlars. Dublin: Bentham & Harvey, 1826.

The Leadbeater Papers. 2 vols. London: Bell & Daldy, 1862. Memoir.

Notes

1. *Poems*, 1808, 115, note.

Leland, Mary
Born: Ireland, 1941
Educated: Ireland.

Mary Leland was born and raised in Cork, where she attended the South Presentation Convent and Miss O'Sullivan's private school. A wonderful teacher of English at Miss O'Sullivan's encouraged her to write, showing her 'connections', and giving her a hearty appetite for drama and the 'nice parts of religion'. This teacher was instrumental in suggesting to her parents that she go into journalism, which she did with the *Cork Examiner*.

She thanks Donal Foley, the news editor of *The Irish Times*, for allowing herself and other women to write 'colour stories' behind the news, and thus allowing them to experiment with unrestricted prose. She sent her first short story to David Marcus for the 'New Irish Writing' page in the *Irish Press*, and she praises his editorial diligence in responding to new writers. 'Displaced Persons' won the Listowel Writers' Short Story Award in 1980. She also received two bursaries from the Arts Council, one in 1985 to help her write *The Little Galloway Girls* (1987) and the other in 1990 when she was working on *Approaching Priests* (1991). She has three children and works as a journalist and feature writer; her work appears in the *Sunday Independent*, *The Irish Times*, and the *Sunday Tribune*.[1]

The Killeen (1985), her first novel, is set in the countryside and city of Cork in the 1930s. The government of the Republican, de Valera, is in power, but the more republican Republicans, who never gave up hopes of a thirty-two-county Ireland, attempt to use England's preoccupation with Germany to reach their goals. Life in impoverished Ireland is grim and harsh, and sensitive characters are especially vulnerable in such an environment. The heroes and priests, who exercise a great deal of influence, discount women, whether wealthy and educated, like Julia Mulcahy, or poor and uneducated, like Margaret Coakley. Maurice Mulcahy, whom the lovely Julia has married in haste in Paris, places his dream of himself as hero above his life and his wife's happiness. Maurice's return, his jailing and subsequent hunger-strike, are welcomed by his vulture-like family, who rebuff Julia's anger at their implicit cheer-leading: 'He feels deeply for the cause, Julia. Very deeply indeed. Who can interfere with a man's right to fight for his country?'[2] But it is not, Leland shows, the cause that compels Maurice so much as the intoxication of becoming 'immortal' through martyrdom.

The Ireland Leland presents is contaminating. Julia will leave Ireland rather than allow her husband's family train her child in a school for 'intellectual and military activists'. (113) But she encourages the unmarried Margaret to leave her child there, repressing her intuition that this 'exchange' will ensure both her own liberty and her son's. Margaret breaks her bargain with Julia and forces her own unmarried brother, Michael, to take her son to the country homeplace. Michael in his turn deserts both his girl-friend and his other sister, sacrificing them to his needs. Throughout, we are conscious of the killeen. The lonely, deserted, unhallowed graveyard to which the Catholic church consigns unbaptised babies serves as appropriate symbol of church and country's care of the tender and vulnerable.

The protagonist in the most recent work, *Approaching Priests*, whose life is enriched through her classical education, finds the Ireland of Post-Vatican II and the EEC a diminished place. This novel 'approaches' new subjects for Leland, and the perspective is unusual in an Ireland that is determinedly European and modern.

Works:

The Killeen. London: Hamish Hamilton, 1985; London: Black Swan, 1986; New York: Atheneum. Novel.

The Little Galloway Girls. London: Hamish Hamilton, 1987. Stories.

Approaching Priests. London: Sinclair Stevenson, 1991. Novel.

Notes

1. Personal communication.
2. *The Killeen*, 105.

Lendennie, Jessie

Born: USA c 20th century
Educated: USA.

An American woman living in Galway, Jessie Lendennie established Salmon Publishing, a press that publishes Irish and international poetry. Salmon Publishing performs a service in opening the way for many new poets and for many non-traditional poets. Salmon gives equal consideration to men and women poets, but is often seen as a women's press, 'an illustration,' Lendennie notes, 'of how few Irish publishers have a significant number of women on their lists.'[1] It has also published one volume of Lendennie's own work, a prose-poem, *Daughter* (1988).

Daughter records the vivid and hurting memories of a young child, memories of exchanges between herself and her mother before her mother's death. Lendennie describes the awful clarity of scenes burned into the child's memory, scenes in which she ignored or complained to her mother, the mother whose love she understands now, the mother she never remembers telling of her love. Although she doesn't know the word 'cancer', the child intuits the threat to her mother and to herself, a threat which is all the more frightening because she cannot articulate it: 'Emma began to hate the sun, the yellow grass, the shadeless trees; hated the smiling girls in their lovely patterned dresses.'[2] There is 'no forgetting' (4) the scenes of rejection:

> 'Emma, where are you going?'
> 'Just across the road, Mom'
> 'Will you stay with me for a little while?'
> Emma shuffled her feet,
> put her hand on the door (56)

The poem itself expresses the child's unstated love, concluding with her cry, 'If you love me, take me with you.' (67)

Works:
Daughter. Galway: Salmon Publishing, 1988. Poetry.

Notes
1. Salmon Publishing Catalogue.
2. *Daughter*, 54.

Lentin, Ronit
Born: Israel, 1944
Educated: Israel, Ireland.
Ronit Lentin was born in Haifa, Israel, attended Reali School in Haifa and the Hebrew University in Jerusalem. She has lived in Ireland since 1969, completed an M Phil in Women's Studies in 1991, and is currently working on a PhD in Sociology/Women's Studies in Trinity College, Dublin. She has worked as a freelance writer for several Irish papers, edited the health section of *IT* magazine, published novels in Hebrew and English, published non-fiction, and had plays broadcast by Israeli and Irish radio.

Her husband, Louis, is a television and theatre producer and director, and they have two children.

Her life has been shaped, she writes, 'mostly by being an Israeli-born daughter of European Jewish parents who left central Europe before the Holocaust but whose families were not spared'. Having grown up in Israel, in 'the first generation to the redemption and with the inculcated beliefs that Jews must be strong or perish, has, paradoxically, brought me, after the '67 war, to the realisation that there is an alternative to wars. I have devoted a lot of my work to trying to grapple with co-existence issues with Palestinians as well as the complex question of my own post-Holocaust Jewish identity.'[1]

Lentin's first two novellas, *Stone of Claims*, and *Like a Blindman*, both in Hebrew and published in Tel Aviv in 1975 and 1977 respectively, explore female Israeli-Jewish identity in relation to Palestinians in the first and to Germans in the second. *Conversations with Palestinian Women* (1982) 'is a series of interviews with Palestinian leaders including Dr Hanan Ashrawi'. Living in Ireland, she notes, has broadened her perception of the Jewish diaspora and of anti-semitism. *Tea with Mrs Klein* (1985), tells of a friendship between a parish priest and a Jewish woman, and 'takes up ethnic and gender issues in the life of Irish Jewry'. Her feminist consciousness was shaped with the development of the women's movement in Ireland, and her academic work reflects her interest in the 'dual consciousness of woman and Jew'.[2]

Night Train to Mother (1989) is the story of Ruth's journey from Israel to Northern Romania, to the childhood home of her mother Carla, grandmother Rosa, and great-grandmother Dora. Chapters are devoted to each of the women, and to Hetti, sister of Rosa, who joins the Communist party in pre-World War II Romania.

Lentin also introduces us to days of sun and happiness, to weddings and dancing, to cooking and feasting, to the good life of middle-class European Jews before both world wars.

Works:
Stone of Claims. Tel Aviv: Siman Kria, 1975. Novel.
Like a Blindman. Tel Aviv: Siman Kria, 1977. Novel.
Tea with Mrs Klein. Dublin: Wolfhound Press, 1985. Novel.
Night Train to Mother. Dublin: Attic Press, 1989; Pittsburgh: Cleis
    Press, 1990. Novel.
Who is Minding the Children? Co-authored with Geraldine
    Niland. Dublin: Arlen House, 1981. Reference.
Conversations with Palestinian Women. Jerusalem: Mifras, 1982.
    Interviews.

Notes
1. Personal communication.
2. Personal communication.

Letts, Winifred M
Born: 1882; Died: 1972
Educated: England, Ireland.

Winifred Letts was born in 1882 and educated in St Anne's
Abbots, Bromley, and at Alexandra College, Dublin. She
was married to W H F Verschoyle. She wrote plays, poetry,
fiction, children's stories, hagiography, and memoirs. Two
of her plays were produced at the Abbey and one at the
Gate.

She wrote of Dublin and the countryside, and, like
many poets of her generation, war. 'Golden Boys'
celebrates, with the optimism typical of the early years of
World War I, the young dead:

Not harps and palms for these, O God,
Nor endless rest within the courts of Heaven, —
These happy boys who left the football field,
The hockey ground, the river, the eleven,
In a far grimmer game, with high elated souls
To score their goals.

The poet prays that these shining boys may 'Still test their manhood's strength' as they 'With Cherubim contend'. Heaven is brighter for their presence:

> Let there be laughter and a merry noise
> Now that the fields of Heaven shine
> With all these golden boys.[1]

Selected Works:
The Mighty Army. New York: Stokes, 1912. Hagiography.
Songs from Leinster. London: Murray, 1913. Poetry.
Halloween and Poems of the War. London: Smith, Elder, 1916. Poetry.
The Spires of Oxford and Other Poems. New York: E P Dutton, 1917. Poetry.
More Songs of Leinster. London: J Murray/New York: E P Dutton, 1926. Poetry.
St Patrick the Travelling Man. London: J Nicholson & Watson, 1932. Biography.
Knockmaroon. London: J Murray, 1938. Memoirs.

Notes
1. In *Halloween and Poems of the War*, 16.

Levine, June

Born: Ireland c 20th century
Educated: Ireland.

June Levine worked as a journalist in the 1970s and was a researcher on *The Late Late Show*, a famed weekly chat show which show-cased many of the contentious issues in Ireland at that time. She was a founder member of the Irish women's liberation movement.

June grew up in Ireland, and went through marriage, breakdown and divorce in Canada. Her earlier work *Sisters* (1982) traces her story and the foundation of the Irish women's liberation movement.

A Season of Weddings (1992) features a heroine who escapes from her marriage into a romantic friendship with a young Indian mother.

Works:
Sisters. Dublin: Ward River Press, 1982. Autobiographical novel.
Lyn. June Levine and Lyn Madden, Dublin: Attic Press, 1987. Non-fiction.
A Season of Weddings. Dublin, New Island Books, 1992. Novel.

Lingard, Joan
Born: Scotland, 1932
Educated: Ireland.

Joan Lingard was born in Edinburgh, her mother's hometown. She grew up and was educated in Belfast, as her father was in the Royal Navy Reserve Service working on a training ship docked in Belfast. Although the family lived in a Protestant stronghold, she did not feel she belonged to either Protestant or Catholic groups because her mother and herself were Christian Scientists. She attended Strandtown Primary School, and at eleven, Bloomfield Collegiate, which was connected with the local Presbyterian Church. Her father was away from home a great deal, but she and her mother had a very close relationship. At sixteen, she faced the trauma of her life when her mother died; this was also the beginning of her rejection of the principles of Christian Science.

'My memory of Belfast', she writes, 'is very much coloured by the war, which impinged a lot on my childhood. I remember the blackout in particular, the air-raid shelters and coming home with a torch, worrying about the dark. Belfast was the city of dark for me at that time, whereas Dublin became the city of light.'[1] Her first published book – she wrote four in copybooks as a child – *Liam's Daughter* (1963), was set in northern Ireland and France; the characters were Irish. After writing six novels for adults, she turned to books for children. Published by Hamish Hamilton and Puffin, the Kevin and Sadie Quintet, *Twelfth Day of July*, *Across the Barricades*, *Into Exile*, *A Proper Place*, and *Hostages to Fortune*, set in contemporary Belfast, are known world-wide. The Maggie Quartet, *The Clearance*, *The Resettling*, *The Pilgrimage* and *The Reunion*, and followed along with many other very successful books for children. *Across the Barricades* won the West German Buxtehuder Bulle Award in 1986. *Tug of War* (1989), inspired by her husband's experiences as a war refugee, was shortlisted for the Carnegie Medal in 1989, the Federation of Children's Book Group Award in 1989, runner up in the Lancashire Children's Book Club of the Year in 1990, and shortlisted in the Sheffield Book Award.

The early adult novels focus on the divides of northern Ireland; her characters are fully developed and sympathetic: they are embroiled in the common problems of their class and political persuasion, but they are always also individuals. Later novels move away from northern Ireland, and continue to present common problems from the perspective of sympathetic, attractive individuals. The most recent, *The Women's House* (1989), introduces three women living together, at different stages of life and from different classes. At eighty-five, Evangeline is failing physically, though mentally the retired writer is fully alive, interested in those around her. Anna is in her mid-forties, a very talented mime artist. Holly is eighteen, has run away from her abusive mother and slum home, and now works in a Pizza joint and devours the books Evangeline gives her. The story revolves about the efforts of a wealthy Italian entrepreneur family to force the women to move out of the house which the Italians have purchased. The friendship of the women is convincing, built on respect and interest, and eventually on affection. As readers, we understand what the women admire in each other, while we sympathize with Evangeline's ageing and growing dependence, with Anna's need for independence and desire for love, and with Holly's pretence of a happy and indulgent home. This is a quiet, impressive story of the enduring friendship of women.

Selected Works:
Liam's Daughter. London: Hodder and Stoughton, 1963. Novel.
The Prevailing Wind. London: Hodder and Stoughton, 1964. Novel.
The Tide Comes In. London: Hodder and Stoughton, 1966. Novel.
The Headmaster. London: Hodder and Stoughton, 1967. Novel.
The Lord on Our Side. London: Hodder and Stoughton, nd. Novel.
The Second Flowering of Emily Mountjoy. Edinburgh: Harris, 1979. Novel.
Sisters by Rite. London: Hamish Hamilton, 1984. Novel.
Reasonable Doubts. London: Hamish Hamilton, 1986. Novel.
The Women's House. London: Hamish Hamilton, 1989. Novel.

Children's Books:
The Kevin and Sadie Quartet:
Twelfth Day of July. London: Hamish Hamilton, 1970. Novel.
Across the Barricades. London: Hamish Hamilton, 1972. Novel.
Into Exile. London: Hamish Hamilton, 1973. Novel.
A Proper Place. London: Hamish Hamilton, 1975. Novel.
Hostages to Fortune. London: Hamish Hamilton, 1988. Novel.

The Maggie Quartet:
The Clearance. London: Beaver, 1981. Novel.
The Resettling. London: Beaver, 1987. Novel.
The Pilgrimage. London: Beaver, 1989. Novel.
The Reunion. London: Beaver, 1989. Novel.

Others:
The Gooseberry. London: Beaver, 1984. Novel.
The Winter Visitor. London: Beaver, 1984. Novel.
The Tug of War. London: Beaver, 1989. Novel.

Notes
1. In *A Portrait of the Artist as a Young Girl*, John Quinn, ed. (London: Methuen, 1986), 102.

Llywelyn, Morgan
Born: c 20th century
Educated: United States of America.

Morgan Llywelyn focuses on the mythic and the historical. She writes of Cuchulain and the Red Branch warriors, of druidic figures and heroes and heroines. Brushed by the 'raven's wing', Cuchulain accepts the goddess of war Morrigan as his talisman and his rage in war is fearsome in *On Raven's Wind* (1990).

Selected Works:
Bard, The Odyssey of the Irish. Boston: Houghton Mifflin, 1984. Novel.
Red Branch. New York: W Morrow, 1989. Novel.
Grania: She-King of the Irish Seas. 1986; rpt. London: Sphere Books, 1987. Novel.
On Raven's Wing. London: Heinemann, 1990. Novel.
Druids. London: Heineman, 1991. Novel.

Longford, Lady Christine
Born: England, 1900; Died: 1980
Educated: England.

Christine Patti Trew was born in Chedder, Somerset, and educated at Somerset College, Oxford. After her marriage to Edward Pakenham, the Earl of Longford, she lived in Ireland and wrote many plays for the Gate Theatre founded by her husband. She translated the Greek classics, adapted Irish and English novels, wrote comedies, histories, and novels.[1]

Selected Works:
Making Conversation. London: Stein & Gollancz, 1931. Novel.
Country Places. London: Gollancz, 1932. Novel.
Mr Jiggins of Jigginstown. London: Gollancz, 1933. Novel.
Printed Cotton. London: Methuen, 1935. Novel.
Mr Jiggins of Jigginstown in Plays of Changing Ireland. Edited Curtins Canfield. New York: Macmillan, 1936. Play.

Lord Edward. Dublin: Hodges, Figgis, 1941. Play.
The United Brothers. Dublin: Hodges, Figgis, 1942. Play.
Patrick Sarsfield. Dublin: Hodges, Figgis, 1943. Play.
The Earl of Straw. Dublin: Hodges, Figgis, 1945. Play.
The Hill of Quirke. Dublin: P J Bourke, 1958. Play.
Mr Supple, or Time Will Tell. Dublin: P J Bourke, nd. Play.
Tankardstown. Dublin: P J Bourke, nd. Play.

Notes
1. For details and a fuller list of works, see *Dictionary of Irish Literature*, Robert Hogan, ed. (Westport, Conn: Greenwood Press, 1979), 378-79.

Lynch, Patricia

Born: Ireland, 1898; Died: 1972
Educated: Ireland.
Writer and suffragist, Patricia Lynch was born in Cork. When her family moved to London after her father's death, she became active in the women's franchise movement. Sylvia Pankhurst asked her to report the 1916 Rising in Ireland for the *Workers Dreadnought*. Her pamphlet *Rebel Ireland* gave an accurate account of the happenings in Ireland and was sold in Europe and America. Her first story was published when she was eleven and her first book, *The Cobblers Apprentice* won the Tailteann Silver Medal for literature in 1932. She published over fifty books, but many o them were non-fiction or children's books. In 1920 she married the writer R M Fox and lived in Dublin until her death.

Selected Works:
The Cobblers Apprentice. Dublin: Talbot Press, 1930. Novel.
The Storyteller's Childhood. Dublin: The Children's Press, 1982. Children's.
The Grey Goose of Kilnevin. Dublin: The Children's Press, 1984. Children's.

Lyons, Genevieve
Born: Ireland, c̲ 20th century
Educated: Ireland.

Genevieve Lyons was born and educated in Dublin. She had a successful career there as actress and founding member of the Globe Theatre. She gave up acting to bring up her daughter, Michele, and now lives in London.

Lyons' first novel, *Slievelea* (1986), chronicles four generations of Irish families, from the famine of 1847, through the 'troubles', to the present. The house itself, Slievelea, plays a large part in this romantic adventure plot. *The Green Years* (1987) continues to tell of Slievelea, and of the friendship of Ashling and Camilla, childhood who help each other through the turbulence of romance and failure.

Works:
Slievelea. London: Futura, 1986. Novel.
The Green Years. London: Futura, 1987. Novel.
Dark Rosaleen. London: Futura, 1988. Novel.
A House Divided. London: Futura, 1989. Novel.

— *M* —

Macardle, Dorothy
Born: 1899; Died: 1958
Educated: Ireland.

Dorothy Macardle, who sometimes wrote as Margaret Callan, was born to the Macardle brewing family of Dundalk, Co. Louth. She was educated at University College, Dublin, and taught at Alexandra College. She became a republican and was arrested during the Troubles (1916) and confined in Kilmainham jail. She chose the republican side in the Civil War and was a friend to Eamon de Valera. Between the two world wars, she worked as a journalist with the League of Nations, and after 1945 worked on behalf of displaced children. She wrote histories, plays, and fiction. She is also noted as an influential film critic for the *Irish Press*.

The Irish Republic (1937), a lengthy and detailed account of the birth of the republic, is her best known work. Praising the work, de Valera notes in the preface: 'She writes as a republican, but constantly refers the reader to sources of information on the opposite side. Her intimate knowledge of the period enabled her to see where close detail was essential for a proper understanding of what occurred, and this detail is given. Her interpretations and conclusions are her own. They do not represent the doctrines of any party. In many cases they are not in accord with my views.'[1]

Macardle's stories often focus on the tensions of the Troubles and their effect on women's lives. 'By God's

Mercy', written during her imprisonment in Kilmainham, is typical. The story gives a young girl's account of her brother's sacrifice of his life to save his 'Chief', who is ill and in hiding. Mother and sister also share in the sacrifice: on hearing that the Chief will shelter in her house, the mother trembles with fear for his safety. "'God help us, Brian," says she, "I'd sooner see yourself slaughtered before my eyes! If the Chief's lost, Ireland's lost!"'[2] Although Brian is shot as he awaits his Chief, his sister Nannie attempts to take the news of the waiting ambush to the Chief's guards. On the way, she must cross the bridge where the would-be ambushers, the Black-and-Tans, are hiding.

> The terror that fell on me was awful. I knew those'd shoot at a shadow; those'd kill a woman as easy as they'd kill a dog ... I thought I'd never move hand or foot again till the world's end. Then all of a sudden the understanding rushed on me — what it meant, like Heaven opening over a lost soul. I knew they hadn't killed the Chief; they were waiting for him; he hadn't come. 'Quick, quick, quick,' I heard it then, Brian whispering in my heart, and the thought came to me what to do. Out into the middle of the bohereen I went, staggering and singing and talking like a drunk woman to myself. Quite slowly I went past them, reeling from one side to another of the road; just as I turned the corner I heard one of them smothering a laugh. I near laughed myself with the lightness and triumph in my heart. (101-102)

Macardle's plays also reveal her interest in the military struggle and its effect on women. Beginning with *Uneasy Freehold* (1942), her novels develop her interest in the supernatural, in intuition, vision, and the power of precognition. *Uneasy Freehold* was made into a film as *The Uninvited*. Another novel, *Fantastic Summer* (1946), which features a large cast and many sub-plots, continues to focus on extra-ordinary powers. The difficulty of interpreting visions is stressed, as Nan, Virgilia's daughter, must decide how to respond to her mother's vision of Nan's impending death.

Selected Works:

Earth-bound: Nine Stories of Ireland. Worcester, Mass: Harrigan, 1924. Short Stories.

Witch's Brew. London: Deane, 1931. Play.

Ann Kavanagh. New York: French, 1937. Play.

The Irish Republic. London: Gollancz, 1937. History.

The Children's Guest. London: Oxford, 1940. Children's Play.

Uneasy Freehold. London: Peter Davies, 1942; as *The Uninvited* in USA, Garden City, New York: Doubleday, Doran, 1942. Novel.

The Loving-Cup. London: Nelson, 1943. Children's Play.

The Seed was Kind. London: Peter Davies, 1944. Novel.

Fantastic Summer. London: Peter Davies, 1946; as *The Unforeseen* in the USA, Garden City, New York: Doubleday, 1946. Novel.

Children of Europe, A Study of the Children of Liberated Countries. London: Gollancz, 1949. Boston: Beacon, 1951. Study of displaced children.

Notes

1. Preface, *The Irish Republic*, 20.
2. From 'By God's Mercy'; reprinted in *Woman's Part, An anthology of short fiction by and about Irishwomen 1890-1960*, ed. Janet Madden-Simpson (Dublin: Arlen House, 1984), 99.

McBreen, Joan

Born: Ireland, 1946
Educated: Ireland.

Joan McBreen was born in Sligo, educated at the Ursuline Convent in Sligo and at Sion Hill in Dublin. Until recently, she worked full-time as a primary teacher. She is also a wife and mother to six children in Tuam, Co. Galway, and a poet who hid her efforts for years. She sees herself as typical of the woman who comes to writing later in life. Prompted by a child's death, she submitted a poem to a local newspaper, but did not reveal her name. The reaction was positive: she contributed more poems and joined the Galway Writers' Workshop, which remains a very important part of her life. Her husband is and has been her 'most important support', enouraging her to write long before she risked publishing.[1] Her work was well-received in Irish and American journals and newspapers: her first volume of poems, *The Wind Beyond the Wall* (1990), received excellent reviews, and she is the first Irish writer to win the prestigious Nicholas Roerich American poetry prize.

The Wind Beyond the Wall introduces the on-going conversation of a child with the child-become-woman. The book is divided into two parts: the first part concentrates on the child as child – but with a sense of the adult looking back; the second, on the child as woman, wife, mother. The voice is always quiet, but insistent, and the moments evoked are the fleeting – bruising or healing – contacts which shape our lives. The wound left by the death of a father is the subject of the first poem, 'The Gift': the loss is unsayable, and thus the poem approaches the wound only indirectly.

And two years is it, since my father died?
My family copy me behind my back,
'God help the one who breaks one of those coffee
                       cups'.

He carried them downtown in brown paper
and I was twenty-one, walking next to him
on the inside of the narrow Sligo streets.

Two years almost, is it? We take coffee
from the small brown and white china cups.
Is it my voice breaks? Am I saying it again?[2]

The father seems a figure of romance and freedom to the child (McBreen's own father was a seaman who spent about two weeks each year at home), and the mother represents restriction. Just as he picks the woodbine which grows beyond the child's reach, the father picks the 'wild rose' the child loves, cursing its thorns. As the mother sweeps 'the petals from the floor', the child sees him pick one up 'and place it carefully/in the small wallet/where he kept her photograph.'[3] He it is who gives his daughter *Wuthering Heights*; the mother recommends *Lives of the Saints*.[4] But the mother also represents security: In 'The Green Quilt' the persona remembers her mother taking the frightened children into her bed on windy nights. Past blends into present as the persona continues:

> I lie awake now nights
> hearing sounds the house makes
> and it is her voice I remember
> between the sheets,
> her voice taking up right
> where she left off.[5]

McBreen is busy on another volume of poems and an Irish/Dutch anthology of translations.

Works:
The Wind Beyond the Wall. Brownsville, Oregon: Story Line Press, 1990, 1991. Poetry.

Notes
1. Personal communication.
2. In *The Wind Beyond the Wall*, 11.
3. 'Wild Woodbine,' in *The Wind Beyond the Wall*, 12.
4. 'The Saints,' in *The Wind Beyond the Wall*, 16-17.
5. In *The Wind Beyond the Wall*, 15.

McCaffrey, Anne
Born: USA, 1926.
Educated: USA

Though born in Cambridge, Massachusetts, Anne McCaffrey moved to Ireland over twenty-one years ago and is now an Irish citizen. She lives in Co. Wicklow and explains that she writes science fiction, not fantasy.[1] She has published numerous books, including two short story collections.

Selected Works:
Restoree. London: NY: Ballantine, 1967. Novel.
Dragonflight. New York: London: Ballantine and Walker and Co., 1968. Novel.
Alchemy and Academe. New York; London: Doubleday and Co, 1970. Short Story anthology. Novel.
To Ride Pegasus. New York; London: Ballantine, 1973. Novel.
Dragonsong. New York; London: Atheneum, 1976. Novel.
Dragonsinger. New York; London: Atheneum, 1977. Novel.
Get Off the Unicorn. New York; London: Del Rey/Ballantine, 1977. Short story anthology.
The White Dragon. New York; London: Del Rey/Ballantine, 1978. Novel.
Moreta, Dragonlady of Pern. New York; London: Del Rey, 1983. Novel.
Dinosaur Planet Survivors. New York; London: Futura/Del Rey, 1984. Novel.
Stich in Snow. Underwood-Miller, 1984. New York; London: Corgi, 1984. Novel.
Dragonsdawn. New York; London: Del Rey, 1988. Novel.
Crystal Line. New York; London: Del Rey, 1992. Novel.
Damia's Children. New York; London: Berkley, 1993. Novel.

Notes
1. Personal communication.

McCarthy, Patricia
Born: England, 1944
Educated: Ireland.

Born in Cornwall, Patricia McCarthy is half English and half Irish, and grew up in England and Ireland. She attended Trinity College, Dublin, from 1962-66, travelled and lived in many countries, and now lives in Sussex. She has published one collection of poems, *A Second Skin*

(1985), from which the following lines of 'Love-Child' are taken.[1]

Child whom I'll not carry,
I'd like you. You'd be a girl,
I think, a lefthanded knockout:
no sin, our only 'ours'.

He who'll never be your father:
one of three, three in one—
is kind and wouldn't insult you
with condemnation.

Works:
A Second Skin. Liskeard, Cornwall: Harry Chambers/Peterloo
   Poets, 1985. Poetry.

Notes
1. Introduction, *A Second Skin*, 1.

McGuckian, Medbh
Born: Ireland, 1950
Educated: Ireland.

Medbh McGuckian's life centres around Belfast, where she was born, attended Catholic schools and Queen's University, and where she lives now with her husband, three sons, and one daughter. Going to Queen's University, 'where there was a ferment of literary activity, meeting poets like Seamus Heaney, Michael Longley, Paul Muldoon, Ciaran Carson', shaped her poetry, as did 'the outbreak of the Troubles in 1969, which confined one to the house and one's own psychological dramas'. Marriage, pregnancy, and birth, she adds, have also 'contributed formatively'.[1]

Medbh McGuckian's poetry: has been widely acclaimed in Ireland, Britain, France, and the USA. She has received many awards: the British National Poetry Society competition in 1979, an Eric Gregory Award in 1980, the Alice Hunt Bartlett Award in 1983. Her most recent volume, *Marconi's Cottage* (1991), was a Poetry Ireland Choice. She was the first woman to be named writer in residence at Queen's (1986-88); her writing, teaching, tours, and family keep her very busy.

Domestic images abound in McGuckian's poetry: houses, flowers, water, the moon. Describing her work, she says, 'It's mostly moody and menstrual in a way a man's poetry never is. Its subject matter is the sea and its flux, the world of water and matter that females dominate, or that dominates them.'[2] But there's always at least a doubleness in the poems. Of the process, she notes, 'I just take an assortment of words, though not exactly at random, and I fuse them. It's like embroidery. It's very feminine, I guess. They are very intricate, my poems, a weaving of patterns of ins and outs and contradictions, one thing playing off another.' At the same time, 'I basically see the role of the poet as a male role which I have adopted', and her poems are thus 'male and female sides of experience'.[3] From an early poem, 'To the Nightingale', to a recent one, 'The Flower Clock', McGuckian's work has become more complex, more intricately wrought. Nuala Archer describes the interiors in McGuckian's most recent poems as 'Escher-like spaces [which] buckle and breathe with a Belfastian difference.'[4] Words slide into images, which shift from female to male, from human to non-human. The experience is that of a musical kaleidoscope.

> I remember our first night in this grey
> And paunchy house: you were still slightly
> In love with me, and dreamt of having
> A grown son, your body in the semi-gloom
> Turning my dead layers into something
> Resembling a rhyme. That smart and
> Cheerful rain almost beat the hearing
> Out of me, and yet I heard my name
> Pronounced in a whisper as a June day
> Will force itself into every room.[5]

As Nuala Archer says, 'Medbh channels linguistic vibrations pluralistically. Rather than creating pendulums, her poems are resonating prisms that amaze the mazes of partition and parturition.'

Works:
Portrait of Joanna. Belfast: Ulsterman Publications, 1980. Poetry.
Single Ladies. Budleigh Salterton, Devon: Interim Press, 1980. Poetry.
The Flower Master. Oxford and New York: Oxford University Press, 1982. Poetry.
Venus and the Rain. Oxford and New York: Oxford University Press, 1984. Poetry.
On Ballycastle Beach. Oxford and New York: Oxford University Press, 1988. Poetry.
Two Women, Two Shores. Galway: Salmon, 1989; Baltimore: New Poets Series Inc., 1989. Poetry.
Marconi's Cottage. Oldcastle, Co. Meath: Gallery Press, 1991. Poetry.

Notes
1. Personal communication.
2. 'An Attitude of Compassions', Interview with Kathleen McCracken, *Irish Literary Supplement*, Fall 1990, 20-21.
3. *Sleeping with Monsters: Conversations with Scottish and Irish Women Poets*, Gillian Somerville-Arjat and Rebecca E Wilson, eds. Dublin: Wolfhound Press, 1990, 2, 4.
4. 'Nuala Archer on Blue Farm', *Two Women, Two Shores*, 7-8.
5. *Venus and the Rain*, 13.

McManus, Liz
Born: Canada, 1947
Educated: Ireland.

Liz McManus worked as an architect from 1969 until 1981, practising in Derry, Dublin, Galway, and Wicklow. Out of a job then, she found herself 'free to write', and has published many short stories. She has participated for years in a monthly workshop of women writers, which she sees as a 'good example of women helping each other to succeed'. Her first published story won a Hennessy New Irish Writing Award. She has also won an Irish PEN Prize and a Listowel Short Story Award. Her novel, *Acts of Subversion* (1991), was nominated for the Aer Lingus/*Irish Times* First Book Award.[1] She is married with four children. She was elected to the Dáil (Irish parliament) as a TD in November 1992.

McManus has a straightforward, energetic approach to her subjects: she takes her readers into the heart of the action without preamble, explanation, or excuse. The reader rarely knows more than the characters, who must make difficult choices based on scant evidence and preparation. In 'Midland Jihad', for example, we enter the mind of a killer, probably an IRA man. It makes no difference what the man's loyalties are because McManus reveals the irony of the zealot's belief that God is on his side, whether he kills for a united Ireland, for union with England, or for Islam. The juxtaposition of the 'religious' killer with the frightened, lonely girl resonates with the implications of prudish Irish Catholic teachings and their resultant tragedies.[2]

Set in Galway in the 1970s, McManus's first novel, *Acts of Subversion*, tells the story of Oran Reidy, a working-class boy who wins a scholarship to university, and of the discontented Jane O'Molloy's confusion as her sister Carol adopts feminist postures. Again without preamble or exaggeration of any kind, McManus reveals the hidden interests that trigger people's responses, the Machiavellian manipulation of the middle-class factory owner, for example, who uses the idealistic Oran and the local IRA to advance his own unjust financial goals. Despite its seriousness, the novel does not lack humour. Initially limited to a minor role in the Republican movement, Oran peers through a window at the secret training: 'Dominick was standing, military-style, hands behind his back, at ease. Facing him, the others were lined up in formation.

Each man wore a black beret and in his hand held a long-handled sweeping brush as a surrogate gun.'[3]

The conflict between the two sisters also receives sensitive and humorous treatment. Noticing how pale her sister looks, Jane asks if she is ill. '"I've never been better." Carol shook her head impatiently. "It's just that I've given up wearing make-up." Peering at Carol's sandy-coloured lashes and open pores, Jane wondered aloud, "Whatever for?"' (118)

As Carol folds her laundry and tells Jane that she intends leaving her family, however, we understand the emotional pull of women's everyday, traditional activities. 'The smell of newly-washed clothes filled the kitchen. It was a comforting domestic smell. It served to reinforce Jane's conviction that what Carol was saying was wrong. Right or wrong. Who knew any more? It was unsafe talk. Dangerous talk, that she knew.' (151) The security that Jane grasps has its rewards and limitations. The adventure that Carol seeks entails both freedom and loss.

Works:
Acts of Subversion. Dublin: Poolbeg, 1991. Novel.

Notes:
1. Personal Communication.
2. 'Midland Jihad', *The Irish Times*, 17 August, 1991.
3. *Acts of Subversion*, 84.

McNeill, Janet
Born: Ireland, 1907
Educated: England.

Janet McNeill was born in Dublin in 1907. In 1913 the family moved to Birkenhead near Liverpool, and she attended school there. She received her MA in Classics from St Andrews University, was very involved in the drama group, and acted and wrote plays. When the family returned to Ireland because of her father's poor health, she took a secretarial course and worked for two years with *The Belfast Telegraph*. She married in 1933 and moved with her husband to Lisburn where she reared her four children.

Her career was halted for eleven years when her children were very young, but the child-rearing years contributed to her writing, especially to the many stories she wrote for children. In 1946 she won a prize for a radio play on northern Ireland BBC, and from then on, was both prolific and successful. She wrote twenty-four popular books for children, eleven adult novels, plays, short stories, articles, and even two opera libretti for children. In 1964 she and her husband moved to England.

McNeill writes about upper-middle-class life; her characters' situations are genteel, their problems are not. *The Maiden Dinosaur* (1964) tends to be read as emotional sterility, but since the heroine Sarah has been in love with her friend for several decades, it is now classed as a lesbian novel.

In *Tea at Four O'Clock* (1956), McNeill dissects family life in bourgeois Belfast, and reveals the distorting, confining nature of the familial and ceremonial patterns. *Tea at Four O'Clock* is at first glance a ritual of gracious, elegant living, but becomes emblematic of all the duties which are exercises in torture for Laura, the victimised younger daughter in the Percival family. The father's severe demands are seen as the principal causes of his son's fecklessness and his younger daughter's nervous misery. But Laura realises that her mother had also some part in fashioning Mildred, the eldest daughter, into a replica of patriarchal repression. The charge that the dying woman laid on the seven-year-old to care for her father, brother, and sister was a heavy, unfair one. But 'care' Mildred did, care becoming synonymous with controlling her sister's every action, impressing on Laura an impossible debt, and making of the girl a robot who anxiously and unquestioningly obeys. Neither does McNeill spare Laura:

the girl's psychological dependence – though pitiable – is also seen as cowardice.

Focusing chiefly on the Percival family, McNeill also presents several incisive character portrayals. Her work at its best is insightful, sensitive, and economical, the prose elegant. As Laura watches a group of emigrants bid farewell to family and friends, the narrator remarks: 'These last farewells – they were only gestures. The passengers for America had all said their farewells a hundred times since their minds were made up and their tickets bought. That boy from the farm – for the last month the lane up to his home has been holy ground and he has trodden it devotedly. The last meal he ate this morning in the farmhouse kitchen – the last farl of soda bread from his mother's griddle – has been a sacrament.' [1]

Selected Works:
Gospel Truth. Belfast: H R Carter, 1951. Play.
A Child in The House. London: Hodder & Stoughton, 1955. Novel.
Tea at Four O'Clock. 1956; rpt. London: Virago Press, 1988. Novel.
The Other Side of the Wall. London: Hodder & Stoughton, 1956. Novel.
A Light Dozen. London: Faber, 1957. Stories.
A Finished Room. London: Hodder & Stoughton, 1958. Novel.
Search Party. London: Hodder & Stoughton, 1957. Novel.
As Strangers Here. London: Hodder & Stoughton, 1960. Novel.
The Early Harvest. London: Geoffrey Bles, 1962. Novel.
The Maiden Dinosaur. 1964; rpt. Dublin: Arlen House, 1984; In USA as *The Belfast Friends.* Cambridge: Riverside Press, 1966; Boston: Houston Mifflin, 1966. Novel.
Talk to Me. London: Geoffrey Bles, 1965. Novel.
The Small Widow. London: Geoffrey Bles, 1967; New York: Atheneum, 1968. Novel.
Switch On Switch Off and Other Plays. London: Faber, 1968. Plays.

Notes
1. *Tea at Four O'Clock,* 97-98.

Madden, Deirdre
Born: Ireland, c 20th century
Educated: Ireland, England.

Deirdre Madden was born in Belfast and studied at Trinity College, Dublin, and at the University of East Anglia. She has written three novels: the first, *Hidden Symptoms* (1986), won the Rooney Prize for Irish Literature in 1987; the second, *The Birds of the Innocent Wood* (1988), received a Somerset Maugham Award in 1989, and *Remembering Light and Stone* was published by Faber and Faber in late 1992.

Hidden Symptoms is the story of Teresa, a student at Queen's University, Belfast, whose twin brother Francis has been murdered. The horror of Francis' death darkens Teresa's life, and the acceptance of the on-going violence gives a natural but horrifying texture to the book. Teresa prefers the Belfast of bombs to the Belfast of her early memories:

> Ulster before 1969 had been sick but with hidden symptoms. Streets and streets of houses with bricked-up windows and broken fanlights, graffiti on gable walls, soldiers everywhere: Belfast was now like a madman who tears his flesh, puts straws in his hair and screams gibberish. Before it had resembled the infinitely more sinister figure of the articulate man in a dark, neat suit whose conversation charms and entertains; and whose insanity is apparent only when he says calmly, incidentally, that he will club his children to death and eat their entrails with a golden fork because God has told him to do so; and then offers you more tea.[1]

The Birds of the Innocent Wood is a tension-filled story about the difficulty of human communication. Jane's loneliness is banished neither by marriage nor by motherhood. But her loneliness is only one face of human loneliness, we realise, as we see her husband, father-in-law, neighbours, and daughters suffer and die without making contact. Strangely, this is not a depressing book: it's full of insights into human behaviour, insights which comfort by suggesting the universality of our experiences. When her twin daughters are sixteen, Jane reflects that they are children no longer: 'What was so frustrating about her daughters was that she felt she ought to understand them, and quite often she almost did, but could never get beyond that "almost". Some little points of knowledge or sympathy always shimmered just out of Jane's access or understanding, and the older her daughters became the more conscious she was of this.'[2] Trying to understand herself in her daughters, Jane wishes she could ask, '"Have I been a good mother to you?" but then felt sad, because she realised the futility of such a question.' (137) The desire for certitude, for definition, is beautifully suggested and always frustrated.

Works:
Hidden Symptoms. Boston/New York: The Atlantic Monthly Press, 1986; London: Faber and Faber, 1988. Novel.
The Birds of the Innocent Wood. London: Faber and Faber, 1988. Novel.
Remembering Light and Stone. London: Faber and Faber, 1992. Novel.

Notes
1. *Hidden Symptoms*, 13-14.
2. *The Birds of the Innocent Wood*, 136.

Maher, Mary
Born: USA, c 20th century
Educated: USA.

Mary Maher published her first novel *The Devil's Card* in 1992. Though born in Chicago, Mary is a fourth generation Irish-American who has lived in Ireland since 1965.

She worked as a journalist with *The Chicago Tribune* before joining *The Irish Times* in 1965. Mary was the first editor of woman's affairs of that paper and has been an activist in the women's movement since the 'sixties. She was a founder member of the Irish women's liberation movement in 1970.

She was the first woman appointed to the sub-editing staff at *The Irish Times* and also the first woman trades union official at that or any national newspaper in Ireland.

She has written and reported widely on women's issues, labour activities and psychological services for children and adults.[1]

Her first novel, *The Devil's Card* (1992), concerns itself with exploring Irish-America in a sympathetic, critical, and admirably unsentimental way.[2] It has been well received as both a murder mystery and a political thriller.[3]

Works:

The Devil's Card. Ireland: Brandon Press, and New York: St Martin's Press, 1992. Novel.

Notes:

1. Brandon Press publicity information.
2. *Sunday Tribune*, November 1992.
3. *The Irish Times*, November 1992.

Manning, Kitty

Born: England, 1936
Educated: Ireland.

Kitty Manning was born in England to Irish parents; her mother was a native of Armagh, her father of Mayo. When she was five, her mother moved with the children to northern Ireland to escape the bombing of World War II. Kitty worked in the northern Ireland Civil Service in Stormont in the 1950s, and although she was one of the few Catholics who worked there and were rarely promoted, she remembers the years there as pleasant. She now lives in Dublin, has five children, and is a hospital administrator. She credits Seán McCann of the *Evening Press* with giving her her first chance to publish and has one novel published to date.[1]

The Between People (1990), opens some time into the recent Troubles with Kate Regan and her mother Harriet revisiting the northern Ireland town in which they had lived until Kate was eighteen. Kate visits, however, not to view the damage caused by the 'unclaimed' bombs, but to remember how it was before the Troubles. The story she tells is similar to Manning's own, and includes bigotry and division between the Catholic and Protestant communities that so uneasily share the town.

Harriet had been cut off by her family when she married a Catholic from the South, so she and her husband had lived in England. During World War II, however, Harriet's husband and son were killed in a London bombing while Harriet and her small daughter were back in Ireland. Having nowhere else to go, Harriet had applied and received a council house in her hometown. Life is bitter here: Harriet's family ignores her, and she feels intellectually and socially superior to the poor Catholic families amongst whom she lives. Kate and Harriet are 'the between people', accepted neither by Catholic nor Protestant community, their house set appropriately between the rival churches.

The atmosphere of the tiny house is claustrophobic: the isolated, introverted Harriet lives in her memories and devours every scrap of information Kate garners on her trips into town. She questions Kate on her return from the Twelfth of July parade, 'Did you see *him*?' Her life is so limited that she need not specify her father. Kate answers yes, and Harriet pursues, 'Where was he? Out at the front? I suppose he was in full dress?' The 'ghost of a smile' crosses Harriet's face, as she tells Kate, 'They all wear white gloves and bowlers,' and confides proudly, 'He always loved a good breakfast the morning of the Twelfth. Porridge, followed by bacon and eggs, soda farls, potato bread. I was the one who cooked him his breakfast. He wouldn't eat it unless I made it for him.'[2]

Manning gives a full picture of life in a northern Ireland town in the fifties, the petty humiliations and snobberies, as well as the material and intellectual poverty, that divide classes and religious groups. The real horror, in fact, is that such pettiness produces tragedy.

Works:
The Between People. Dublin: Attic Press, 1990. Novel.

Notes
1. Acknowledgments, *The Between People*.
2. *The Between People*, 38-39.

Manning, Mary
Born: 1906
Educated: Ireland, England, USA

Mary Manning was born in Dublin and educated at Morehampton House School and Alexandra College, Dublin. She studied acting in the Abbey school, and art in London and Boston. She worked with the Irish Players in England and with the Abbey in Dublin before joining the Gate theatre, where she acted as publicity manager and editor of their shortlived magazine. She moved to Boston when she married, raised her family there, and was one of the founders of the Cambridge Poets' Theatre. After her husband's death she returned to Ireland.

Manning wrote plays, novels, and short stories. Her first play, written for the Gate, *Youth's the Season* (1936), was a witty and successful story of middle-class Dubliners; her next two plays, *Storm over Wicklow*, and *Happy Family*, were produced in the Gate, but were less successful. In Boston, she turned to novels, again witty depictions of middle-class society. Her adaptation of *Finnegans Wake* was first produced by the Cambridge Poets' Theatre in 1955, and has been produced successfully since as *Passages from Finnegans Wake* or *The Voice of Shem*. Back in Ireland, she became a theatre critic and returned to play-writing, adapting Frank O'Connor's novel *The Saint and Mary Kate*, which the Abbey produced in 1968. *The Last Chronicles of Ballyfungus* (1978), her first volume of short stories, is a satirical glance at contemporary Ireland.[1]

Works:
Youth's the Season in *Plays of Changing Ireland.* Curtis Canfield, ed. New York: Macmillan, 1936. Play.
Mount Venus. Boston: Houghton, Mifflin, 1938. Novel.
Lovely People. Boston: Houghton, Mifflin, 1953. Novel.
Passages from Finnegans Wake by James Joyce. Cambridge, Mass.: Harvard, 1957. Play.
The Last Chronicles of Ballyfungus. Boston: Houghton, Mifflin, 1978. Stories.

Notes
1. *Dictionary of Irish Literature*, Robert Hogan, ed. (Westport, Conn.: Greenwood, 1979), 436-37.

Manning, Olivia

Born: 1908; Died: 1980
Educated: England.

Olivia Manning's father was a British naval officer; her mother was from Ulster. She trained at art school, worked for a time painting furniture in London, and then moved to book production. She published the first of a long list of novels, *The Wind Changes*, in 1937. In 1939, she married R D Smith, a lecturer for the British Council, and later professor at the New University of Ulster. A distinguished novelist, she is best known for her Balkan and Levant trilogies.[1]

Selected Works:
The Wind Changes. 1937; rpt. London: Virago, 1988. Novel.
Artist Among the Missing. 1949; rpt. London: Heinemann, 1975. Novel.
The Doves of Venus. 1955; rpt. London: Virago, 1984. Novel.
The Balkan Trilogy: The Great Fortune. 1960; rpt. New York: Penguin Books, 1981. Novel.
The Spoilt City. 1962; rpt. New York: Penguin Books, 1981. Novel.

Friends and Heroes. 1965; rpt. New York: Penguin Books, 1981. Novel.

A Romantic Hero and Other Stories. London: Heinemann, 1967. Stories.

The Play Room. London: Heinemann, 1969. Novel.

The Levant Trilogy: The Danger Tree. London: Weidenfeld and Nicolson, 1977. Novel.

The Battle Lost and Won. London: Weidenfeld and Nicolson, 1978. Novel.

The Sum of Things. London: Weidenfeld and Nicolson, 1980. Novel.

Notes:
1. Isobel English, 'Introduction', *The Doves of Venus*, Virago edition.

Martin, Joy
Born: Ireland, 1937
Educated: Ireland.

Joy Martin was born in Limerick in 1937 and educated at Laurel Hill Convent, Limerick. Her mother was an Irish Catholic, her father an English Protestant, wounded in the war. The family lived, she writes, 'as rather poor relations on my grandfather's land in County Limerick. My parents were immensely tolerant people to whom religious bigotry was as much anathema as "class" ... Still, as a child I was deeply conscious of being neither this nor that; now I realise that I gained valuable insight into three worlds – that of the well-to-do, landed Catholics of the south-west of Ireland; the English middle classes; and what we then termed "The Poor" – and learned that a lingering sense of "not belonging" has its compensations.'[1]

Like many another only child, she read 'voraciously', and was privy to adult conversation. She always wanted to write and published her first short story when she was only seventeen. 'Like its author,' she notes, 'it was pretentious and precious.'[2] She wished to study English at university, but her family could not afford this, so she turned to journalism. The editor of the *Limerick Weekly Echo*, now defunct, took her on as a trainee reporter, and after two years she moved to the *Evening Press* in Dublin. After she married, she lived in South Africa and worked for the liberal *Rand Daily Mail*, was assistant editor of *Femina* magazine, and wrote two non-fiction books before turning to novels. The first, *Twelve Shades of Black*, interviews with twelve men and women from black townships around Johannesburg, was a runner-up for the South African Literary Award. The second, *Myth and Magic*, analysed the beliefs of the Shona people of Zimbabwe. Between two spells in Africa, she worked for the BBC, writing news for the Home and World Service. She has two children and three step-children, lives in Chelsea, London, and whenever possible, in the family's holiday home in Whitegate, Co. Clare.

The Moon is Red in April (1989), based on the founding of the House of Hennessy Cognac, is set in eighteenth-century Ireland and France. Richard O'Shaughnessy flees from Cork to France to escape the penal laws and to fight in the Irish Brigade. The Hennessy family assisted in the research for this novel, providing letters and documents relevant to the period. *Ulick's Daughter* (1990) is also based on a true story, and is set in Ireland and Russia. Ulick, John de Burgh, fourteenth Earl of Clanricarde in Co. Galway, has an illegitimate child by the daughter of one of his tenants. When Ulick's son inherits, he evicts mother and child, forcing them to live on the roadside.

Image of Laura (1992) is a three-generational story set in Berlin from 1930-39, in London in the 1950s and 1960s, in South Africa in the 1970s, and in London of the present. In this present, the seventy-five-year-old Laura holds a retrospective exhibition of her photography, and an unusual birthday present brings back the past.

Works:
A Wrong to Sweeten. London: Weidenfeld and Nicholson, 1986. Novel.
The Moon is Red in April. London: Weidenfeld and Nicholson, 1989. Novel.
Ulick's Daughter. London: Grafton Books, 1990. Novel.
A Heritage of Wrong. London: Grafton Books, 1991. Novel.
Image of Laura. London: HarperCollins, 1992. Novel.

Notes
1. Personal communication.
2. Personal communication.

Martin, Mary Letitia (Mrs Martin Bell);
Born: Ireland, 1815; Died: 1850
Educated: Ireland.

Mary Letitia Martin was born in Co. Galway, when the Martin family was still a great landowning one. She herself was known as 'The Princess of Connemara' and inherited 200,000 acres in 1847. She was the daughter of 'Humanity Dick Martin'.[1] The land which she inherited was heavily mortgaged, however, so she emigrated with her husband to Belgium, where she supported herself and her husband by writing romances. Pregnant in 1850, she sailed with her husband to America and died in childbirth in New York. Her most interesting novel is the autobiographical *Julia Howard* (1850), which deals with the famine and the west of Ireland.[2]

Selected Works:
Julia Howard. 3 vol. London: Bentley, 1850. Novel.

Notes
1. Riana O'Dwyer, Department of English, University College, Galway; Personal communication.
2. *A Biographical Dictionary of Irish Writers*, Anne M Brady and Brian Cleeve, eds. (Mullingar: Lilliput Press, 1985), 159.

Maude, Caitlín
Born: Ireland, 1941; Died: 1982
Educated: Ireland.

Caitlín Maude was born in Connemara, educated at Mount Mellick Convent, and took her degree in Arts at University College, Galway. She worked as a teacher, an actor, and a *sean-nós* (traditional) singer. Her interpretation of the great love songs particularly *Donal Og* was perhaps the most distinguished of this century.[1] She married in 1969, had one son, and with her husband, Cathal O Luain, was active in setting up an Irish school in Tallaght; Her poetry was well received when published in journals during her lifetime, and collected and published after her death. Several poems are translated into English in *Pillars of the House* and *The Bright Wave: An Tonn Gheal*.[2]

These lines are from the short lament of the housewife, 'Caoineadh na Mná Tí'

A theach bhoicht
i do fhothrach
ceal lámh
a shlíocfadh do dheann
fulaingíonn tusa freisin
fís[3]

The lovely 'Aimhréidhe' is translated by Joan Trodden Keefe as 'Tangled'; the first verse in Irish and translation follows.

Siúil, a ghrá,
Cois trá anocht—
Siúil agus cuir uait
na deora—
éirigh agus siúil anocht

Wander, my love
along the shore tonight—
wander and stop
your weeping—
rise up and wander tonight

ná feac do ghlúin feasta
ag uaigh sin an tsléibhe –
tá na blátha sin feoite
agus tá mo chnámhasa
dreoite ...

bend your knees no more
at that mountain grave –
those flowers are withered
and my bones are
mouldering ...

(Labhraim leat anocht
ó íochtar mara –
labhraim leat gach oíche
ó íochtar mara ...)

I speak to you tonight
from sea-depth –
I speak to you every night
from sea-depth ...[4]

Works
Caitlín Maude, Dánta. edited Ciarán O Coigligh, Baile Atha
   Cliath: Coiscéim, 1984. Poetry.
Dramaíocht agus Prós, Caitlín Maude, edited Ciarán O Coigligh,
   Baile Atha Cliath: Coiscéim, 1988. Plays and Prose.

Notes
1. *Breithiunas*, Máiread Ní Ghráda, Oifig an tSoláthair, 1978.
2. See 'Brollach', Caitlín Maude. *Dánta*, 7-11; and Caitlín Maude,
   Pillars of the House, A A Kelly, ed. (Dublin: Wolfhound, 1988),
   129.
3. In Caitlín Maude, *Dánta*, 67.
4. In *Pillars of the House*, 130.

Medbh, Máighréad
Born: Ireland, 1959
Educated: Ireland.

Máighréad Medbh was born in Co. Limerick, and attended
school in Newcastle West, Co. Limerick. She lived in
Dublin with her two children for a time, but currently lives
in Belfast.

Poetry breaks the silence that surrounds us, Medbh
says. 'Communication isn't a circle. It's more like sending
up flares and taking pot luck with whether they'll be seen

or not. When I produce poetry I'm trying to make a circle, trying to feel less alone. And maybe in the process of doing that I help other people to feel less alone too. I hate to think that so many of us are lost in an enforced silence, wandering in a bare land which has no mirror to reflect us.'[1]

Her first volume, *The Making of a Pagan* (1990), poems and prose poems, covers her life from the womb, through growing up, loving, having children, and living in a patriarchal world. Stages of a little girl's life, and stages of a woman's life, all are there. Medbh laments the nebulous borders that inevitably limit the young girl who was once free to be child – not boy or girl – to play and do and think as child.

The language of her poetry sings love, curses hypocrisy, is filled with aggression. The target of the curse is often Roman Catholic doctrine. In 'Original Sin', for example, the pregnant woman reflects on the doctrine that her child is a sinner 'while upside down/in a bag of water ... staring down/at the evil crown/of the pagan goddess, Quim.' But the girl baby will reverse matters:

But it makes no odds
because my child's a bud
and she'll burst onto earth
like a flower should.
She'll shut up the church
like a jack-in-the-box
and she'll shout 'up yours'
to the Pope and John Knox.

The Original Witch
will pick up the switch
and turn off the lights
in the steeple's sight.
She will laugh Ha Ha
She will laugh Ho Ho
And the walls will go
just like in Jerico.[2]

Máighréad Medbh performs as a rap/rock poet.

Works:
The Making of a Pagan. Belfast: Blackstaff Press, 1990. Poetry.

Notes
1. Personal communication.
2. In *The Making of a Pagan*, 44-45.

Meehan, Paula
Born: Ireland, 1955
Educated: Ireland; USA

The eldest of six children, Paula Meehan spent most of her childhood in the family flat at the corner of Seán McDermott and Gardiner Streets. Paula was fortunate in belonging to a family which prized education: she was very close to her grandparents, and her grandfather taught her to read before she went to school; her aunts, uncles, and family members fed her voracious reading appetite; and her mother, whom she sees as 'extremely intelligent and very frustrated ... by the role assigned her as mother and housewife ... ranked education, especially for her daughters, as a priority'. Although she has lived in many countries, the landscape of the north inner city is 'the nurturing landscape' for much of her poetry.

Paula Meehan demonstrated her independence early: expelled from Holy Faith Convent in Finglas — where her family had moved into a new corporation estate during her teens — she studied for the Intermediate Certificate on her own, and then spent two happy years at Whitehall House Senior Girls' School, a vocational school, preparing for the Leaving Certificate. Her adolescence was troubled; she was perceived as a 'rebel, or a right handful'. She left Finglas and returned to the city during her first year at college, and was involved in street and experimental theatre. She received a BA from Trinity College, Dublin, in

English, History and Classical Civilisation, and a Master of
Fine Arts from Eastern Washington University. She lives in
Dublin.

She always wrote and considers writing a 'natural
occupation'. Toward the end of the 1970s, however, while
living in a small croft in the Shetland Islands, she began to
shape her poetry with the idea of art rather than self
expression. She has taught in schools and universities, in
poetry workshops, in prisons, and with community
groups, working part-time, rather than full-time.
Particularly drawn to American poets, 'possibly for the
vigour and centrality of the vernacular in their work', she
also 'learned a vocabulary of terror' from the Russians. She
loves Irish poets, especially 'those poets pushing up behind
me', and has herself been encouraged by Brendan Kennelly
and Eavan Boland. Several bursaries from the Arts Council
saved her sanity, certainly her 'bacon'.[1]

She composes her poetry aloud, and believes it should
be performed, either in a reader's mind or recited. I think
we can agree: the strong voices and the graphic, colloquial
idioms invite recitation. 'Don't Speak to Me Of Martyrs'
suggests the contemporary Irish woman's sense of the
irrelevance of the Irish political candidate's litany of Irish
history. 'Up there on the platform a man/speaks of the
people: of what/we need, of who we really are, of
how/we must fight to liberate ourselves.' But the woman's
mind retreats to the school of her childhood, a 'ghost
place', 'littered with our totems;/a tattered Plough and
Stars,/a bloodstained Proclamation,/Connolly strapped
wounded to a chair,/Mayblossom in Inchicore.' And from
there to the National Museum with her father, to her
mother's nursing her to sleep, and to the prayers with the
schoolgirls in the Pro-Cathedral. The 'mourning and
weeping' embraced by the 'poor banished children of Eve'
in the prayer is ironically and appropriately followed by a
rejection of the 'macabre rosaries' of the martyrs.[2]

The most recent volume, *The Man Who Was Marked by
Winter*, shows the range of Meehan's voice: soft memories

of childhood, sad songs for dead children, complex portraits of parents, and tears for an unloving society. Everything now suggests the loss of the child to the mother in 'Elegy For a Child'. 'Clouds move over the river/Under the sun – a cotton sheet shook out.' And the mother's voice weeps: 'You were but a small bird balanced/ Within me/ ready for flight.'[3] The statue of Mary, in 'The Statue of the Virgin at Granard Speaks', expresses the bitterness of being unable to help the fifteen-year-old girl, who came all alone on a cold winter's night to deliver the baby no one knew she carried, and then died at the feet of the helpless statue.

> and though she cried out to me in extremis
> I did not move,
> I didn't lift a finger to help her,
> I didn't intercede with heaven,
> nor whisper the charmed word in God's ear.[4]

Works:
Return and No Blame. Dublin: Beaver Row, 1984. Poetry.
Reading the Sky. Dublin: Beaver Row, 1986. Poetry.
The Man Who Was Marked By Winter. Dublin: Gallery, 1991. Poetry.

Notes
1. Personal communication.
2. In *Wildish Things*, Ailbhe Smyth, ed. (Dublin: Attic Press, 1989), 74.
3. In *The Man Who Was Marked By Winter*, 27, 28.
4. In *The Man Who Was Marked By Winter*, 42.

Mhac an tSaoi, Máire (Máire MacEntee);
Born: Ireland, 1922
Educated: Ireland, France.

Máire Mhac an tSaoi was born Máire MacEntee in Dublin, in 1922; she publishes her work in Irish under Máire Mhac an tSaoi. She was educated at Alexandra School, Dublin, Scoil Ghobnait, Dún Chaoin, and Beaufort, Rathfarnham. Her university education is extensive and varied: she took her BA Degree at University College, Dublin, in Celtic Studies and Modern Languages, taking first place in Modern Irish, French, and English. She studied law at King's Inns, Dublin, and was called to the Irish Bar in 1944. In 1945, she received her MA degree in classical modern Irish, with a thesis on Pierce Ferriter, a seventeenth century Irish poet. Meanwhile she was a scholar at the Dublin Institute for Advanced Studies, 1942-45, and published *Two Irish Arthurian Romances* in 1946. From 1945-47, she studied at the Institut des Hautes Etudes en Sorbonne, University of Paris.

A career in Foreign Affairs followed: she entered the Dublin Ministry in 1947, as Third Secretary, and served in Paris and Madrid from 1949-51. She served as Secretary of the Irish Cultural Relations Committee, 1951-52, and was seconded to the Department of Education to work on the compilation of a modern English/Irish dictionary, 1952-56. From 1956 to 1961, she served at the International Organisations Desk in the Department of Foreign Affairs, and from 1957-60 she was a member of the Irish delegation to the General Assembly of the United Nations. In 1961, she was appointed Permanent Representative of Ireland to the Council of Europe in Strasbourg and resigned to marry Conor Cruise O'Brien in 1962. She accompanied him during his periods of residence in Africa, London, and the USA.[1]

Máire Mhac an tSaoi also taught Irish at various levels in Ireland and abroad, instituted and taught a course on the Irish background to Anglo-Irish literature at Queen's College, New York, 1969-70, with Dr Liam and Dr Máire de Paor, and was visiting lecturer in the Department of Folklore and Folklife at the University of Pennsylvania in 1989.

Modest about her achievements, Máire Mhac an tSaoi writes, 'I am that anachronism, the middle-class

Irishwoman of the twenties, conditioned to a quietism so absolute that, until I was thirty, I did not make a single independent decision as to what course my life should take; authority and ineluctable circumstances dictated what I did and what I became.'[2] Poetry came naturally to her: both sides of her family bought, read, and wrote poetry, and she cannot remember 'not having an absolute facility for metrical form'. (22) Emotion translates into poetry in her mind, she notes, so that the finished product functions as 'autobiographical notes', though there may be no obvious connection between poem and initial emotion. 'The process is entirely aural – I hear my poems before I write them – it is also almost automatic, with very little conscious choice involved and very little revision.' (22) She does not see her own poetry as a 'primary occupation', but describes herself as a 'housewife who writes verse'. However, she draws on the vast store of poetry she knows by heart to endure the often 'soul-destroying monotony that goes hand in hand with the quasi-sacramental nature of home-making.' (23) Her self-respect as a writer rests on the belief that her own work will in the future similarly refresh the weary. While she set her early poetry in Arcadia, 'the climate of my prolonged and protected adolescence,' she has written since her marriage 'as myself, myself as perceived by society, middle-class, middle-aged, suburban'. But, she notes, 'the Dublin housewife is as much a dramatic creation as the earlier rural colleen.' (24)

To this point, she has published three volumes of poetry in Irish, a selection of translations from classical Irish poetry, a monograph on the life and work of Gerald FitzGerald, Third Earl of Desmond, a fourteenth-century Hiberno-Norman magnate who appears to have originated the practice of courtly love-poetry in Gaelic, and many articles, stories, and poems in newspapers and journals. Her collected poetry was published under the title *An Cion go Dtí Seo* in 1988, and her work has been translated into French, Japanese, and Hebrew.

Best known popularly as a writer of love lyrics, Máire Mhac an tSaoi presents an ironic definition of woman based on society's treatment of her in 'Cad is Bean':

Gránna an rud í an bhean,
hOileadh casta,
Díreach seach claon ní fhéadair,
Bréag a n-abair;

Níl inti ceart ná náire,
Níl inti glaine,
An ghin ón gcléibh tá meata,
Mar is baineann;[3]

Máire Mhac an tSaoi was the editor of *Poetry Ireland Review* and is engaged in a translation into Irish of Rainer Maria Rilke's *Duino Elegies*.

Selected Works:
Margadh na Saoire. Baile Atha Cliath: Sairséal & Dill, 1956. Poetry.
A Heart Full of Thought. Baile Atha Cliath: Sairséal & Dill, 1959. Translations from Classical Irish Poetry.
Codladh an Ghaiscígh. Baile Atha Cliath: Sairséal & Dill, 1973. Poetry.
An Galar Dubhach. Baile Atha Cliath: Sairséal & Dill, 1980. Poetry.
An Cion go Dtí Seo. Baile Atha Cliath: Sairséal O Marcaigh, 1988. Collected Poetry.

Notes
1. Personal communication.
2. Máire Mhac an tSaoi, 'At Work: Poet as Housewife'.
3. In *An Cion Go Dtí Seo*, 54.

Millar, Florence Norah
Born: Ireland, 1920
Educated: Ireland, England.

Florence Millar was born in Co. Dublin and educated in Dublin and England. She studied music at the Royal Irish

Academy of Music. She has written novels, stories, and plays.[1]

Selected Works:
Fishing is Dangerous. London: Gifford, 1946. Novel.
Grant's Overture. London: Gifford, 1946. Novel.
The Lone Kiwi. Dublin: Dawson, 1948. Novel.

Notes
1. *A Biographical Dictionary of Irish Writers*, Anne M. Brady and Brian Cleeve, eds. (Mullingar: Lilliput Press, 1985), 163.

Milligan, Alice
Born: Ireland, 1866; Died: 1953
Educated: Ireland, England.

Alice Milligan was born in Co. Tyrone, the daughter of an Irish antiquary, Seaton M.[1] She edited *Shan Van Vocht* with Ethna Carbery from 1896-99, and wrote plays, poems, and a novel. Her subjects were patriotic, or tales from Irish legend and myth. She wrote The *Last Feast of the Fianna* a Celtic Twilight play, for the Irish Literary Theatre in 1900. The following lines are from 'Finnula', a poem about the daughter of King Lir, turned into a swan by a jealous stepmother.

> Among the reeds round waters blue
> White wings are spread,
> And she is seen who should have been
> For centuries dead,
> She, who ice-pierced on perilous coasts
> To land and sky
> Lifted the swan-song of her grief
> But could not die.[2]

Selected Works:
A Royal Democrat. London: Simpkin, Marshall; Dublin: Gill, 1892. Novel.
The Life of Theobald Wolfe Tone. Belfast: J W Boyd, 1898. History.

The Last Feast of the Fianna. London: David Nutt, 1900. Play.
The Daughter of Donagh, a Cromwellian Drama in Four Acts. Dublin: Lester, 1920. Play.
Hero Lays. Dublin: Maunsel, 1908. Poetry.
We Sang for Ireland. [Poems of Ethna Carbery, Seamus Macmanus, Alice Milligan]. Dublin: Gill, 1950. Poetry.
Poems by Alice Milligan. Edited Henry Mangan. Dublin: Gill, 1954. Poetry.

Notes
1. *A Biographical Dictionary of Irish Writers,* Anne M Brady and Brian Cleeve, eds. (Mullingar: The Lilliput Press, 1985), 163.
2. In *We Sang for Ireland,* 133.

Mitchell, Geraldine
Born: Ireland, 1949
Educated: Ireland, France.

Geraldine Mitchell, a freelance journalist, was born in Dublin, but has lived and worked in France, Algiers, and Spain. She contributes regularly to *The Irish Times,* and has worked on travel guides to Spain. We follow the adventures of a group of French teenagers in Connemara in her first book for young adults, *Welcoming the French.*

Works:
Welcoming the French. Dublin: Attic Press, 1992.

Mitchell, Julie
Born: England, c 20th century
Educated: Ireland, England.

Julie Mitchell was born in Cheshire and moved with her family to northern Ireland when she was seven. She was educated at the Methodist College, Belfast, and Bristol University.

Her novel, *Sunday Afternoons* (1988), tells the story of a friendship in the divided communities of northern Ireland.

Works:
Sunday Afternoons. London: Penguin, 1988. Novel.

Mitchell, Susan Langstaff
Born: Ireland, 1866; Died: 1926
Educated: Ireland.

Susan L Mitchell was born at Carrick-on-Shannon in 1866. She was a friend to William Butler Yeats and in 1901 became assistant editor of *The Irish Homestead*, later *The Irish Statesman*. Much of her poetry is religious, but she was also a critic and her wit is apparent in her satires and study of George Moore.

Her poem, 'A Lament for George Moore', catches some of this wit as the poet calls on Moore to return to Ireland and reminds him of 'the Stellar Zodiac' of 'Virgo Magee, Leo AE,/And Edward Martyn'.

Who hailed your firstlings as they grew
Chapter by chapter;
And when we showed our Muse to you
You did adapt her!

The poem concludes:

Now Yeats suggests (with Goethe) here
The likeliest measure of a mind
Is — what we can't find anywhere —
The girls it leaves behind.

O bad gray head good women knew,
There comes a thought unmixed with sadness,
In that the worst that you could do
Was hardly badness!

O hazardous and harmless lover,
Come back to Ireland, come back and bring
(What though your writings are all passed over)
In your person a Playboy unguessed at by Synge.[1]

Works:
*Aids to the Immortality of Certain Persons in Ireland: Charitably
Administered.* Dublin: The New Nation, 1908; with additions,
Dublin: Maunsel, 1913. Satires.
The Living Chalice. Dublin, London: Maunsel, 1908. Poetry.
Frankincense and Myrrh. Dundrum, Dublin: Cuala Press, 1912.
Frontpiece hand-coloured by Jack B Yeats. Poetry.
Secret Springs of Dublin Song. Dublin: Talbot, 1918. Poetry.

Notes
1. In *Secret Springs of Dublin Song*, 47-48.

Molloy, Frances
Born: Ireland, 1947; Died: 1991
Educated: Ireland.

Frances Molloy was born in Derry, where she received 'a
patchy education'. She left school at fifteen to work in a
local factory. She also spent some time as a nun. After
living in England for eighteen years, she returned to
Ireland in 1988. She married and had two children.[1] In
1989, she described herself as 'worn out by many flittings',
a description unfortunately confirmed by her early death
in 1991.[2] She published many stories in magazines in
England, several of which have been anthologised, and
one novel.

Her work is pervaded by a sense of humour at once
wild and intimate: in the short story, 'Women are the
Scourge of the World', she assumes the voice of a paranoid
wife-beater, justifying both his suspicions and his
behaviour at the inquest on his dead wife. 'Depressed,
indeed,' he concludes of his wife, 'a quare lot she had to be
depressed about I can tell you, with a mug like me out

humping bricks on his back all day long to keep her in style. Carpets in every room that woman had.' A sinister note creeps in, suggestive of the cycle of violence against women, as he thinks of his daughter, Una. 'Una is turned into a right snotty wee brat, and she will need to mind her step. She'll not always have the old granny's skirts to hide behind. Just let her wait till all this fuss dies down. A man has a legal right to his own wains.'[3] The same concern is evident in the bitterly funny 'An Irish Fairy Tale', in which Molloy sees Saint Kevin of Glendalough, celebrated for throwing the temptress (the woman who loved him) off the mountain into the lake, as 'the patron saint of woman beaters'.[4]

Molloy's novel, *No Mate for the Magpie* (1985), is a belly-laughing, largely autobiographical account of the adventures of Ann Elizabeth McGlone. Told in Northern Irish dialect, the book takes us through Ann's formal education, which is very patchy indeed, her encounters with the Catholic church, with Protestant and Catholic bigotry, her jobs and experiences as a nun, to her eventual decision to leave Ireland. Her real education occurs as she cares for her mother's wains, deals with injustice, and becomes involved in the civil rights marches of the late 1960s. Through Ann's eyes, we see the northern Ireland situation as a shock to common sense and the butt of a great deal of laughter.

A was no good at sins till a started school,' Ann notes, 'but maybe that was because a didn't know any. Wance a got te know them though, it was hard te avoid them — especially sins of the flesh, touchin' the body — which was the biggest sin of all.' [5] Confession comes around, and the kind priest who has put Ann at ease suddenly becomes 'wile cross' as she tells her sins: 'god give me strength or wan day a'll swing for that oul bat. Then he toul me that a couldn't do sins of the flesh atall an' that the teacher wanted te be locked up in the big house for scarin'

poor wee wains stiff an' if me bum iver got itchy
again a was to give it a good scratch. (14)

Works:
No Mate for the Magpie. London: Virago, 1985. Novel.

Notes
1. Author Introduction in *No Mate for the Magpie.*
2. 'Contributors' Notes', in *Wildish Things,* Ailbhe Smyth, ed. Dublin: Attic Press, 1989, 225.
3. 'Women are the Scourge of the Earth', in *Wildish Things,* 24, 23.
4. 'An Irish Fairy Tale', in *The Female Line: Northern Irish Women Writers,* Ruth Hooley, ed. Belfast: northern Ireland Women's Rights Movement, 1985, 148.

Morgan, Lady (Sydney Owenson);
Born: 1776; Died: 1859
Educated: Ireland.

The date and place of Sydney Owenson's birth are uncertain; the writer did her best to conceal the first and to romanticise the second, claiming to be born on a boat between England and Ireland. Her ancestry is the material of romance: her mother, a respectable English woman, married the unconventional Irish actor, Robert Owenson; her grandmother, daughter of a Protestant baronet eloped with her grandfather, a Catholic farmer from the west of Ireland. This grandmother would make a name for herself playing the harp. When Sydney's mother died in 1789, Robert Owenson sent his daughters to school in Clontarf, Dublin, and then on to a 'finishing school' in Earl Street, Dublin. The girls also spent time in Kilkenny, where their father established a theatre. Sydney became a governess in 1801 and published her first work, a book of poems, the same year.

Her literary output was enormous: novels, dramas, poems, melodies, and travel books. In 1812, she married Sir Charles Morgan. The couple lived in Ireland until 1837, travelled in Europe, and spent their final years in London. Lady Morgan's novels, which relentlessly exposed the injustices of English rule in Ireland, were very popular in her lifetime, perhaps because the material was so unusual, but were also harshly attacked by critics in the *Quarterly Review.*

Although her novels are long, dramatic, and romantic, Lady Morgan still has a readership today. She pioneered Irish freedom in her work when such a stance was unpopular. In work after work, she exposes the poverty of Irish people, both urban and rural, and the injustices perpetrated against the Catholic population. English misrule is shown to be the source of Irish problems. Further, popular stereotypes are often avoided, an impoverished Irish noble being depicted realistically, rather than romantically. Despite her own romanticism, Lady Morgan also reveals the danger inherent in the emotional embrace of uncertain versions of history, often promulgated by seanachies, songs, and stories. Lady Morgan shows both a broad intellectual grasp of the complexities of the Irish situation and a sympathetic response to that situation.

Selected Works:
Ireland: From the Act of Union, 1800, to the Death of Parnell, 1891. New York and London: Garland Publishing, 1979; Includes: *The Wild Irish Girl,* 3 vol, 1806; *O'Donnel: A National Tale,* 3 vol, 1814; *Florence Macarthy: An Irish Tale,* 4 vol, 1816; *The O'Briens and the O'Flahertys,* 4 vol, 1827; *Dramatic Scenes from Real Life,* 2 vol. 1833. Novels.
St Clair: or, The Heiress of Desmond. London: Highley and Archer, 1802. Novel.
The Novice of St Dominick. London: Richard Phillips, 1805. Novel.
Woman: or, Ida of Athens. London: Longman, 1809. Novel.
Patriotic Sketches of Ireland, Written in Connaught. Baltimore: Bobin and Murphy, and Callender and Wills, 1908. Stories.
The Missionary: An Indian Tale. New York: Franklin, 1811. Novel.
The Book of the Boudoir. London: Colburn, 1829. Autobiographical.
The Princess, or, The Beguine. Paris: Gagliani, 1835. Novel.
Woman and her Master. 2 vol. London: Colburn, 1840. Study of Women.

An Odd Volume. London: Bentley, 1859. Extracts from Autobiography.

Passages from my Autobiography. New York: Appleton, 1859. Autobiography.

Lady Morgan's Memoirs: Autobiography, Diaries, and Correspondence. Edited by W Hepworth Dixon. London: Allen, 1862. Autobiography.

Morrissy, Mary
Born: Ireland, 1957
Educated: Dublin.

Mary Morrissy was born in Dublin. She won the Hennessy Award for short stories in 1984 and her work has appeared in several magazines, newspapers and anthologies. She reviews fiction for *The Irish Times* and *The Independent* on Sunday. She currently lives in Dublin and is working on a novel.

Mary's stories deal with modern life. Her direct style and use of unusual subjects are illustrated admirably in the story 'Divided Attention', in which the former lover of a married man has an unusual relationship with a silent phone caller.

> I've told all this to my caller. I've named him Larry in your honour. I've had to battle against his groaning and heaving but I've persisted. He keeps ringing so it must do something for him. It's therapy for me, you could say. Therapy, indeed! I can see you wrinkle your nose disdainfully. I needed to tell someone. I needed to tell you – but he's a good second best. I address the noisy static that is his frustration. I am happier that he is preoccupied – as you were in your way – and that he is not listening exclusively to me. I could not bear your undivided attention.[1]

Works:
A Lazy Eye. London: Jonathan Cape, 1993. Short Stories.

Notes:
1. From 'Divided Attentions' in *A Lazy Eye*. 1993.

Morton, May

Born: Ireland, 1876; Died: 1957
Educated: Ireland.

Mary (May) Elizabeth Morton was born in Co. Limerick, but lived in Belfast from 1900. She was chairwoman of Belfast PEN and also a founder of the Young Ulster Society. She was vice-principal of a girls' model school in 1934. Her verse was published and broadcast widely and she won the Festival of Britain Northern Ireland Award for poetry. Many of her poems recreate an excellent picture of weaving and spinning, one of the crafts of women practised over centuries.[1]

Selected works:
Dawn and Afterglow. Quota Press, Belfast, 1936. Poetry.
Sung to the Spinning Wheel. Quota Press, Belfast, 1952. Poetry.

Notes
1. From A A Kelly's Pillar of the House, 90.

Mulholland, Rosa, Lady Gilbert

Born: 1841; Died: 1921
Educated: Ireland.

Rosa Mulholland was born in Belfast and married John T Gilbert in 1891. Her many novels, short stories, and poetry were Irish, religious, and romantic, and very popular during her lifetime.

Mulholland typifies the upper-middle-class writer so dominant in Irish Catholic fiction in the late nineteenth century. Her significant novels seek to advance a version of Irish Catholic life acceptable to Victorian sensibilities. Her novel *The Tragedy of Cris* (1903) is about a girl going to London to save her romantic friend from prostitution.

Selected Works:
Marcella Grace. London: Kegan Paul, 1896. Novel.
The Wicked Woods. London: Burns & Oates, 1897. Novel.
Nanno, A Daughter of the State. London; Grant Richards, 1899. Novel.
Onora. London: Grant Richards, 1900. Novel.
The Tragedy of Chris. London, Edinburgh: Sands, 1903. Novel.
Our Boycotting. Dublin: Gill, 1907. Play.
The Return of Mary O'Murrough. Edinburgh & London: Sands, 1908. Novel.
Father Tim. London & Edinburgh: Sands, 1910. Novel.
Old School Friends. London: Blackie, 1914. Novel.
The Daughter in Possession. London: Blackie, 1915. Novel.
Narcissa's Ring. London: Blackie, 1916. Novel.
O'Loghlin of Clare. London & Edinburgh: Sands, 1916. Novel.

Mulkerns, Val
Born: Ireland, 1925
Educated: Ireland.

Val Mulkerns was born and educated in Dublin. She published her first stories in *The Bell* magazine, and later became associate editor of this literary magazine. She won the Allied Irish Banks Prize for Literature in 1984 for *Antiquities* (1978), *An Idle Woman* (1980), and *The Summerhouse* (1984). A member of the Irish Academy of Letters, she is married and has one daughter and two sons.[1]

The stories in *An Idle Woman* examine areas of contemporary life, usually life as experienced by the middle-class wives of professional men. When we first meet the rich, idle, unsatisfied Joanna in the title story, she anxiously awaits a call from Michael, her husband's partner, with whom, she hopes, she has begun an affair.

Mulkerns focuses on both Joanna's anxiety and frustration, and on Brendan's — her husband — generosity to his wife. When her would-be lover — guilty over betraying his friendship with Brendan — refuses to contact her, she thinks, 'Michael was, after all, only prepared to let her suffer in the interests of his own conscience. Brendan was prepared to let her have a lover if that was what she wanted.'[2] 'Humane Vitae' in the same volume concentrates on the frustrations engendered by the Catholic Church's position on birth control.

The Summerhouse is a careful dissection of the family life of a wealthy Catholic extended family. In this, as in many Anglo-Irish 'Big House' novels, the destruction of house and family is the work of the family itself, not of any outside forces. The O'Donohoe family comes together every summer in the house that their father bought to show their success in the world. Husbands, children, and in-laws are subjected to the three O'Donohoe daughters' standards, standards which seem dictated by a fear of sinking back into their roots. Con, an unapproved in-law, reflecting on the sisters' dislike and abuse of Andrew, their nephew and his adopted son, thinks they see him as 'an unsalvageable lout, some sort of throwback to the family's peasant origins'.[3] Married to the beautiful Eleanor, Con is totally unable to protect Andrew or Julia, his and Eleanor's daughter, from the family's attacks. Con has no prestige because, despite his success in the diplomatic corps, he is still seen by Hanny as a jumped-up peasant from the wrong end of the town, one who has no rightful place in the O'Donohoe home.

Works:
A Time Outworn. London: Chatto and Windus, 1951; New York: Devin-Adair, 1952. Novel.
A Peacock Cry. London: Hodder and Stoughton, 1954. Novel.
Antiquities. London: Deutsch, 1978. Stories.
A Friend of Don Juan. London: Murray, 1979. Stories.
An Idle Woman. Dublin: Poolbeg, 1980. Stories.
The Summerhouse. London: Murray, 1984; London: Futura Publications, 1985. Novel.

Very Like a Whale. London: Fontana, 1986. Novel.

Notes
1. Notes. *The Summerhouse.*
2. In *An Idle Woman,* 25.
3. *The Summerhouse,* 46.

Murdoch, Iris
Born: Ireland, 1919
Educated: England.

Iris Murdoch was born in Dublin to Anglo-Irish parents. She studied classics at Somerville College, Oxford, from 1938 until 1942, when she became involved in the war effort, serving as assistant principal in the Treasury from 1942-44. In 1944 she became an administrative officer with the United Nations Relief and Rehabilitation Administration and worked with refugees until 1946. After the war, she studied philosophy in Newnham College, Cambridge. She was named Fellow at St Anne's College, Oxford, in 1948, and Honourable Fellow in 1963. She is married to the novelist and critic John Bayley, and lives outside Oxford.

Sartre: Romantic Rationalist (1953) was Murdoch's first book, followed in 1954 by her first novel, *Under the Net.* Philosophical and literary essays and twenty-four novels have appeared since 1954. The novels have all been highly acclaimed – *The Sea, the Sea* (1978) won the Booker Prize – and was published widely (though only the first publisher is listed here).

The adjectives most often applied to Murdoch's novels are 'philosophical' and 'intellectual'; they are also deeply-imaginative, complex, and moral. Despite the veneer of realism and good-manners, a Murdoch novel is profoundly disturbing: enacting bitter cruelties, the middle-class characters always behave politely, and Murdoch usually resists closure, leaving the characters exposed to new circumstances. Thus, she emphasises the partial nature of art, and rather than leaving her readers satisfied, Murdoch forces us to realise the impossibility of ever seeing, much less understanding, the entire picture, and hence we must contemplate the dangerous and contingent nature of all action.

The nature of good in a chaotic world is a central concern in Murdoch's work. Her exploration goes deeper with each novel, as she unravels layers of deceits which mimic goodness. The Irish connection seems unimportant in her novels, though she introduces Irish characters in several, and sets *The Red and the Green* (1965) in the Ireland of 1916. Her character portrayals convince, but Murdoch is ultimately concerned with something that transcends individual human beings, or nationalities. Her most recent novel, *The Message to the Planet* (1989), presents Marcus Vallar: a genius who excels in maths, painting, and philosophy, a Jew who although physically unscathed by the Holocaust attempts to identify with the suffering of the victims, a man who draws friends and the neglected alike to his side, a man who may even raise his friend from the dead. His daughter Irina, not a follower, berates Marcus to his friend:

> he did visit Auschwitz and distinguished himself by fainting. He should have remembered he was just a tourist. And he went to India to look at all the suffering on show there, perhaps he thought that *they* would see that he was really a god, but all he got was hepatitis. And another thing is, he's got to be a great sinner and understand evil as well as good and be the victims and Hitler too and Christ and anti-Christ.[1]

Marcus's death at the end of the novel fails to resolve the question Irina implicitly poses on the nature of good, on the nature of Marcus. The scope of this, like most Murdoch novels, is huge; the scope of her corpus, immense.

Selected Works:
Sartre: Romantic Rationalist. Glasgow: Fontana, 1953.
Under the Net. London: Chatto and Windus, 1954. Novel.

The Flight from the Enchanter. London: Chatto and Windus, 1956. Novel.

The Sandcastle. London: Chatto and Windus, 1957. Novel.

The Bell. London: Chatto and Windus, 1958. Novel.

A Severed Head. London: Chatto and Windus, 1961. Novel.

An Unofficial Rose. London: Chatto and Windus, 1962. Novel.

The Unicorn. London: Chatto and Windus, 1963. Novel.

The Italian Girl. London: Chatto and Windus, 1964. Novel.

The Red and the Green. London: Chatto and Windus, 1965. Novel.

The Time of the Angels. London: Chatto and Windus, 1966. Novel.

The Nice and the Good. London: Chatto and Windus, 1968. Novel.

Bruno's Dream. London: Chatto and Windus, 1969. Novel.

A Fairly Honourable Defeat. London: Chatto and Windus, 1970. Novel.

An Accidental Man. London: Chatto and Windus, 1971. Novel.

The Black Prince. London: Chatto and Windus, 1973. Novel.

The Sacred and Profane Love Machine. London: Chatto and Windus, 1974. Novel.

A Word Child. London: Chatto and Windus, 1975. Novel.

Henry and Cato. London: Chatto and Windus, 1976. Novel.

The Sea, the Sea. London: Chatto and Windus, 1978. Novel.

Nuns and Soldiers. London: Chatto and Windus, 1980. Novel.

The Philosopher's Pupil. London: Chatto and Windus, 1983. Novel.

The Good Apprentice. London: Chatto and Windus, 1985. Novel.

The Book and the Brotherhood. London: Chatto and Windus, 1987. Novel.

The Message to the Planet. London: Chatto and Windus, 1989. Novel.

Notes
1. *The Message to the Planet*, 105.

Nelson, Dorothy

Born: Ireland, c 20th century
Educated: Ireland.

Dorothy Nelson was born and educated in Bray, Co. Wicklow. She worked in many offices in Dublin and London, while writing her first novel, *In Night's City* (1982). She read from her novel at the first International Feminist Book Fair; it was televised for Channel 4 and won the Rooney Prize in 1983. She received an Arts Council Bursary in 1981.

In Night's City captures two cries of agony, the cries of a mother and her daughter, both of whom are abused by the same man, the husband and father. The story moves from mother's to daughter's consciousness and covers twelve years, years of Sara's growth from child to woman, until the father's death. Esther, the mother, Sara, and the father share the same bedroom; the three sons occupy the only other bedroom in the working-class household. There is no hiding from the father's activities, and Esther seems to hate him as much for his violations and beatings of herself, as for his abuse of their daughter.

Esther escapes temporarily into bitterness and schemes of revenge: 'So I gave him four children. But I said he would pay for them. He would never pay the way I had to but he would pay as much as he was able. That nourished me and gave me the strength to go on. It was like a beacon of light in the dark nights drawing me closer and closer to the wild churning of my own blood until I was so consumed that the nights ceased to exist and all that mattered was that light. I worked it just right. I lay beside him and I could hear the uneasy silence in him, eating him up as he tried to find the words that would tell him.'[1]

Sara escapes through schizophrenia, allowing 'Maggie' – her other self – to experience the horror rather than Sara. 'I'm not three-and-a-half. I just told you, I'm four now. He tickled me again an' I was laughin' into his colours. Then it was dark. I felt the Dark touchin' me funny an' I was cryin' so Maggie came an' he touched Maggie funny not me. Not me. Not me.' (7)

The narrative is structured through stream-of-consciousness and almost surrealistic movements, techniques which depict very effectively the nightmarish quality of the lives of mother and daugther.

A second novel, *Tar and Feathers* (1987), compares the hopeless poverty of unemployment with the almost shocking optimism of the young.

Works:
In Night's City. Dublin: Wolfhound, 1982. Novel.
Tar and Feathers. Dublin: Wolfhound, 1987. Novel.

Notes
1. *In Night's City*, 64.

Ní Bhrolcháin, Muireann
Born: Ireland, 1955
Educated: Ireland.

Born in Galway to an Irish speaking family, Muireann Ní Bhrolcháin attended Scoil Fhursa, an all-Irish school, and Salerno Convent. She received her BA degree from University College Galway, in History and Old-Irish, and completed an MA and doctorate in Celtic Studies while on scholarship at the Dublin Institute for Advanced Studies.

She began writing while at college and won prizes for poetry and short stories in the Gael-Linn organised competition, *Slógadh*. She was an active member of the Irish Drama Society in University College, Galway, and spent six years with An Taibhdhearc, the Irish language theatre in Galway, as an actress, singer, and finally producer. She works in the Old-Irish Department of St Patrick's College, Maynooth.

As there was little or no reading material for teenagers in Irish, she decided that there was a market for light, modern novels for the ten-to eighteen-year-old age group and for adults learning Irish. Since 1989 she has published three such novels: *An Bád sa Chuan*, *Eachtraí Samhraidh*, both for teenagers, and *Ar Ais Arís*, aimed at the adult learner. Written in simple Irish, it has the adult theme of a woman terrorised by a mysterious telephone caller. A fourth, *An Solas sa Chaisleán*, awaits publication. All four have been awarded prizes by the Oireachtas, the primary annual Irish literary and performing arts competition.

She has also received awards for a book of short stories for the adult learner, and for one stage play and two radio plays in the Oireachtas. Two of these have been performed by the Radio Éireann players. One deals with the problem of undetected and untreated post-natal depression, and the second with tense mother-daughter relationships. Both are unpublished.

Although most of her work for adults deals with the world of women and children, she maintains that she does not make a conscious effort to write for girls and women but that this is what her own experience of life offers as an inspiration.[1]

Works:
An Bád sa Chuan. Cló Iar-Chonnachta, 1990. Teenage fiction.
Eachtraí Samhraidh. Cló Iar-Chonnachta, 1991. Teenage fiction.
Ar Ais Arís. Cló Iar-Chonnachta, 1992. Fiction.

Notes:
1. Personal communication.

Ní Chinnéide, Máire
Born: Ireland, 1880; Died: 1967
Educated: Ireland.

Máire Ní Chinnéide was born in Dublin and educated at the Dominican Convent, Sion Hill and in Ardscoil Mhuire, a Dominican college in Merrion Square where women could take a degree from an Ollscoil Ríoga. (They were not allowed to attend university lectures.) She took a degree in Modern Literature in 1900. She was professor of Irish in Ardscoil Mhuire in Donnybrook from 1903. A very active member of the Gaelic League, she played Una in the Gaiety production of Douglas Hyde's play *Casadh an tSúgáin*. In 1906 she married Seán Mac Gearailt.

In the early twenties she was an active member of Conradh na Gaeilge. She is well known as the editor of two books by Peig Sayers, *Peig* and *Macnamh Sean-Mhná*. As a visitor to the Great Blasket Island, she encouraged Peig, who was an excellent storyteller, to tell her own story. She herself was one of the first playwrights in Irish. She wrote *Gleann na Sidheog* in 1902; *An Dúthchas* in 1908 – this play was staged by An Comhar Dramaíochta in the Abbey and *Sidheoga na mBláth*, a play for children was staged in 1909. *Cois Abhann Araglainn*, a four-act play, was staged during the Oireachtas (Irish Literary Festival) in 1911, but the play was not published. Her other works include An *Cochall Draoidheachta* (1938), *Cáit Ní Dhuibhir* (1938), a play for young girls and *Scéal an Tí* (1952). From 1903-35 she published essays, translations, critical articles and plays for children in *An Claidheamh Soluis*, *Banba*, *An Branar*, *Misneach*, *The Irish Rosary* and *Ar Aghaidh*.[1]

Works:
Gleann na Sidheog. Baile Atha Cliath: Muintir na Leabhar Gaeilge, 1902. Play.
An Dúthchas. Baile Atha Cliath: Conradh na Gaeilge, 1908. Play.
Sidheoga na mBláth. Baile Atha Cliath: Conradh na Gaeilge, 1909. Play.
An Cochall Draoidheachta. Baile Atha Cliath: Brún agus O Nualláin, 1938. Play.

Cáit Ní Dhuibhir. Baile Atha Cliath: Brún agus O Nualláin, 1938. Play.

Scéal an Tí. Baile Atha Cliath: Oifig an tSoláthair, 1952. Play.

Notes
1. *Beathaisnéis a Dó 1882-1982*, D Breathnach and M Ní Mhurchudha, Clóchomhar, 1986.

Ní Chonaill, Eibhlín Dubh
Born: Ireland, c.1748; Died: 1800
Educated: Ireland.

Eibhlín Dubh was the daughter of Domhnall Mór O Connaill of Derrynane, the grandfather of Daniel O'Connell, known as 'The Liberator', and credited with achieving Catholic Emancipation. Her first husband died six months after the wedding, and Eibhlín Dubh married Colonel Art O'Leary of the Irish Brigade. As Catholics subject to the penal laws, the O'Learys could not own a horse worth more than five pounds, and O'Leary got into trouble when he refused to sell his mare to a Protestant neighbour who offered the maximum sum. O'Leary was shot as he attempted to escape the law, and the story goes that the riderless horse returned to Eibhlín Dubh and brought her to the Colonel's dead body.[1]

Eibhlín Dubh composed a lament for her husband, *Caoineadh Airt Uí Laoghaire*, often cited as the best lament in Irish in the eighteenth century. Women were the composers, custodians, and performers of *Caoinea* or keen. The significance of this genre of women's oral poetry has been explored and elucidated by Angela Bourke.[2]

Mo chara go daingean
      tú!
Is cuimhin lem aigne
An lá bhreá earraigh úd
Gur bhreá thíodh hata
      dhuit
Faoi bhanda óir
      tarraingthe,
Claíomh cinn airgid –
Lámh dheas chalma –
Rompsáil bhagarthach –
Fír-chritheagla
Ar namhaid chealgach –
Tú i gcóir chun
      falaracht,
Is each caol ceannan fút.
D'umhlaídís Sasanaigh
Síos go talamh duit,
Is ní ar mhaithe leat
Ach le haon-chorp
      eagla,
Cé gur leo a cailleadh
      tú,
A Mhúirnín mh'anama.[3]

My friend forever!
My mind remembers
That fine spring day
How well your hat
      suited you,
Bright gold banded,
Sword silver-hilted –
Right hand steady –
Threatening aspect –
Trembling terror
On treacherous enemy –
You poised for a canter
On your slender bay
      horse.
The Saxons bowed to
      you,
Down to the ground to
      you,
Not for love of you
But for deadly fear of
      you,
Though you lost your
      life to them,
Oh my soul's darling.[4]

Works:

Caoineadh Airt Uí Laoghaire. Edited Seán O Cuív. Baile Atha Cliath: Brown and Nolan, 1923.

Caoineadh Airt Uí Laoghaire. ed. Seán O Tuama, Baile Atha Cliath: Clóchomhar, 1961.

Notes

1. *A Biographical Dictionary of Irish Writers*, Anne M. Brady and Brian Cleeve, eds. (Mullingar: Lilliput Press, 1985), 320-321.
2. 'Performing - not writing' by Angela Bourke, in *Graph II* winter 1991/2, 28-31. Also Angela Bourke, *Working and Weeping: Women's Oral Poetry in Irish and Scottish Gaelic Poetry*. Women's Studies Working Papers No. 7 (Dublin: UCD Women's Studies Forum, 1988).

3. *Caoineadh Airt Uí Laoghaire* ed. Seán O Tuama. Baile Atha Cliath: Clóchomhar, 1961, 33-34.
4. 'Eibhlín Dhubh Ní Chonaill', in *Pillars of the House*, A A Kelly, ed. (Dublin: Wolfhound, 1988), 31.

Ní Chuilleanáin, Eiléan

Born: Ireland, 1942
Educated: Ireland, England.

Eiléan Ní Chuilleanáin was born in Cork, the daughter of Cormac O Cuilleanáin, Professor of Irish literature, and Eilís Dillon, the novelist. She was educated at University College Cork, and Oxford. She is a senior lecturer in Renaissance Literature at Trinity College, Dublin, and the co-editor of *Cyphers*, a literary magazine. She is married to the poet Macdara Woods, and has one son.

'Being born into a family with an Irish Republican tradition' helped shape her life; 'my father fought in the War of Independence and was imprisoned in the Civil War; my mother's uncle was executed in 1916 and her mother arrested and imprisoned when she was a small child,' she notes. Learning Irish at home was also important: she found it 'an opening to a world of strangeness in the past, to hearing the voice of Gaelic submerged in the English spoken in Ireland, and to other European languages'. A member of a musical family, she learnt to play the viola and to sing Schubert lieder. She was exposed to two very different sides of Irish life: her father had 'six unmarried sisters, three of whom escaped from home into convents while the others stayed at home and lived a more-than-conventual life of prayer and domesticity'. Her mother, on the other hand, 'wrote and published, so that I knew it was a valid way of making a living'. She also credits the 'very lively literary scene' of Dublin in the sixties and seventies with encouraging her work, and the fact that one can teach in a university there and not be 'constantly surrounded by academics'.[1]

Eiléan Ní Chuilleanáin's poetry soaks up feminine and precise natural images, and welds Irish and classical history and myth. A poem like 'The Lady's Tower' suggests and celebrates tower and house as metaphors of the feminine: 'Hollow my high tower leans/Back to the cliff; my thatch/Converses with spread sky,/Heronries.' 'Wash' attempts to establish female identity as distinct from, not opposite to, male. 'Wash the man out of the woman:/The strange sweat from her skin, the ashes from her hair./Stretch her to dry in the sun/The blue marks on her breast will fade.'[2]

'Site of Ambush' flies high over the whole countryside from which the enemy parties will emerge, to the precise point of the ambush, and streams back through all history, and forward into a future beyond the ambush. As the 'asthmatic engines' wheeze up the hill, the country waits: 'The pine trees looked up stiff;/At the angle of the road, polished stones/Forming a stile, a knowing path/Twisting away; the rough grass/Gripped the fragments of the wall.' The poignancy of the innocent becomes part of history: 'Nearer; a boy carried a can to the well/Nearer on the dark road./The driver saw the child's back,/Nearer; the birds shoaled off the branches in fright./ Deafly rusting in the stream/The lorry now is soft as a last night's dream./The soldiers and the deaf child/Landed gently in the water'. The poem moves through ages before and after history until 'The child came back from the well./Symmetrical breasts of hills criss-crossed./The trees grew over the sun.'[3]

Acts and Monuments (1972), her first volume, won the Patrick Kavanagh Award, and her work has increased in strength, music, and complexity ever since. *The Magdalene Sermon* (1989) was shortlisted for *The Irish Times*/Aer Lingus Award in 1990.

Works:
Acts and Monuments. Dublin: Gallery Press, 1972. Poetry.
Site of Ambush. Dublin: Gallery Press, 1975. Poetry.

The Rose-Geranium. Dublin: Gallery Press, 1981. Poetry.

The Second Voyage. Dublin: Gallery Press; Newcastle upon Tyne: Bloodaxe Books, 1986; Revised Edition, Winston-Salem, Wake Forest University Press, 1991. Poetry.

The Magdalene Sermon. Dublin: Gallery Press, 1989; Winston-Salem: Wake Forest University Press, 1991. Poetry.

Notes

1. Personal communication.
2. In *The Second Voyage*, 11-67.
3. In *The Second Voyage*, 14-21.

Ní Dhómhnaill, Nuala
Born: England, 1952
Educated: England; Ireland.

Nuala Ní Dhómhnaill was born in England to Irish parents, but most of her schooling took place in Ireland, through the medium of Irish. She received a BA from University College, Cork, in Irish and English in 1972, and completed the Higher Diploma in Education there in 1973. She has taught part-time in several secondary schools, and in universities in Turkey and Ireland. She runs seminars, workshops, engages in broadcasting, and in the past ten years has given over 300 poetry readings, in Ireland, Scotland, Wales, England, France, Italy, Austria, Belgium, Canada, and the USA. She spent seven years on the *seachrán* in Turkey and Holland. Her husband is Turkish and she speaks Irish, English, Turkish, French, German, and Dutch.

As a young woman she took Joyce's dictum to heart and fled the nets of nationality, language, and religion. After several years, however, she realised that she had as much right as anyone to live in Ireland: 'So I upped and broke up the family, sold all my earthly possessions and brought my two children home to Ireland with me, determined to make my way as a writer in Irish in Ireland.'[1] Ten years later, she is still on course; her work has been recognised and received many prizes, including the American Ireland Fund's Literary Award in 1991.

She writes creatively in Irish. 'I think I'm very lucky in being Irish because the Irish language wasn't industrialised or patriarchalised. And many things, including this idea of a deeper quality, this negative femininity, this Hag Energy, which is so painful to mankind, hasn't been wiped from our consciousness, as it has in most cultures. Irish in the Irish context is the language of the Mothers, because everything that has been done to women has been done to Irish.'[2] An event which severely traumatised her at 19, and on which she 'brooded for twenty years', forced her into poetry and myth. 'It is like the way rocks are subjected to great pressure in the bowels of the earth,' she notes, 'so that limestone is metamorphosed into marble and even common carbon into diamonds. The metamorphosis which occurs when disparate psychic entities are held together in the closed vessel of the psyche is poetry.'[3]

Many of her poems are anthologised and translated into English. The poetry is filled with exact natural descriptions, with the reality of contemporary women in Ireland, and with images which resonate into a mythic unity with land, with the 'Hag Energy', with Ireland as muse. 'Aubade' beautifully and precisely pictures 'the bickering of jackdaws', 'the green mallard's/Stylish glissando among reeds,' 'the moorhen/Whose white petticoat flickers around the boghole;' but at the same time, the poet notes, regretfully, the contrast between the indifference of nature and the human desire to make life different, better.[4] While 'As Fragile As a Shell' captures the loneliness of the woman who peers through a letter box into the house of her desired one, but expects no miracle, no dove, for 'it is only inwardly, in the psyche/that miracles happen', 'Without Your Clothes' presents the humorous musing of the woman who most admires her lover naked, but before they go out dancing reluctantly advises, 'I suppose you had better/put your clothes on/rather than have half the women of Ireland/totally undone.'[5]

These lines from 'Scéala' — translated as 'Annunciations' — are typical of the wit and subversion of Ní Dhómhnaill's poetry.

O, a mhaighdean rócheansa,	Remember
nár chuala trácht ar éinne riamh	o most tender virgin Mary that never was it known
ag teacht chughat sa doircheacht	that a man came to you in the darkness alone,
cosnocht, déadgheal	his feet bare, his teeth white
is a shúile lán de rógaireacht.[6]	and roguery swelling in his eyes.[6]

Works:

In Irish

An Dealg Droighin. Corcaigh: Cló Mercier, 1981. Poetry.
Féar Suaithinseach. Má Nuat: An Sagart, 1984. Poetry.
Feis. Maigh Nuad: An Sagart, 1991. Poetry.

In Translation:

Selected Poems. Dublin: Raven Arts Press, 1986. Translated by Michael Hartnett. Poetry.
Selected Poems/Rogha Dánta. Dual Language Text. Dublin: Raven Arts Press, 1988. Translated by Michael Hartnett. Poetry.
Pharoah's Daughter. New and selected poems. Dublin: The Gallery Press, 1990. Translated by many Irish poets. Poetry.
The Astrakhan Cloak. Poems in Irish, Translations, Paul Muldoon, 1992. Meath: Gallery Press, 1992.

Notes
1. Personal communication.
2. In *Sleeping with Monsters*, Gillian Somerville-Arjat and Rebecca E Wilson, eds. (Dublin: Wolfhound Press, 1990), 154.
3. Personal communication.
4. In *Sleeping with Monsters*, 155.
5. In *Wildish Things*, Ailbhe Smyth, ed. (Dublin: Attic Press, 1989), 211, 214.
6. In *Selected Poems*, 44-45.

Ní Dhuibhne, Eilís

Born: Ireland, 1954
Educated: Ireland, Sweden

Eilís Ní Dhuibhne has been interested in writing since she became 'totally addicted to fiction' at age seven or eight. She attended school in Dublin at Scoil Bhríde in Earlsfort Terrace, St Mary's Haddington Road, and Scoil Chaitríona, Eccles Street, and acknowledges the early encouragement of English teachers. Along with many Irish women, she is grateful to David Marcus, who – while Eilís was still at University College, Dublin – published several of her short stories in his 'New Irish Writing' page in the *Irish Press*. David Marcus was one of the first to recognise that 'women's writing was the important literary phenomonen of this era'. She berates herself for lack of awareness at college: failing to note that all the writers assigned were men. However, she did use a pseudonym herself because she wrote of love and sexual relationships, and at some level felt these topics would trouble the nuns who had encouraged her writing. She took a MPhil and PhD in Folklore, a subject she found fascinating, because she has 'always been concerned with discovering the secret of storytelling'. Although she did not write fiction while working on her PhD, she is grateful for the discipline gained in that writing. She has published one novel, two collections of short stories, and two children's books, as well as scholarly work.

Very interested in being Irish, in the linguistic doubleness, and in Irish folklore, Ní Dhuibhne particularly likes the Icelandic writer Halldor Laxness, finding similarities in the Icelandic and Irish experiences. She enjoys, wishes to write – and does write – accessible texts, and is particularly attracted to Alice Munroe, whose work she finds subtle, feminine, unpretentious, entertaining and serious.[1]

Situations and characters are complex in Ní Dhuibhne's work. *The Bray House* (1990) is a haunting story of a Swedish archaeologist's visit to Ireland following the devastation of Ireland, Britain, and much of western Europe by a nuclear explosion and chain reaction. The novel is set in the twenty-first century, but social, political, and environmental attitudes have not advanced. In response to the 1990s greenhouse threat of global warming, most countries, we hear, either turned to nuclear power entirely, or sacrificed the environment in an attempt to avoid nuclear accidents. When the disaster — innocuously called the 'Ballylumford Incident' — occurs, the prime minister of Britain, a Margaret Thatcher-clone, Ms Bennet, is meeting with the president of the USA and the Irish premier in California to discuss a new Anglo-Irish agreement. By coincidence, the British royal family is also out of the country. Initially the IRA is blamed, a scapegoat, the narrator suggests, admitting that by that time, the organisation had become 'both sophisticated, disgruntled, and callous enough to perpetrate such an act'. Nothing, you see, has changed. 'Tears in her brilliant eyes,' the prime minister speaks from a Beverly Hills mansion, 'We must now try to build on what we have left to us. We must not give in or despair, but remember that Great Britain has always been the leader among all nations. There will always be an England.' She did not, the narrator notes, 'mention Ireland'.[2]

Works:
Blood and Water. Dublin: Attic Press, 1988. Short Stories.
The Bray House. Dublin, Attic Press, 1990. Novel.
The Uncommon Cormorant. Dublin: Poolbeg, 1990. Children's Book.
Eating Women is not Recommended. Dublin: Attic Press, 1991. Short Stories.
Hugo and the Sunshine Girl. Dublin: Poolbeg, 1991. Children's Book.
Viking Ale. Editor, with Professor Séamas O Catháin. Festschrift for Professor Bo Almqvist. Boethius Press, 1991.

Notes
1. Personal communication.
2. *The Bray House,* 64-65.

Ní Fhaircheallaigh, Una
Born: Ireland, 1874; Died: 1951
Educated: Ireland.

Una Ní Fhaircheallaigh was born in Co. Cavan. She studied at University College, Dublin, where she took an MA. She actively sought equal opportunities for women in the universities and was a member of the first governing body of UCD (NUI). She began her study of Irish in 1896, and she was appointed as a lecturer in Modern Irish in 1909 in UCD, on the foundation of the National University of Ireland. She succeeded Douglas Hyde as professor of Modern Irish Poetry in 1932, and she was a prominent and very active officer of the Gaelic League.

She was president of the Irish Industrial Development Association and of the Homespun Society; she was an administrator of the John Connor Magee Trust for the establishing of industries in Gaeltacht areas and President of Cumann Camógaíochta na hÉireann. She was associated with the foundation and running of Irish Colleges in Cloch Cheannfhaola (Donegal), Tourmaceady (Mayo) and of Coláiste Laighean.

She was present at the first meeting of Sinn Féin in November 1905, but she believed that the Gaelic League should stay out of politics. However, she chaired the meeting in April that year in Wynnes Hotel, when Cumann na mBan was founded. She published her work in English as Agnes O'Farrelly.

Works:
Out of the Depths. Dublin: Talbot Press, 1921. Poetry.
Aille an Domhain. Baile Atha Cliath: Brún agus O Nualláin, 1927. Poetry.
Grádh agus Crádh. Baile Atha Cliath: Conradh na Gaeilge, 1901. Novel.
Smuainte ar Arainn. Baile Atha Cliath: Conradh na Gaeilge, 1902. Non-fiction.
An Cneamhaire. Baile Atha Cliath: An Clóchumann, c.1902. Novel.
Filidheacht Sheághain Uí Neachtain. Baile Atha Cliath: Conradh na Gaeilge, 1911.

Leabhar an Athar Eoghan. Baile Atha Cliath: Gill, 1903.

Notes:
1. *Beathaisnéis a Dó 1882-1982*. B Breathnach agus M Ní Mhurchú, Clóchomhar, 1986.

Ní Fhoghludha, Aine
Born: Ireland, 1880; Died: 1932
Educated: Ireland.

Aine Ní Fhoghludha was born in Ring, Co. Waterford, (a Gaeltacht), and educated there and at the Convent of Mercy in Dungarvan. She took a degree in Irish at University College, Cork. She spent some years teaching at primary and secondary levels. She was sacked, it is believed, for expressing nationalistic opinions in the classroom after the 1916 Rising. She married Séamus O Néill in 1917 and went to live in Cashel, became an active member of Cumann na mBan and was known as a good musician.

Her writing shows her concern with political affairs as in the extract below from 'Athchuinghe an Oglaoich' (The Warrior's Petition) in which the ideal *pro patria mori* is combined with religious sentiment. Many of her poems are in traditional song metres and her love lyrics and nature poetry are conventional.

A Dhia, bí liom ar mhaigh an áir,
Do ghrásta im' chroidhe!
Cuir brígh is neart is lúth im' lámha
An namhad do chlaoidheadh
Go bhfeicfear Éire arís fé cháil,
Bí liom, a Dhia![2]

Works:
Idir na Fleadhanna. Baile Atha Cliath: Oifig Díolta Foilseacháin Rialtais, 1922. Poetry.

Díthreabhach an Tobair. Baile Atha Cliath: Oifig Díolta Foilseacháin Rialtais, 1934. Translation.

Bréigríocht Apollo. Baile Atha Cliath: Oifig Díolta Foilseacháin Rialtais, 1934. Translation.

Breacadh an Lae. Baile Atha Cliath: Oifig Díolta Foilseacháin Rialtais, 1934. Translation.

Róis Dhearga. Baile Atha Cliath: Oifig Díolta Foilseacháin Rialtais, 1934. Translation.

Notes
1. *Beathaisnéis a Dó 1882-1982,* D Breathnach and M Ní Mhurchú, Clóchomhar, 1986.
2. *Idir na Fleadhanna,* 7.

Ní Ghlinn, Aine
Born: Ireland, 1955
Educated: Ireland.

Aine Ní Ghlinn was born in Tipperary, attended the Presentation Convent in Thurles, and University College, Dublin. She is a freelance journalist / broadcaster / writer /poet, and works mainly for RTE and Raidió na Gaeltachta. Her first collection of poetry, *An Chéim Bhriste* (1984), went into two editions in 1984. Her second collection of poetry, *Gairdín Pharthais* (1988), won the Bord na Gaeilge Award at Listowel Writers' Week in 1987 when still in manuscript form. *Mná as an nGnáth* (1990), a collection of non-fiction stories based on the lives of well-known women, won an Oireachtas award in 1989, and *Déithe Is Daoine,* a collection of myths from all over the world, was published in 1992. Her work has also been broadcast on radio and television and has appeared in a variety of anthologies.[1]

A translation of 'An Chéim Bhriste', 'The Broken Step', by the author appears in *Pillars of the House.*

I hear you coming up the stairs. You walk on the broken step. Everyone avoids it but you walk on it always.

You asked me my name. We were together and you said I had blue eyes.

If you see the sunlight at the end of the day
and it awakens a poem in you ...
That is my name.[2]

The same suggestive quality is in much of her poetry, 'Deireadh an Bhóthair', for example:

Cé hí an bhean a shiúlann leat?
Braithim a scáil romhat amach.

Níl ann ach an ghaoth
ag dalladh do shúl[3]

'Tochailt' leaves aside the gentle suggestion and reveals the effects of too much probing, digging, into the other's mind:

Ní raibh fágtha os mo chomhair ansan
ach meangadh gáire nach raibh gá aige
le hútamáil na bhfocal
ná le fústráil na gcorp.[4]

The title poem in *Gairdín Pharthais* is a humorous revision of, and a deletion of gender bias in, the Garden of Eden story.

Works:
An Chéim Bhriste. Baile Atha Cliath: Coiscéim, 1984. Poetry.
Gairdín Pharthais. Baile Atha Cliath: Coiscéim, 1988. Poetry.
Mná as an nGnáth. Baile Atha Cliath: An Gúm, 1990. Biographical Sketches.
Déithe Is Daoine. Baile Atha Cliath: An Gúm, 1992. Myths.

Notes
1. Personal communication.
2. In *Pillars of the House*, A A Kelly, ed. (Dublin: Wolfhound Press, 1988), 163.
3. In *An Chéim Bhriste*, 19.
4. In *An Chéim Bhriste*, 9.

Ní Ghráda, Máiréad

Born: Ireland, 1896; Died: 1971
Educated: Ireland.

Máiréad Ní Ghráda was born in Kilmaley, Co. Clare, at a time when Irish had not quite disappeared from the area as a spoken language. She was educated at the Convent of Mercy, Ennis. She was awarded a scholarship to University College, Dublin (UCD), where she took a degree in Irish, French and English. She taught in a private school for a short time and as a member of the Gaelic League she worked as a *timire* (a peripatetic teacher). She was also a member of Cumann na mBan. She was secretary to Ernest Blythe during the first Dáil and during the Civil War. In 1923 she married Risteard O Cíosáin, a civil servant. She spent the next couple of years teaching and, in 1926 started work with RN (*Radio Éireann*). She spent nine years there as a producer and was the first woman broadcaster in Ireland. Later she worked as an editor with Browne and Nolan, publishing house.[1]

Ní Ghráda is a well-known woman playwright in Irish. She wrote her first play, *An Uacht* (1935), for her students; Mícheál Mac Liammóir produced it in the Gate Theatre. A prolific writer, her work gives evidence of a feminist awareness of women's issues, and she created strong roles for women, especially for young women. *An Triail* (The Trial) is based on the story of a young girl who had to leave home because of being pregnant, while the man she was involved with went on with his life. It was staged at the Eblana Theatre in 1964 and shown on television later that year. It was a very successful play, praised by the critics, notably by Harold Hobson. As well as the works listed below, she wrote many school textbooks, school plays and dictionaries.[2]

Works:
Mícheál. Dublin: Oifig an tSoláthair, 1933. Play.
An Uacht. Dublin: Oifig an tSoláthair, 1935. Play.
An Grá agus an Garda. Dublin: Oifig an tSoláthair, 1937. Play.

An Bheirt Dearthár agus Scéalta Eile. Dublin: Oifig an tSoláthair, 1939. Stories.
Manannan. Dublin: Oifig an tSoláthair, 1940. Children's Stories.
Giolla an tSolais. Dublin: Oifig an tSoláthair, 1945. Play.
Lá Buí Bealtaine. Dublin: Oifig an tSoláthair, 1953. Play.
Ull Glas Oíche Shamhna. Dublin: Oifig an tSoláthair, 1955. Play.
Súgán Sneachta. Dublin: Oifig an tSoláthair, 1959. Play.
Stailc Ocrais. Dublin: Oifig an tSoláthair, 1966. Play.
Mac Uí Rudaí. Dublin: Oifig an tSoláthair, 1963. Play.
An Triail/Breithiúntas. Dublin: Oifig an tSoláthair, 1978. Plays.

Notes
1. *Beathaisnéis a Aon 1882-1982,* B Breathnach and M Ní Mhurchú, Clóchomhar, 1986.
2. Máiréad Ní Ghráda agus a saothar liteartha, Eámon O Cíosáin, in *An Triail, Breithiúnas,* 1978.

Ní Laoghaire, Máire Bhuidhe
Born: Ireland, 1774; Died: c 1847
Educated: Ireland.

Máire Bhuidhe Ní Laoghaire was born in West Cork. She eloped with Séamus de Búrca when she was eighteen and lived near Keimaneagh for the rest of her life. They had 150 acres of land and were known for their generosity to the less well-off. The editor of her poems states that she could neither read nor write. Her poetry belongs in the oral literary tradition: the songs she composed have been known and sung throughout Gaeltacht areas since her time to the present day. The published edition of her poetry is based on manuscripts written at the beginning of this century and on versions collected by the editor.

Máire Bhuidhe's poetry is conventional — she composed in the *aisling* tradition, wrote laments, and tried, in the manner typical of poets who saw themselves as responsible for public morale, to instil hope for freedom into her people. Very few women are known to have composed in this tradition. Her best known poem/song is

Cath Chéim An Fhia, a celebration of a battle during agrarian unrest. This extract shows how she conveys the turmoil and confusion of a fight:

Níor fhan bean ná páiste i mbun aítribh na tighe aca
Ach na gártha do bhí aca, agus mílte ologón,
Ag féachaint ar an ngarda ag teacht láidir 'na
dtimcheall
Ag lámhach is ag líonadh is ag scaoileach'na dtreo;
An liú gur lean abhfad i gcian,
Sé dubhairt gach flaith gur mhaith leis triall:
'Gluaisidh mear tá an cath dhá rian
Agus téimis 'na chomhair.'[1]

Works:
Filíocht Mháire Bhuidhe Ní Laoghaire ed. D O Donnchú. Baile Atha Cliath, Oifig an tSoláthair, 1931. Poetry.

Notes
1. *Filíocht Mháire Bhuidhe Ní Laoghaire*, 56.

Ní Mhóráin, Bríd
Born: Ireland, c 20th century
Educated: Ireland.

Bríd Ní Mhóráin was born in Co. Cork but moved to Camp in the Dingle peninsula with her family at the age of four. She later spent two years in Dublin, one as a junior executive officer in the civil service, and one as a student of linguistics. She also spent a year in France, as a teacher of English. She is now married and lives in Camp. She teaches languages in Tralee, Co. Kerry. In 1990 she took an M Lit degree in Irish in Trinity College, Dublin.[1]

In 1985 Bríd attended an Arts Council workshop for Writers in Irish, directed by Seán Mac Mathúna. Writing produced in that workshop was published a *Imeachtaí na Ceardlainne 1985*. Bríd Ní Mhóráin has two pieces in it – a short story, 'An t-ardán rince', and a short piece entitled 'O,

Lios Dún Bhearna'. She took part in the 1988 workshop which was directed by Nuala Ní Dómhnaill. She has won Oireachtas prizes for her poetry and for research into the history of the Irish language. Her poetry has been published in *Innti 12* and in *Innti 13*, in *An tUltach*, and in *Women's Work.*[2]

Works:
Ceiliúradh Cré. Baile Atha Cliath, Coiscéim, 1992. Poetry.

Notes
1. Personal communication.
2. Personal communication.

Ní Shéaghdha, Nóra
Born: Ireland, 1905; Died: 1975
Educated: Ireland.

Nóra Ní Shéaghdha was born in Baile an Mhordhaigh in the West Kerry Gaeltacht. She was educated in Cill Chluain primary school, and in Moyderwell Secondary School in Tralee and later attended Mary Immaculate Training College in Limerick. She took up a teaching post on the Great Blasket Island. Her first book, *Thar Bealach Isteach* (1940), is an account of her seven years there. She translated plays by Lady Gregory, Synge, M J Molloy, B G McCarthy and John Murphy, for local production in Irish. Her own play, *Dún an Oir*, was broadcast on Radio Éireann in 1960. She has written one romantic novel *Peats na Baintrighe* (1945).[1]

Works:
Thar Bealach Isteach. Dublin: Oifig an tSoláthair, 1940. Memoir.
Peats na Baintrighe. Dublin: Oifig an tSoláthair, 1945. Novel.

Notes:
1. *Beathaisnéis a Dó 1882-1982*, D Breathnach agus M Ní Mhurchú, Clóchomhar, 1986.

Ní Shúilleabháin, Siobhán
Born: Ireland, 1928
Educated: Ireland.

Siobhán Ní Shúilleabháin was born in Ballyferriter in the Kerry Gaeltacht and educated at the local primary school, at Coláiste Ide Preparatory School, and trained as a primary teacher in Carysfort Training College in Dublin. She taught in a school in Cabra, Dublin, for four years and worked as a language advisor on de Bhaldraithe's English-Irish dictionary 1952-1955. She attended painting and sculpture classes in the National College of Art, studied the History of Art under Francoise Henry in UCD, and took a diploma in the History of the Fine Arts in TCD. She married in 1955 and lived in Dublin, Belfast and Connemara. She has lived in Galway since 1965.

Her writing has won her numerous awards: an Irish Life Award for *Cití* in 1974, twice winner of first prize at the Listowel Writers' Week, and her work has taken first prize in the Oireachtas literary competitions for drama, novels, short stories and teenage fiction. Her plays have been staged in the Taibhdhearc theatre, in University College Galway, and by local theatre groups. Radio Éireann produced the following plays: *Cití, Go scara an bás sinn, Céad Grá Mná, An dubh ina geal, Meaisín liom leat, Marmaléid ar an dtoast, Diail agus deamhain, Oighre mic, Mise agus Spock*. Three of her television plays have been produced by Telefís Éireann: *Teacht is imeacht, Saolaíodh Gamhain*, and *An Carabhan*. Another three have been accepted for future production: *Oiche Shamhna, Oileán* and *Siúracha*. She has had short stories published in many Irish periodicals and translations of a selection of these are being prepared for publication.[1]

Works:
Ospidéal. Baile Atha Cliath: Foilseacháin Naisiúnta Teoranta, 1980. Novel.
Cití. Baile Atha Cliath: Sairséal agus Dill, 1975. Play.
Triúr Againn. Baile Atha Cliath: Sairséal agus Dill, 1955. Teenage Fiction.

Cursaí Randolf. Baile Atha Cliath: Sairséal agus Dill 1957. Teenage Fiction.

Dúinne an Samhradh. Baile Atha Cliath: An Preas Talbóideach, 1957. Teenage Fiction.

Mé Féin agus Síle. Baile Atha Cliath: An Gúm, 1978. Teenage Fiction.

Mise mé féin. Cló Iarchonnachta, 1987. Teenage Fiction.

Eoghan. Cló Iarchonnachta, 1992. Teenage Fiction.

Notes:
Beathaisneás a Dó 1882-1982. D Breathnach agus M Ní Mhurchu. Clochomhair, 1986.

Nic Ghearailt, Máire Aine
Born: Ireland, c 20th century
Educated: Ireland.

Máire Aine Nic Ghearailt was born in Corca Dhuibhne, the Kerry Gaeltacht (Irish-speaking area) and trained as a primary schoolteacher in Mary Immaculate Training College in Limerick. She has written five collections of poetry, including one for children, *An tUlchabhán agus Dánta eile* (1990).

Her subjects range from traditional to contemporary, from laments for the exile to dreams of space. The second stanza of 'Deireadh Oíche' compares the persona's children, or Irish exiles, to the children of Lir:

Mar Chlann Lir, a scaradh ó chéile
Ar uiscí fiaine Mhaoile,
Is ansin ar Iorras uaigneach;
I bhfoscadh a chéile
Nuair a buaileadh Clog na Saoirse.[1]

In 'Brionglóid', the persona dreams of being an astronaut, abandoned in space when her rocket explodes.

Pléascadh mo roicéad i bhfad ó shin
Ní raibh sa dúthaigh seo ach mé
Gan aon teacht as agam.

Shiúil mé liom fad chosáin righne an uaignis
Ní chloífinn raon na siúlóide seo go deo.[2]

Works:
Eiric Uachta. Baile Atha Cliath: Clóchomhar Teoranta, 1971.
Poetry.
Leaca Liombó. Baile Atha Cliath: Coiscéim, 1990. Poetry.
An tUlchabhán agus Dánta Eile. Baile Atha Cliath: Coiscéim, 1990.
Poetry.
Mo Chúis a Bheith Beo. Baile Atha Cliath: Coiscéim, 1991. Poetry.
O Ceileadh an Bhreasail, Baile Atha Cliath: Coiscéim, 1992. Poetry.

Notes
1. In *Leaca Liombó,* 23.
2. In *Leaca Liombó,* 37.

Norton, Caroline Elizabeth Sarah

Born: England, 1808; Died: 1877
Educated: England
Caroline Norton was born and raised in England. She
separated from her husband in 1840, and her writings
reflect her deep unhappiness in marriage. She remarried
after the death of her first husband, but died herself three
months later. Her sister is Helina Selina Blackwood (Lady
Dufferin).[1]

Selected Works:
The Dream and other Poems. London: Henry Colburn, 1841.
Poetry.

Notes:
1. see A A Kelly *Pillars of the House,* (Dublin; Wolfhound, 1987),
   40.

— O —

O'Brien, Charlotte Grace
Born: Ireland, 1845; Died: 1901
Educated: Ireland, USA.

Charlotte Grace O'Brien was born in Cahirmoyle. One volume of poetry was published during her life, and her nephew, Stephen Gwynn, published a selection of her writings with a memoir after her death. [1]

Works
Lyrics. London: Kegan Paul, Trench, 1886. Poetry.

Notes
1. See *Pillars of the House*, A A Kelly, ed. Dublin: Wolfhound Press, 1988, 56-57.

O'Brien, Edna
Born: Ireland, 1930
Educated: Ireland.

Edna O'Brien was born in Tuamgraney, Co. Clare, educated at the National School in Scarriff, the Convent of Mercy at Loughrea, and the Pharmaceutical College in Dublin. She was married from 1951-64, and she has two sons. In 1959 she moved to London, but returns to Ireland for frequent visits.

O'Brien has written novels, short stories, plays, and non-fiction. Her novels often feature the Clare she loves and young women in situations similar to those she herself experienced. 'A lot of my life', she writes of her time in convent school, 'was as portrayed in *The Country Girls* — certainly the actual bleakness of the convent and the regimented life found their way into that book. But the narrative is not true'[1]. 'In my mind,' she notes,'I still live in the locality of my early childhood and when I write I do so with the greatest ease when I set stories there. I am not "cataloguing" the people of the village — my writing is an imaginative re-inventing of those people.'(142)

Books were very scarce in her childhood: she recalls a copy of *Rebecca* being passed around the village, page by page. But she always wanted to be a writer: 'for as long as I can remember I knew that I would write. I didn't know what it meant to be a writer but I knew that my reality, my life and my fate would be lived out through words.'(142)

Love — the experience of sexual love, the bitterness of its loss, and the love of parents and children — is central to O'Brien's work. *The Country Girls* (1960), written very shortly after she moved to London, and its sequels, *The Lonely Girl* (1962) and *Girls in Their Married Bliss* (1964), created a stir when first published, because the frank approach to a woman's wakening desire was rare in Irish fiction and they featured some eroticism between girls. Later work is formally more experimental: one woman's stream-of-consciousness structures *Night* (1972), for example, as Mary Hooligan drifts from scenes of childhood, mother and father, to lovers, and the son she loves. The young girls in the early novels are vulnerable, easily bruised by love. The women in the later work are still hurt by love, but not defeated.

In 'Long Distance,' in a recent collection of short stories, *Lantern Slides* (1990), a woman meets again the man she loved, the man who left her. All her old feelings surface, her love, insecurity, vulnerability.

"Did you ever dream of me?" she asked lightly, in a bantering way. "All the time," he said in the softest of voices. Now what did that mean? What was he saying?

Were they good dreams, bad dreams, crowded
dreams?'² As they talk she thinks it doesn't matter
what they say, only what they are thinking. 'They were
merely skimming the surface of the years, hiding all
the urgent parts of themselves, she hiding the
vengeances that indeed she had conceived because she
had been jilted, and he believing that she had betrayed
him with that bilious letter.' (161)

When she finally 'teases' him about love, he invites her to
come with him to Thailand.

Every bit of her wanted to say yes. Her eyes said it and
the eyes at the tip of her fingertips said it and the flesh
at the back of her throat ached at the thought of these
new sensations. ... His touch on her knee was like a
little electric shock, but pleasant. If only they could go
there and then. If only he stood up and carried her. Yet
her answer was firm. She knew what she must say. The
little beads of ecstasy in her throat were turning to
tears, salt tears. It came back in a blinding guttural
flash, the pain when he had left, the savagery of it, his
deafness to her pleas, his refusal even at Christmas to
answer a telephone call, his forgetting her address.
(162-3).

Works:
The Country Girls. London: Hutchinson, 1960. Novel.
The Lonely Girl. London: Jonathan Cape/New York: Random
  House, 1962. Reprinted as *Girl with the Green Eyes*, London:
  Penguin, 1964. Novel.
Girls in Their Married Bliss. London: Jonathan Cape, 1964/New
  York: Simon & Schuster, 1968. Novel.
August is a Wicked Month. London: Jonathan Cape/New York:
  Simon & Schuster, 1965. Novel.
Casualties of Peace. London: Jonathan Cape, 1966/New York:
  Simon & Schuster, 1967. Novel.
The Love Object. London: Jonathan Cape, 1968/New York: Alfred
  A Knopf, 1969. Short Stories.
A Pagan Place. New York: Alfred A Knopf, 1970. Novel.
Zee & Co.. London: Weidenfeld & Nicholson, 1971. Novel.

Night. London: Weidenfeld & Nicholson, 1972/New York: Alfred A Knopf, 1973. Novel.

A Pagan Place. London: Faber, 1973. Play.

A Scandalous Woman. London: Weidenfeld & Nicholson/New York: Harcourt, Brace, Jovanovich, 1974. Novel.

Mother Ireland. London: Weidenfeld & Nicholson, 1976. Nonfiction.

Johnny I Hardly Knew You. London: Weidenfeld & Nicholson, 1977. Novel.

The Collected Edna O'Brien. London: Collins, 1978. Stories.

Virginia. New York and London: Harcourt Brace Jovanovich, 1984. Play.

Lantern Slides. London: Weidenfeld & Nicholson, 1990. Short Stories.

Notes

1. In *A Portrait of the Artist as a Young Girl*, John Quinn, ed. (London: Methuen, 1986), 141. Following references noted in parenthesis in text.
2. *Lantern Slides*, 159.

O'Brien, Kate

Born: Ireland, 1897; Died: 1974
Educated: Ireland.

Kate O'Brien was born in Limerick in 1907. Her mother died when she was five years old, and she was sent to join her older sisters at the French convent of Laurel Hill in Limerick. Later she received a scholarship to University College, Dublin, where she took her BA degree. After college she tried her hand briefly at several things: the foreign page of the *Manchester Guardian*, teaching, and governessing in Spain. Although she fell in love with Spain, she returned to London and was married for a short time before finally finding herself as writer, dramatist initially, then novelist. She lived most of her life in either Ireland or England – with lengthy trips to the USA – and was denied entry to her beloved Spain after the publication of her travel book, *Farewell, Spain*, in 1937. Not until 1957 was she allowed to return. She died in Kent in 1974. *Presentation Parlour* (1963) gives a whimsical account of the O'Brien origins, the sheltering and sheltered aunts, and the Presentation nuns who watched over the young family.[1]

O'Brien's first successes were in drama, but she soon moved to novels, and would also turn to journalism, criticism, travel books, and a life of Teresa of Avila. Her first novel, *Without My Cloak* (1931), in which gay relationships between men feature, won the Hawthornden Prize and the James Tait Black Memorial Prize. Later novels also won critical acclaim and popular audiences, despite the banning of *The Land of Spices* (1941) by the Censorship of Publications Board; the acclaim was the reward of the well-crafted work, and the popularity may have been a response in part to the new content, the realistic focus on the woman's situation in the Irish Catholic middle-class. O'Brien's protagonists are torn between familial and religious duty and individual desire, and while the conflict is usually resolved in favour of duty, O'Brien makes no bones about the price this duty extorts from women. *The Flower of May* (1953), *Mary Lavelle* (1936), and *As Music and Splendour* (1958) all feature romantic female friendship and the latter two have lesbian heroines.

The Land of Spices (1941), presents the development of a young woman from child to adult, and seems to invite comparisons with Joyce's *Portrait of the Artist as a Young Man*, as O'Brien's heroine, Anna Murphy, undergoes trials similar to those of Stephen Dedalus. O'Brien suggests, however, that women are faced with more obstacles in their quest for intellectual freedom than are men. Indeed, the battle against family and tradition is so tough that in order to succeed, Anna needs all the courage and discipline she can muster, as well as a powerful friend. The Mother Superior of the French convent of Sainte Famille becomes Anna's ally, a nurturing replacement of the negligent and incompetent biological mother. Anna's story intertwines with Mother Superior's, and we see the nun finally forgive herself her own youthful intolerance as she encourages, advises, and fights for Anna. While Stephen in *Potrait of the Artist as a Young Man* moves toward isolation and exile, Anna comes to an intuitive understanding and appreciation of the wisdom and detached maternal guidance of her unsentimental mentor.

O'Brien also analyses the parochialism of Irish nationalism in *The Land of Spices*. The English suffragette whom Anna befriends is suspect in the nationalist and religious climate of early twentieth-century Ireland. The young priests are very narrow-minded, and even the more enlightened bishop finds the French Catholic convent 'too European for present-day Irish requirements. Its detachment of spirit seems to me to stand in the way of nationalism.'[2] But Mother Superior resists attempts to distort education into nationalist service. 'Indifferent alike,' the narrator notes, 'to the needs of Gaelic Leaguer or British officer, she still thought it necessary to train girls, for their own sakes and for the glory of God, to be Christians and to be civilised.'(187)

That Lady (1946), perhaps her most popular work, presents the romance of Ana de Mendoza and Antonio Perez, and the place in their lives of Philip II of Spain. As so often in O'Brien novels, Ana is a Catholic of conscience, in love with a man forbidden by her religion. Again as so often, O'Brien probes the deep psychological recesses of Ana and of Philip, as well as the excruciating conflict between desire and constraints imposed by religion.

Kate O'Brien had a distinguished career as novelist, dramatist, scholar, and travel writer. She was a fellow of the Royal Society of Literature and a member of the Irish Academy of Letters.

Works:
Distinguished Villa: A Play in Three Acts. London: Benn, 1926. Play.
Without My Cloak. 1931; rpt. London: Virago, 1986. Novel.
The Anteroom. 1934; rpt. London: Virago, 1989. Novel.
Mary Lavelle. 1936; rpt. London: Virago, 1991. Novel.
Farewell, Spain. 1937; rpt. London: Virago, 1985. Travel Book.

Pray for the Wanderer. London: Heinemann, 1938; Garden City: Doubleday, Doran, 1938. Novel.

The Land of Spices. 1941; rpt. London: Virago, 1988. Novel.

English Diaries and Journals. London: Collins, 1934. Memoir.

The Last of Summer. 1943; rpt. London: Virago, 1990. Novel.

That Lady. 1946; rpt. London: Virago, 1985; In USA, *For One Sweet Grape*. Garden City: Doubleday, Doran, 1946. Novel.

That Lady: a Romantic Drama. New York: Harper, 1949. Play.

Teresa of Avila. London: Parrish, 1951; New York: Sheed & Ward, 1951. Religious Life.

The Flower of May. London: Heinemann, 1953; New York: Harper, 1953. Novel.

As Music and Splendour. London: Heinemann, 1958; New York: Harper, 1958. Novel.

My Ireland. London: Batsford, 1962; New York: Hastings House, 1962. Travel Book.

Presentation Parlour. London: Heinemann, 1963. Memoir.

Notes

1. *Presentation Parlour*.
2. *The Land of Spices*, 233, Doubleday Edition.

O'Brien, Kate Cruise

Born: Ireland, 1948
Educated: Ireland, USA

Kate Cruise O'Brien was born in Dublin to Conor Cruise O'Brien and Christine Foster, who came from northern 'Protestant stock', had a 'great sense of fun', and left Belfast for Trinity College, Dublin, before World War II. Her father, the writer and diplomat, is son of Kathleen Sheehy, who along with her sisters, Hannah Sheehy Skeffington and Mary Kettle, played a prominent part in the Ireland of 1916. Kate Cruise O'Brien was baptised a Catholic, though her parents were not believers, and 'educated at eccentric Protestant schools': Rathgar Junior School, where she learnt little, because she 'regarded all formal learning as an interruption to a vivid fantasy life inspired by Enid Blyton's *Famous Five* and *Secret Seven*'; and Park House

School in Morehampton Road, which was 'less tolerant and more Protestant'.[1]

After Park House, she spent a year in the USA, eligible to attend New York University because her father was on the faculty, but barred from doing so because she refused to have her weight checked and photograph taken. In 1972 she graduated in English from Trinity College, Dublin. Male efforts to exclude women from clubs in Trinity and male 'hysteria' at her resistance to such exclusion turned her into a feminist. Her first story, 'Henry Died', was published in 1971 in the 'New Irish Writing' page of the *Irish Press* and won the Hennessy award. After marriage and the birth of her son, Alexander, she returned to writing, and *A Gift Horse*, a collection of short stories, was published in 1978. Several of the stories from this collection have been anthologised and published in magazines in England, Denmark, Sweden, and Africa. Besides writing a weekly column for the *Irish Independent* and reviews for several papers and magazines, and doing TV interviews and radio broadcasts, she also enjoys her involvement in the Arts Council's Writers in Schools programme.

'The qualities which are disadvantages in the job market become positive strengths in a writer,' she notes, and 'neuroses which are deeply embarrassing to meet on the street aren't embarrassing at all when you meet them on the page. I mean, would you invite Heathcliff to dinner?'[2] Many of O'Brien's stories and her novel, *The Homesick Garden* (1991), are told from the perspective of an intelligent, observant and sensitive child or teenager. The family background is often eccentric. In 'Sackcloth', for example, the young Sarah feels alienated in schools where headmistresses talk of empire and religion, because her mother's lack of belief and her unconventionality are a difficult burden. In a moment of insight, however, Sarah realises that her mother is more generous than the conformers.

Humour makes the real pain and insights of the young more bearable. The child in 'A Sunday Walk' nostalgically remembers the time she couldn't move her legs: 'Her mother had come, shaken and anxious, and bent over the stretcher lovingly. Like a mother in a book.'[3] This child also remembers the man who often exposed himself to her, and the difficulty she had in deciding how to behave: 'It seemed rude to run away. It might make the man embarrassed about not being properly dressed.' (11)

Antonia in *The Homesick Garden* is older and more analytical. She constantly ponders the interactions of her mother and father, her mother and grandmother, and everyone's reaction to her Aunt Grace, her mother's unconventional — single and pregnant — sister. The novel explores the paralysis of manipulative relationships: Antonia understands that her mother partakes, almost conspires, in her own victimisation by her mother. And as Antonia begins an emotional relationship with a boy, she sees that she is her 'mother's daughter': 'I kept on listening for the insult behind the words.'[4] The grandmother correctly realises the destructiveness of her daughter's always wanting 'to please', but viciously plays on this very trait.(25) Finally, however, mother and daughter achieve some small sense of autonomy, in large measure through perceiving and responding to the partial self-image they see in the other.

Works:
A Gift Horse. Dublin: Poolbeg, 1978. Short Stories.
The Homesick Garden. Dublin: Poolbeg, 1991. Novel.

Notes
1. Personal communication.
2. Personal communication.
3. In *A Gift Horse*, 10.
4. *The Homesick Garden*, 117.

O'Brien, Mary

Born: Ireland, c 18th century
Educated: Ireland.
Mary O'Brien published one play, a comedy, and a volume
of poetry. Her wit can be seen in these lines from *Paddy's
Salutation to the Right Honorable William Pitt.*

> Now Billy, my dear,
>   Accept Teague's salutation,
> For the care of the Prince,
>   And the good of the nation;
>
> Now forgetting your wits,
>   When in council they sit,
> To make a Prince Regent,
>   While you reign King Pitt.[1]

A few stanzas on, she praises:

> Sure the fame of our Billy
>   No tongue can unravel —
> He exceeds all the heroes
>   At home or on travel;
>
> Old Grandams unborn
>   Shall in aftertimes sing,
> The glories and wisdom
>   Of Billy Pitt, King. (10-11)

Works:
The Political Monitor, or *Regent's Friend.* Dublin: W Gilbert, 1790.
    Poetry.
The Fallen Patriot. Dublin: W Gilbert, 1794. Play.

Notes:
1. In *The Political Monitor,* 9.

O'Callaghan, Julie
Born: USA, 1954
Educated: USA; Ireland.

Julie O'Callaghan works in Trinity College, Dublin. She published a volume of poetry in 1983, *Edible Anecdotes*. In 'Bookworm', the persona cannot understand his/her partner, who sweeps the carpet, polishes the furniture, does everything in fact with a book in her hand. The poem concludes:

> As I point the car towards work
> you sit beside me with American Poetry Review.
> Everyone is tired, waiting in a traffic jam;
> I brake and honk and swear,
> but you are reading 'Words are everywhere.'[1]

The quick movement, connections, and flights of a child's mind seem to structure 'A Small Australian Girl in a Large Irish Farmhouse', written for Susannah. 'Would you like to see my favorite room?' the poem asks and immediately describes. 'It's rather scary, but it has a little window/where you can see the horses./I keep my dragons in it.' From the dragons, she moves to a giant, to the little sister who wails for yogurt, to the bicycle she can't bring back to Australia, and finally to the comforting fantasy of the cake:

> I'll show you my pretend cake—
> it's my lunch container and inside
> the ingredients are empty orange juice cartons
> and a piece of chalk; I've put a red
> plasticine cherry on top.
> Would you care for a bite?[2]

Works:

Edible Anecdotes. Portlaoise: Dolmen, 1983. Poetry.
Taking My Pen for a Walk. London: and New York: Orchard Books: 1988. Poetry for Children.
What's What. Newcastle-upon-Tyne: Bloodaxe Books, 1991. Poetry.

Notes
1. In *Edible Anecdotes*, 52.
2. In *Edible Anecdotes*, 53.

O'Connor, Clairr

Born: Ireland, 1951
Educated: Ireland.

Clairr O'Connor was born in Limerick and received her early education at St Mary's Convent there. She graduated from University College, Cork, in 1972, with a degree in Medieval History and English. She taught in London from 1972-77, and in Ireland since 1978. She took the Higher Diploma in Education in 1978, a Master's in Education in 1982, and a Diploma in Japanese Studies in 1986, all in St Patrick's College, Maynooth, where she lives with her husband and son.

She has written plays, poetry, short stories, and one novel – so far. *Getting Ahead* was a Monday Play in October, 1987, on BBC Radio 4; *House of Correction* was staged in Cork, in May 1989, as part of the Cork Arts Theatre Club Festival, and her radio play, *Costing the Coffins*, was produced by RTE in 1990. She received a Ragdale Foundation scholarship in 1987, was the Irish Exchange Writer at New Dramatists, New York, 1988, and was also funded by Poets and Writers Inc. to give readings in New York. Her poetry has appeared in newspapers, journals, and anthologies.[1]

O'Connor's stories are filled with a particularly pungent humour, which springs from situations – though extreme examples of these situations – familiar to many. 'For The Time Being' tells of a childhood dominated by memories of the past and anxieties for the future. 'My parents gave the impression that the present was a gauzy, insubstantial thing. People who lived there, they implied, were somehow lightweight.' Her father worked in a morgue, the narrator tells us, and the family's Sunday outings were spent in graveyards: 'Photographs were taken of the happy family perched on tombs.' Dead bodies were a commonplace – the little girl often played under a 'sheeted table', making a 'cold man' colder by her use of his sheet to cover her doll. 'Years later, in drama school, I appalled my class mates when, asked to improvise a happy scene from childhood, I enacted the burial service.'

Her first novel, *Belonging* (1991), nominated for *The Irish Times*/Aer Lingus award in 1991, probes the mystery of identity. When Deirdre Pender returns to Ireland from New York for her parents' funeral, she reads a journal which suggests that she may be the daughter of a Hungarian refugee. Distraught, she journeys to Hungary in search of proof of her parentage. She finds her identity, however, not in archives, but in the often traumatic relations with friends and family.

Works:
When You Need Them. Galway: Salmon, 1989. Poetry.
Belonging. Dublin: Attic Press, 1991. Novel.

Notes
1. Personal communication.
2. In *Wildish Things*, Ailbhe Smyth. ed. (Dublin: Attic Press), 1989, 65-72.

O'Connor, Kathleen
Born: Ireland, 1934
Educated: Ireland.

Kathleen O'Connor was born in Blackpool, a village on the north side of Cork city. She attended St Vincent's Convent, loved the nuns – the Irish Sisters of Charity – and joined the order herself when she was seventeen.

Professed in 1957, she taught school in Dublin, but left the order in 1958. In 1963, when she was ready to re-enter the convent, she met the man who became her husband.

The couple had three boys in three years, and after nine miscarriages, she had a fourth baby boy.

Her husband was an engineer, and the couple ran a very successful business which employed over 100 people. Unfortunately her husband suffered a coronary in 1982 and the factory went into liquidation in 1985. During the trauma of 1985, she began writing, 'as a release from tension and a therapy'. She regards herself as a storyteller rather than a writer, and her experiences are the bases of her novels. She planned nothing in her life, except becoming a nun. She sees God as shaping her perspectives, does her best, and leaves everything else to Him.[1]

The first O'Connor novels, *A Question of Heaven* (1990), tells the story of the marriage of Hugh O'Grady and Peggy O'Flaherty, brought together through passion, despite class differences. Class snobbery is rife in the small village of Glenbeg; Peggy allows it to control her life, even to tear her family apart. The story and tragedy of the mother reverberates in the daughters' lives as Deirdre becomes pregnant and Alanna must leave her beloved convent to care for her. *Stepping Stones* (1990) continues the story, focussing on Alanna, and on adventures and situations more extreme than anything Peggy and Hugh faced. *Mags* (1991) is the third novel in the sequence.

Works:
A Question of Heaven. Cork: Emperor Publishing, 1990. Novel.
Stepping Stones. Cork: Emperor Publishing, 1990. Novel.
Mags. Cork: Emperor Publishing, 1991. Novel.

Notes
1. Personal communication.

O'Donnell, Mary
Born: Ireland, 1954
Educated: Ireland.

Mary O'Donnell always wanted to be a writer, a desire her family nurtured. Indeed, she notes that key-people in her life have always been encouraging, especially her husband. Born in Monaghan, she attended the St Louis Convent there, then took a degree in German and Philosophy, and the Higher Diploma in Education, at St Patrick's College, Maynooth. She has worked as teacher, translator, library assistant, drama critic for the *Sunday Tribune*, and has published a volume of poetry, a volume of short stories and one novel, to date.

Mary O'Donnell credits feminism with shaping her perspective. Brotherless herself, she was shocked as an adult to discover that many young men 'subscribed to the pregnant, barefoot and in-the-kitchen theory of Coupledom!' and that some women also saw marriage as a 'meal-ticket'. Angered by the 'insidious sexism which denies the humanity of both women and men, forcing each gender towards premature emotional death,' she condemns the callous dismissal of married women's activities as 'time-fillers' which must not interfere with her real motherly and wifely duty. The subjects of her poems and short stories are often drawn from her 'responses to the different facets of what being a woman means', and entail a rejection of traditional, limited and stereotypical images. Although she thinks women have been excluded from literary history, and that their work is subjected to more severe scrutiny than men's, she wishes to avoid the exclusionary tendencies of the past and to have men and women participate and work together.

For technical innovation, she looks not to her own culture, but to the Poles, Zbigniew Herbert and Tadeusz Rozewicz, and to American poets.[1] Her poetry has received many prizes; most recently *Reading the Sunflowers in September* was nominated for an *Irish Times*/Aer Lingus

282

award. Her fiction was awarded the William Allingham Award for short stories in 1989.

The poems in *Reading the Sunflowers in September* (1990) cover a wide range of subjects: female and male sexuality, the emotional vulnerability of young girls, of women and men, infertility, betrayal, relationships between mothers and daughters, between friends, scars of history from Babi Yar to Derry – and more. Sometimes richly clotted with images, sometimes simple and bare, the poems are patterned both formally and informally. The poet thinks 'Excision' – a poem full of images of the maiming of women in 'civilisations' as diverse as Ireland, Sudan, Iran, India, and Japan – her most important political poem. The language moves from beautiful: 'She grapples in child innocence, mad/with hysteric hurt as the women hold/her down and bind with florid pain:/The cropping of pink lips, curling/coral from screaming girls,' to brutal: 'It rots/the brightest soul until she/is too cuntless to dare,' revealing the poet's sympathy and anger.[2]

The world of *Strong Pagans and Other Stories* (1991) is that of contemporary Ireland, a country where intellectual acceptance of the mores of western society does little to calm the demands of the emotions. Again the range is wide and we are invited to enter the world of transvestites, adulterers, pederasts, married priests, 'happily-married' women, and more. But O'Donnell does not simply illustrate the variety that is Ireland; she moves certainly to reveal the contradictory impulses that enrich and torment.

Set in contemporary Dublin and Egypt, the first-person, present tense novel, *The Lightmakers* (1992), veers between the present and the past. Hanna Troy, a successful press photographer, faces a series of crises, among them the destructiveness of her relationship with her husband Sam, an idealistic architect. She wanders around Dublin one afternoon, recalling an idyllic childhood in rural Ireland, but wracked with guilt and rage about the failures of her adult life, and in particular the betrayals. How she comes to terms with herself and how she reconciles the past with the present, forms the crux of this novel.[3]

Works:

Reading the Sunflowers in September. Galway: Salmon, 1990. Poetry.

Strong Pagans and Other Stories. Dublin: Poolbeg, 1991. Stories.

The Lightmakers. Dublin: Poolbeg, 1992. Novel.

Notes

1. Personal communication.
2. In *Reading the Sunflowers in September*, 15, 16.
3. Personal communication.

O'Driscoll, Kathleen

Born: Ireland, 1941
Educated: Ireland.

Kathleen O'Driscoll lives in Galway, and received her BA degree and her diploma in Higher Education from University College, Galway. She has worked as a teacher and reads in schools under the Arts Council Writers in Schools Scheme. She has published a volume of short stories and a volume of poems, both with Caledon Press.

Ether, the volume of short stories, usually examines the dark side of life, but doesn't exclude the whimsical. 'The Powers' tells the story of a young child's adventure with learning: her unconventional and practical approach to fairies, religion, history, and romance collides with the traditional wisdom of her elders. Reporting on her First Communion, she tells the nun, 'It tasted like soap and I thought it was going to taste lovely.' Her honesty is greeted with a typical reprimand, 'Child, that's a sacrilege.' The next girl has already learnt to conform: 'I felt like a saint,' she says, her smug hypocrisy winning the nun's approval.[1]

The destructiveness of this early training in hypocrisy is seen in later stories and in *Goodbye Joe*, the volume of poems. The persona in 'The Defeated' is a free-spirited woman, much like the adult we might expect the persona of the earlier story to become. This woman has fun with her own children and offers rooms to the 'lads' – the boys involved in IRA activities. When she discovers that they have killed a Protestant Loyalist, however, she is furious, seeing them as murderers. The deceitfulness and indulgence of church and IRA ritual at a funeral for one of the lads killed during a raid in the North upsets the woman so much that the 'authorities' place her in a mental institution. Her clarity of vision is destructive to her murderous society. Catholic metaphor pervades the poetry, as the mother in 'Credo' worries about the fearful god she can be to her child. The title poem is addressed to the friend who has taken weedkiller and died. Life in O'Driscoll's work is intense and painful; escape into over-medication or suicide is understandable.

Works:
Goodbye Joe. Dublin: Caledon, 1980. Poetry.
Ether. Dublin: Caledon Press, 1981. Short Stories.

Notes
1. In *Ether*, 11.

O'Faolain, Eileen (née Gould)

Born: Ireland, 1901; Died: 1988
Educated: Ireland

Eileen Gould was born in Cork and even as a child she recalls her fascination for folktales and folklore.[1] In 1928 she married author and biographer Sean O'Faolain and they had two children.

She has had numerous children's books published as Eileen O'Faolain. Her daughter is the writer Julia O'Faolain.

Selected Works/Children's books:
Miss Pennyfeather and the Pooka. Dublin: Browne & Nolan, 1944.
The Children of Crooked Castle. Dublin: Browne & Nolan, 1945.
Children of the Salmon and other Irish Folktales. Dublin: Longman, 1945.
Irish Sagas and Folk Tales. London: OUP, 1954.
High Hang the Sword. London: OUP, 1959.

Notes:
1. See preface of *Children of the Salmon*. Dublin: Longman, 1945.

O'Faolain, Julia
Born: England, 1932
Educated: Ireland.

Julia O'Faolain was born into a family of writers and romantics; her mother, Eileen Gould O'Faolain, wrote children's stories; her father, Seán O'Faolain, edited *The Bell*, a journal for new Irish writing, and was himself a distinguished Irish writer. Seán and Eileen signalled their commitment to the ideals of the 1916 Rising by learning the Irish language and changing their name from Whelan to the Irish O'Faolain. Disillusioned when their leader Eamon de Valera compromised on a twenty-six-county free state, the O'Faolain parents still set out to expose their children to what their daughter calls 'the romantic Ireland of his [Seán's] youth. Which did and didn't exist.' She recalls great evenings of open house for poets and writers in the family home in Killiney, a beautiful — almost rural in those days — hilly village overlooking Dublin Bay.[1]

O'Faolain took her degree at University College, Dublin, spent time in Rome and Paris, and back in Ireland talked to her father about a career. He advised writing of her experiences abroad, and the result was *Godded and Codded* (1970), a novel about Irish women in Paris. Four more novels have followed, several collections of short stories, and a documentary history of women. Already O'Faolain's cold eye is at work in the first novel, exposing the confined condition of those bound by the stifling social strictures of middle-class Irish society in the 1960s. O'Faolain's language is vigorously alive and colourful; all her characters, but particularly the sexually repressed irrationals, are bruisingly memorable. Their language is evocative of their characters: Patsy, the grotesque carry-over from 1916 in *No Country for Young Men* (1980), for example, christens the American film-maker who makes love to the Irish heroine, the 'Californicator'.

Set in Ireland, England, Italy, and the USA, O'Faolain's short stories reflect her cosmopolitan life style: married to an Italian-American, the writer spends part of the year in London and part in Los Angeles. The pompous, the smug, and the venal are the targets of satire in the short stories. O'Faolain's gift is to juxtapose the boundaries of class, national, and gender conventions with the desires of an average human being. As in the best of satire, she distances her readers from the characters and thus renders the clash of expectations, the situation rather than the human disappointment, uproariously funny.

While something of the savage irony and brilliance of Swift runs through the short stories, something that castigates because it cares deeply, a deeper understanding and sympathy for human complexities pervades the novels. *Women in the Wall* appeared in 1975, a fiction about historical characters, nuns, poets, kings, set in sixth-century Gaul. Here, O'Faolain reveals familiar human motivations propelling the most barbarous and/or ascetic of actions, and allows us to see the complex human beings behind the almost incomprehensible historical figures of that chaotic period.

O'Faolain next turned her critical intelligence and cold eye on 'the Troubles'. Through the eyes of a seventy-five-year-old nun, we see the civil war in which she was a young girl; we also see her confuse the violent characters around her with those in that early war. Nominated for the prestigous Booker McConnell Prize, *No Country for Young Men* tells a typical twentieth-century story of revolutionary turned politician turned reactionary. Foregrounded on this intricate historical tapestry is the modern love-story, the dance that will be danced though the world fall. O'Faolain's compassion is revealed here: the elderly nun is never the object of ridicule, the drunk is never just a drunk, and the beautiful woman is rarely a heroine.

The intertwining of personalities in a long-term marriage is explored in *The Obedient Wife* (1982), and once again, O'Faolain eschews any ideological or conventional solution. Although the Italian heroine Carla finds love, respect for her opinions, and consideration in her American lover, she returns to Italy and her macho husband. Carla's motives are complex and not always clear even to herself: her husband's insistence on his need for her seems to confirm her belief in their relationship, while her lover's acceptance of her refusal seems to suggest his lack of conviction as to that relationship. And finally, O'Faolain suggests that a husband – like a wife – is only one part of the tapestry of a life. Carla's life in Italy, her job there as lawyer, her role as mother, as wife, as daughter-in-law, as member of a cosmopolitan, sophisticated society, is ultimately more important to her than is a particular lover.

Works:
We Might See Sights. London: Faber & Faber, 1968. Short Stories.
Godded and Codded. 1970. In U.S. *Three Lovers*. New York: Coward, McCann & Geoghegan, 1971. Novel.
Man in the Cellar. London: Faber & Faber, 1974. Short Stories.
Women in the Wall. 1975; rpt. London: Virago, 1985; New York: Carroll and Graf, 1988. Novel.
Melancholy Baby and Other Stories. Dublin: Poolbeg, 1978. Short Stories.
No Country for Young Men. Middlesex: Penguin, 1980; New York: Carroll and Graf, 1986. Novel.
Daughters of Passion. Middlesex: Penguin, 1982. Short Stories.
The Obedient Wife. 1982; rpt. Middlesex: Penguin, 1983; New York: Carroll and Graf, 1985. Novel.
The Irish Signorina. Middlesex: Viking, 1984. Novel.
Not in God's Image: Women in History from the Greeks to the Victorians. Edited with Lauro Martines 1973; rpt. London: Virago, 1979. History.

Notes
1. Brenda Maddox, Interview with Seán and Julia O'Faolain in *Sunday Times Magazine* (1 April, 1984), 8-9.

O'Farrell, Kathleen
Born: Ireland, c̲ 20th century
Educated: Ireland.
Kathleen O'Farrell has written one historical novel set in Ireland c̲1780.

Works:
Kilbroney. Kerry: Brandon, 1992. Novel.

O'Hagan, Sheila
Born: Ireland, c̲ 20th century
Educated: Ireland, England.
Sheila O'Hagan left Ireland for London when she was nineteen. She settled, married, and raised three children before taking degrees in art, English literature, and theatre. She began writing poetry at Birkbeck College in 1984, and since then has three times won prizes at Listowel Writers' Week, as well as the Goldsmith Award in 1988, and the Patrick Kavanagh Award in 1991. She lives in Dalkey, Co. Dublin, and Clapham, London, and is a member of the Dublin Writers' Workshop.[1]

Her poetry has appeared in journals and newspapers from Canada to Australia; the first volume, *The Peacock's Eye*, was published in 1992. The volume is divided into three parts: the first examines childhood and family ties, the second presents a more independent, mature and confident persona, and the third moves into a world of myth and art. Poems in Part One deal with loss and dependence, often the lost opportunities of communication. 'The Watermark' describes the agony of the unspoken, 'my mouth full of words/that will not come', in saying goodbye to one's mother:

Now I grow thin,
my robe bundles
as I turn to the light
to touch you again,
all the lost words
filling my mouth.[2]

Again, 'You Call to See Me' notes the invisible gap which separates mother and daughter, a gap breached only in the imagination, only in the other's absence.(10) The departed father is also addressed:

And when no drinks no friends left,
don't leave me you say. But I do just that.
I walk out on you. Now I would break down doors
for one look of your face.[3]

In Parts Two and Three insight transforms and replaces the agony of loss as the first poem, 'River', shows.

So bright beneath yourself
unstitching and unstitching
your amber strands
your shadow slats

those bits of you
that spin
their watery embroidery

the bits of me
that rush with you
retracing my tapestry (21).

Works:
The Peacock's Eye. Galway: Salmon, 1992. Poetry.

Notes
1. Introduction in *The Peacock's Eye*.
2. In *The Peacock's Eye*, 9.
3. 'Father', in *The Peacock's Eye*, 16.

O'Mahony, Norah Tynan
Born: Ireland, 1905; Died: 1932
Educated: Ireland.

The sister of Kathleen Tynan, Norah wrote novels and poetry.

Works:
The Fields of Heaven. London: Erskine Macdonald, 1915. Poetry.
Desmond's Foster-Child. Dublin: np, 1915. Novel.

O'Malley, Mary
Born: Ireland, c 20th century
Educated: Ireland.

Mary O'Malley was born in Connemara and educated at University College, Galway. She lived eight years in Portugal where she taught English at the New University of Lisbon. She now works as a part-time journalist in Galway, where she lives with her husband and two children. Her poetry has appeared in many magazines and journals and was shortlisted for the 1989 *Sunday Tribune*/Hennessy Awards.

O'Malley's first volume of poems, *A Consideration of Silk* (1990), spans a wide variety of subjects and places. She sympathises with victims of history and women, from Hiroshima to Angola to Chile. Solemn, bardic language resonates in 'Revolt', as the first bird to fly over 'outraged Hiroshima' bears 'witness/To the second sin'. 'I am here to stop man (or history book)/Shifting the blame for this one/Between any woman's legs.'[1] 'Veronica' chronicles the horrors women faced in Chilean prisons; opening the poem with the image of European astronomers journeying to Chile 'To stare at the most distant stars', and closing by noting the place in Chile

Where no-one dares to look
For vanishing stars,

> A black hole in the hearts
> Of ordinary men,[2]

the poem implicitly condemns the Europeans, willing to search for stars, yet blind to human misery.

Heavy, dignified language charts human suffering, but O'Malley picks up her pace with irony and humour when the situation warrants. 'Skipping Song' catches the rhythm of children's chants as it gaily fantasises a world destroyed by the nuclear power station at Sellafield, which pours its poison into the Irish sea.

> Strange flowers grow on Sellafield Green,
> The loveliest meadow that ever was seen.
> Oh pluck me a flower
> From up there so high,
> A pretty fireblossom
> To light up the sky.[3]

O'Malley's language is precise, rich, and evocative, perhaps nowhere more lovely than in the tender 'Wordgames', dedicated to her son, 'A small stumbling Columbus', who dips his exploring toe into 'slithery S words'.[4]

Works:
A Consideration of Silk. Galway: Salmon Publishing, 1990. Poetry.

Notes
1. In *A Consideration of Silk*, 6.
2. In *A Consideration of Silk*, 38.
3. In *A Consideration of Silk*, 32.
4. In *A Consideration of Silk*, 15.

O'Neill, Joan
Born: Ireland, c 20th century
Educated: Ireland.

Joan O'Neill lives in Bray with her husband and five children. Late to the writing scene, she credits workshops and particularly Mary Rose Callaghan with giving her a start. Her novel, *Daisy Chain War* (1990), was an immediate success in Ireland and she began work at once on a sequel.

Daisy Chain War evokes a sense of life in Ireland during World War II and the 'Emergency', when food was rationed. The protagonist associates the pleasure of eating with life in the country, recalling in vivid detail the fragrance, taste, and abundance that greets the girls when they visit their farming cousins. Family life is warmly described: Lizzy's cousin Vicky is sent over from England for the duration of the war, and Lizzy and Vicky compete first for girlfriends, then for boyfriends. Lizzy's older sister Karen marries an American soldier, and the family endures heartbreak when he is missing in action. Warm family relations extend to the grandmother and cousins, and transcend sibling rivalries. From the theatre-playing games of children and competition of neighbours, the story moves to an unresolved love story. The author had many queries from young people eager to know the outcome of the romance.[1]

Works:
Daisy Chain War. Dublin: Attic Press, 1990. Novel.
Promised. Dublin: Attic Press, 1991. Novel.

Notes
1. Personal communication.

O'Neill, Mary Devenport
Born: Ireland, 1879; Died: 1967
Educated: Ireland.

Mary Devenport was born in Loughrea, Co. Galway, and attended the National College of Art in Dublin. She kept a salon in Rathgar, and knew many of the writers of her day.

Her poems appeared in her husband's play, *The Kingdom-Maker*, in *The Irish Times*, *The Bell*, and *The Dublin*

Magazine, and in one collection, *Prometheus and Other Poems (1929)*. She also wrote verse plays, one of which, *Bluebeard*, appears in this collection and was performed by Austin Clarke's Lyric Theatre Company in 1933.[1] Her voice is distinctive and original:

> Something whinges to me
> When spring is beginning,
> Or when the leaves are grown
> Heavy and dull,
> Or light is streaked in the sky,
> Or the slim moon turned fully,
> 'OVER AGAIN TILL YOU DIE.'[2]

Works:
Prometheus and Other Poems. London: Cape, 1929. Poetry/Play.

Notes
1. *Dictionary of Irish Literature*, Robert Hogan, ed. (Westport, Conn.: Greenwood, 1979), 538.
2. 'Something Whinges to Me', in *Prometheus and Other Poems*, 11.

O'Neill, Moira
Born: Ireland, c 1870; Died: 1955
Educated: Ireland.

Moira O'Neill was the pen name of Agnes Nesta Shakespeare Skrine, *née* Higginson, originally from Co. Antrim. She was, according to her daughter Molly Keane, the novelist and playwright, 'practically a recluse', not at all interested in the 'social life about her', but popular with friends and family for all that. She lived with her husband and five children on country estates in Kildare and Wexford. *Blackwoods*, one of the best literary magazines of its time, would, Keane says, publish 'almost anything' her mother wrote. Although she published many literary reviews, she was best known as a poet. 'They were jolly good poems, too,' her daughter says, 'romantic sort of poems about the peasant life.'[1]

O'Neill wrote poems and songs to children, translations of Italian poems, nature poems. Some poems catch the accents of rural Ireland, and the wit reminds us occasionally of her daughter's lively sense of humour. Two different views on marriage are presented in 'Her Sister' and 'Never Married'; one sees the institution as natural for women, the other sees it as a severe trial. Both are typical of O'Neill's style and humour.

Ah, no use o'talkin'! Sure a woman's born to wed,
An' not go wastin' all her life by waitin' till she's dead.[2]

Oh, never think I'm wantin' to miscall the race o'men,
There's not a taste o' harm in them, the cratures!
They're meddlesome, an' quarrelsome, an'
troublesome, but then
The Man Above He put it in their natures.[3]

Selected Works:
An Easter Vacation. London: Lawrence & Bullen, 1893; New York:
Dutton, 1894. Poetry.
Songs of the Glens of Antrim. Edinburgh and London: Blackwood,
1901. Poetry.
More Songs of the Glens of Antrim. Edinburgh and London:
Blackwood, 1921. Poetry.
Collected Poems of Moira O'Neill. Edinburgh and London:
Blackwood, 1933. Poetry.

Notes
1. In *A Portrait of the Artist as a Young Girl*, John Quinn, ed.
   (London: Methuen, 1986), 66.
2. 'Her Sister', in *More Songs of the Glens of Antrim*, 15.
3. 'Never Married', in *More Songs of the Glens of Antrim*, 11.

— P —

Pearse, Mary Brigid
Born: Ireland, 1884; Died: 1947
Educated: Ireland.

Mary Brigid Pearse wrote one novel and edited the life of her brother, the leader of the 1916 Rising. Her novel, *The Murphys of Ballystack* (1917), is a humorous tale of the Murphy family, grocers in Ballystack, and of various members of the community, the priest, parson, doctor, etc. The humour rests on gentle whimsy and fairly stereotypical characterisations. The Murphy store advertises 'Fresh eggs received daily', but as Pat Casey notes when an egg breaks open of its own accord, 'To my sarten knowledge ... that is the thirteenth egg that burst itself, for all the world like a German bombshell, before the dacent customers of this shop! That's on week days. Mebbe they do be doin' it on Sundays as well; but I hope they have the common dacency to behave thimselves on the day ov rest.'[1]

Works:
The Murphys of Ballystack. Dublin; Gill, 1917. Novel.
The Home Life of Padraig Pearse: As told by himself, his family and friends. Dublin: Browne and Nolan, 1935. Memoir.

Notes
1. *The Murphys of Ballystack*, 7-8.

Pender, Margaret T
Born: Ireland, 1865; Died: nd
Educated: Ireland.

Margaret T Pender was born in Co. Antrim and educated at home, at Ballyrobin National School, and at the Convent of Mercy in Belfast. She married shortly after she left school and thereafter contributed poetry under various pen-names to many journals. After she won a fifty pound prize for a short story in the *Weekly Freeman*, she turned to novel-writing. Her death date is not known.

Selected Works:
The Green Cockade: A Tale of Ulster in 'Ninety-Eight. Dublin: Martin Lester, 1920. Novel.
The Spearmen of the North. Dublin: Talbot, 1931. Novel.

Pilkington, Laetitia
Born: Ireland, 1712; Died: 1750
Educated: Ireland.

Laetitia Pilkington married a clergyman named Matthew Pilkington and from 1730-1737 the Pilkingtons were friends to Jonathan Swift. Mrs Pilkington fled to England after a scandal which caused her husband to expel her from his house. Her poetry was published in England, but debts mounted and she was imprisoned for debt in 1742. A pamphlet war ensued between the Pilkingtons when she returned to Ireland to collect subscriptions to write her memoirs. She is best known for the memoirs, and Swift's biographers are indebted to her for anecdotes of his later life. Included in her memoirs is her poetry, re-written from memory.

Her friend Colley Cibber warned her of the rumour that her husband was the poet and that she had merely stolen his lines. He advised her to publish on a subject never-before written about to prove her abilities.[1] The first lines of the poem follow:

When you advised me, Sir, to choose
Some odd new subject for the muse,
From thought to thought unpleased I changed,
Through Nature, Art, and Science ranged,
Yet still could naught discover new,
Till, happily, I fixed on you.
Your Stoic turn, and cheerful mind
Have marked you out of all mankind,
The oddest theme my muse can find.[2]

Works:
Memoirs of Mrs Laetitia Pilkington. Introduced by Iris Barry.
1748; rpt. London: Routledge, 1928.

Notes:
1. Iris Barry, 'Introduction', in *Memoirs of Mrs Laetitia Pilkington*.
2. *Memoirs*, 178-9.

Power, Marguerite, Lady Blessington
Born: 1789; Died: 1849
Educated: Ireland.

Marguerite Power was born in Clonmel, the daughter of a
Catholic family. Her father urged her marriage with a
Captain Farmer when she was only fifteen. She left Farmer
after three months, and married the Earl of Blessington
when Farmer died in 1818. She travelled with her husband
in Europe and met Byron; her *Conversations of Lord Byron
with the Countess of Blessington* (1834) were very popular.
Impoverished after the Earl's death, she turned to writing
fashionable travel books and novels. Although her work
was popular and financially successful, she died bankrupt
in Paris in 1849.[1]

Selected Works:
Grace Cassidy, or, The Repealers. 3 vol. London: Bentley, 1833.
   Novel.
The Two Friends. 3 vol. London: Saunders, 1835. Novel.

Confessions of an Elderly Gentleman. 8 vol. London; Longman, 1836.

Conversations of Lord Byron with the Countess of Blessington. 1834 rpt, Princeton, New Jersey: Princeton University Press, 1969. Non-fiction. Edited with introduction and notes by Ernest de Lovell, Jr.

Notes
1. *A Biographical Dictionary of Irish Literature*, Anne M. Brady and Brian Cleeve, eds. (Mullingar: Lilliput Press, 1985), 206-207.

Purcell, Deirdre
Born: Ireland, 1945
Educated: Ireland.

Deirdre Purcell was born in Dublin and educated there and in Mayo. She worked for the civil service and Aer Lingus and, after an appearance on an amateur stage, was invited to join the Abbey Theatre as one of its permanent company. In 1968 she went to Loyola University, Chicago, as actress-in-residence for the theatre department, stayed on in Chicago, married, and performed a variety of jobs. She returned to Dublin in 1973, joined RTE as a radio continuity announcer, switched to newsreading in 1977, became a television journalist in 1979, and was anchoring the station's *Nine O'Clock News* when she left in 1983. She began writing for the *Irish Press* in 1983, and then spent seven years with the *Sunday Tribune*, with which she won the two most prestigious awards in Irish journalism, the Benson and Hedges Award and the Cross Award. She is the Taoiseach's nominee to the Board of the Abbey Theatre, is on the Council of the Credit Institutions' Ombudsman, and has published several non-fiction books as well as two novels. She lives in Dublin with her two sons.[1]

A Place of Stones (1991), Purcell's first novel, an instant bestseller, tells the story of Molly Ní Bhriain, the famous and successful actress from the island of Inisheer off the west coast of Ireland. Born in the USA to Maggie and Cal Smith, the baby Susannah Smith was on route to Ireland with her wealthy parents when their chartered plane ran out of fuel in a storm and crashed in the Atlantic Ocean. That same night, Sorcha and Micheál O Briain's baby daughter, Molly, died. Susannah takes the place of the dead Molly. Ignorance of Molly's true identity leads to complications and tragedy; final revelations, however, untangle the plot to the satisfaction of the majority of the characters.

The novel moves with ease from quiet, poor Inisheer to London and Chicago. The tensions of the early homelife in Inisheer are paralleled with the tensions of life back in Chicago where Molly's brother Christian clashes with his grandfather. In London and Chicago, the scene shifts to elegantly clothed characters in luxurious restaurants and lovely homes. The tensions and potential violence remain just under the rich veneer, however, suggesting an essential similarity in human personality despite appearances.

The second novel, *That Childhood Country* (1992), is set in Co. Monaghan and in Prince Edward Island in Canada. It covers the years 1953-79 and follows the story of twin brothers who emigrate to Canada.

Works:
A Place of Stones. Dublin/London: Townhouse/Macmillan, 1991. Novel.
That Childhood Country. Dublin, London: Townhouse/ Macmillan, 1992. Novel.

Notes
1. Personal communication.

— *R* —

Redmond, Lucile
Born: Ireland, 1949
Educated: England, Ireland, USA.

Lucile Redmond was born in Dublin and educated in England, Ireland, and the USA. She has received both the Hennessy New Irish Writing Award and the Allied Irish Banks Award. She has one collection of stories, *Who breaks up the old moons to make new stars* (1978).[1]

'The Shaking Trees' is an imaginative depiction of a woman's death as movement from human to plant life.

The season grew colder and the trees talked less often. Gradually a yawning silence spread through the grove. Sometimes small animals scuttled through the trees with amazing rapidness. Then it came that they moved so fast that they were like irritating buzzing. She wondered vaguely whether this was a seasonal change. She was too sleepy to bother reasoning it out. Her leaves began to itch at about the same time as the wind became gusty and blew them off in molting tufts. She cradled the nests in her branchforks and hunched against the cutting gale. The snow blew to bank around her shivering trunk. She became warm and dozy. The aspens slept for the winter.[2]

Works:
Who breaks up the old moons to make new stars. Dublin: Egotist Press, 1978. Short Stories.

Notes

1. Introduction, 'The Shaking Trees', in *Stories by Contemporary Irish Women*, Daniel J Casey and Linda M Casey, eds. (Syracuse: Syracuse UP, 1990) 151.
2. 'The Shaking Trees', 155.

Reid, Christina

Born: Ireland, c̲ 20th century
Educated: Ireland.

Christina Reid was born and educated in Belfast, where she lived until 1987. She was writer-in-residence at the Lyric Theatre, Belfast, 1983-84, and also at the Young Vic, London, 1988-89. She lives in London with her three daughters.

Reid's plays for television, radio, and stage have been produced and acclaimed in Ireland, England, Scotland, Europe and America. *Tea in a China Shop*, her first play, won the Thames TV Playwright Scheme Award in 1983, and was runner-up in *The Irish Times*/Dublin Theatre Festival/Women's Play Competition, 1982. *Did You Hear the One About the Irishman ... ?* won the Ulster TV Drama Award in 1980; *The Belle of the Belfast City* won the George Devine Award in 1986, and *The Last of a Dyin' Race* won the Giles Cooper Award in 1986. The Young Vic commissioned *Lords, Dukes and Earls* in 1989, and Reid has also written for schools and children, as well as specials and serials for television and radio.[1]

The world of Reid's plays is contemporary Belfast. She writes sympathetically about both extremists and moderates. Narrow perspectives often mark extremists, but humour plays a large part in all her work. In *The Belle of the Belfast City*, Dolly, the matriarch, keeps her home humming to the slightly naughty numbers and the partisan ballads she once sang in music-halls. Unlike the extremists, however, Dolly responds warmly to many in need, including her grand-daughter, also named Belle, taken in by Dolly when their severe, sin-fearing parents died.

Joyriders, one of Reid's most successful plays, presents the interactions between four Catholic unemployed teenagers and Kate, the thirty-four-year-old, middle class social worker in charge of the Youth Training Programme that the teenagers attend. When Arthur, described as a 'skinhead by accident rather than choice ... accidentally shot by the army ... injuries have left him with a shaven head, a scarred face and a limp,' is awarded seventy thousand pounds compensation, Kate invites the four teenagers to dinner at her house to celebrate.[2] Sandra is cynical, Tommy quotes Marx and steals, Arthur wants to be a chef, and he and Maureen, who lives with and worries about her twelve-year-old, glue-snuffing, joyriding brother, admire Kate and her surroundings. After dinner, Kate serves a liqueur:[3]

Maureen: It's lovely roun' here. No army nor police nor nuthin'.

Tommy: No need. They don't make petrol bombs roun' here, just money.

Sandra (sniffing the liqueur): What's this?
Kate: It's a coffee liqueur.
Sandra swallows a large mouthful, coughs, splutters.
Sandra: Jeesus!
Arthur: Yer supposed to sip it slow, ye ignoramous.
Maureen (sipping hers): It's lovely.
Sandra: It beats glue.
Kate: Do you sniff glue, Sandra?
Sandra: Nigh an' again.
Kate: Why?
Sandra: Why do flies eat shite?
Tommy: Because they can't afford gin and tonic.
Kate: Do you all do it?
Arthur: I usta. After the accident I never bothered no more.

Sandra: He's afraid it'll rust the oul steel plate. (61)

Reid graphically presents the horrors of the present violence in northern Ireland, and the bigotry and prejudice woven over generations. Her plays, however, are very funny: the resilience and humour of her characters are notes of optimism in a grim situation.

Works:
The Last of a Dyin' Race. Best Radio Plays. London: Methuen, 1986. Play.
Tea in a China Cup and *Joyriders*. London: Methuen, 1987. Plays.
The Belle of the Belfast City and *Did You Hear the One About the Irishman ... ?* London: Methuen, 1989. Plays.

Notes
1. Personal communication.
2. *Joyriders*, 39.
3. *Joyriders*, 39.

Richards, Maura
Born: Ireland, 1939
Educated: Ireland.

Maura Richards was born in Mitchelstown, Co. Cork, and attended St Mary's Presentation Convent and the Vocational School there. Her daughter, Carol, was born in Dublin in 1970, and in 1977 Maura married an Englishman and has lived in England since. She trained as a counsellor and works as Child Protection Administration Area Co-Ordinator in Social Services.

The 'whole ethos of Catholicism in Ireland', she believes, shaped her perspective. Her schooldays were 'the beginning of the end of the stranglehold of the Catholic Church in Ireland', a hold that was thus 'all the more vicious.' 'So of course', she writes, 'a lot of the struggle of my writing is about trying to release myself from that background. The birth of my daughter in Dublin in 1970, when I was not married, produced *Nine Months and No*

Man which was my title for *Two to Tango* (1981) and the aim of the exercise was to try and reproduce the feelings and experiences of that nine months.'[1]

Irish poets, Irish mythology, and Irish history comprised her early reading, also the writers her mother read: Elliot, the Brontës, Henry Woods, and Elizabeth Bowen. Although her own knowledge of the Irish language is poor now, she notes that she 'was reared in a very nationalistic background where Ireland with all her sorrows and triumphs of a thousand years was part and parcel of every day. It's only in recent years that I've realised that a large part of the sadness with which I live was made up of the eternal yearnings of that constantly aborted United Ireland.'[2]

Two to Tango is the story of Brig O'Mahony's pregnancy and the birth of her daughter. Richards details the experience of the unmarried mother sympathetically and humorously, from the moment Brig tries to tell herself that she's not pregnant, through the anxiety of telling her family and finding the money to pay the nursing home, until the triumphant arrival of the baby. Despite the opposition she faces, Brig is confident of one thing: 'my loyalty lay with the child inside me, not with any grown-ups who should be well able to look after themselves.'[3]

Richards gives an accurate and detailed account of the panic, rejection, and isolation of the young mother left alone in a cold hospital room, as well as the details of labour and the mother's feeling of incompetency with the new and tiny baby. The humour, too, rings true. Disappointed a few days after the birth because her daughter's lovely colour seems to have changed, Brig is teased by the nurse: 'Ye all think yeer babies had sunray lamps in there. The child was slightly jaundiced, that's all; most babies are born like that.' (181)

Richards' second novel, *Interlude* (1982), differs very much from the first in its eroticism, but is similar in that it too 'blew up a storm of contradictory reviews'.[4] Another novel remains unpublished and a fourth is in progress.

Works:

Two to Tango. Dublin: Ward River Press, 1981. Novel.
Interlude. Dublin: Ward River Press, 1982. Novel.

Notes

1. Personal communication.
2. Personal communication.
3. *Two to Tango*, 90.
4. Personal communication.

Robertson, Olivia

Born: England, 1917
Educated: England, Ireland.

Olivia Robertson was born in London in 1917. She attended Heathfield School in Ascot and Alexandra College in Dublin, and studied art at the Grosvenor School of Modern Art in London and the Royal Hibernian Academy in Dublin. Her novels and stories are set in Ireland and combine elements of the ancient and mysterious with the everyday. Pagan altars, for example, robbers, fairies, and cures are all part of the romantic world of *Field of the Stranger* (1948). Her interest in the supernatural was not, however, simply a literary ploy to lure readers: Olivia Robertson became a priestess in the Fellowship of Isis, which she founded with her brother, in a castle near Enniscorthy.[1]

Besides novels, Robertson wrote of Dublin and of Isis, illustrating her work herself.

Works:

St Malachy's Court. London: Peter Davies, 1946; New York: Odyssey, 1947. Stories.
Field of the Stranger. London: Peter Davies, 1948; New York: Random House, 1948. Novel.
The Golden Eye. London: Peter Davies, 1949. Novel.
Miranda Speaks. London: Peter Davies, 1950. Novel.
It's an Old Irish Custom. London: Denis Dobson, 1953. Essays.
Dublin Phoenix. London: Jonathan Cape, 1957. On Dublin.

The Call of Isis. Enniscorthy: Cesara, 1975. On rites of Isis.
The Isis Wedding Rite. Enniscorthy: Cesara, 1976. On rites of Isis.

Notes
1. *Dictionary of Irish Literature,* Robert Hogan, ed. (Westport, Conn.: Greenwood Press, 1979), 568-69.

Roche, Regina Maria
Born: 1764; Died: 1845
Educated: Ireland, England.

A sentimental novelist, Regina Maria Roche's popularity rivalled Lady Morgan's during their lifetimes. Jane Austen mentions her very popular novel, *The Children of the Abbey* (1796), in *Emma,* and satirised Clermont in *Northanger Abbey.* The latter was reprinted as a result in Jane Austen's *Horrid Novels* in 1968.[1] Roche published at least fifteen novels.

Selected Works:
The Children of the Abbey. 4 vol. London: Newman, 1796. Novel.
Anna; or, Edinburgh. 2 vol. London: Hill, nd. Novel.
Castle Chapel. 3 vol. London: Newman, nd. Novel.
Clermont. 4 vol. London: Newman, nd. Novel.

Notes
1. Riana O'Dwyer, Department of English, University College, Galway; Personal communication.

Roddy, Moya
Born: Ireland, c 20th century
Educated: Ireland, England.

Moya Roddy was born in Dublin and studied media at the Central London Polytechnic, where she obtained a First Class Honours Degree in 1983. She worked on *Diverse*

Reports, a current affairs programme, for Channel Four, was commissioned to write a screenplay for the British Film Institute in 1987, and has written several screenplays for Hollywood since. She has also published several short stories, one in *The Irish Times'* Summer Fiction Series in 1991, and one novel to date. She lives with her daughter in Ireland.

The novel, *The Long Way Home* (1992), tells the story of Jo Nowd, a young woman growing up in early 1960s Dublin. Jo's parents moved to Dublin from the country, determined to save money, give their children an education, and raise them above the working-class neighbourhood in which they live. Teased as a 'culchie', Jo needs friends desperately and falls into stealing and lying to ensure companionship. Her struggle for independence is waged against the dreary world of her mother's and society's limited expectations and the bullying habits of her father. Working-class Dublin of the 1960s is a dull and mean place and offers little in the way of fun or excitement. But despite every setback, Jo determines to free herself and become a famous and wealthy dress-designer.

Works:
The Long Way Home. Dublin: Attic Press, 1992. Novel.

Ros, Amanda McKittrick
Born: Ireland, 1860; Died: 1939
Educated: Ireland.

Amanda McKittrick Ros was born Anna Margaret McKittrick in Drumaness, Co. Down. She attended Marlborough Training College in Dublin from 1884-86 before taking a post as teacher in Larne. There she met Andrew Ross, the stationmaster whom she married and aggrandised, as she did herself, claiming, for example, that her full name was Amanda Malvina Fitzalan Anna

Margaret McLelland McKittrick Ros. For their tenth wedding anniversary, her husband had her first novel, *Irene Iddesleigh* (1897), privately printed. After Andrew Ross died in 1917, she married Thomas Rodgers, but was widowed again in 1933 and died in 1939.[1]

Delighting in extravagances of alliteration, surprising metaphor, startling descriptions, and preposterous coincidences, her novels have been the objects of ridicule and an almost cult-like delight. In *Helen Huddleson*, an unfinished novel completed by McKittrick Ros's biographer Jack Loudan in 1969, Lord Rasberry takes Helen to the house of his dead aunt. 'It had been untenanted since the death of Lady Dolly Dray, his aunt, the novelist whose fat resources were diminished by the scurrilous, scandalising, spiteful critic scions of bastardom, found always trampling upon the heels of fame.'[2] Lord Rasberry pleads his case:

'Will you love me, my fond girl?' he panted. 'Will you?' She remained immobile – taciturn.

'Ah, darling – speak,' he pleaded plaintively. 'I am mad with excitement, wild with expectancy, awaiting those sweet lips of yours to open and act their part in conveying to me that for which I have yearned for years.'

He pressed his hot forehead with his hand.

'Will you be my wife, Helen Huddleson?' the sweat drops pebbling his brow as he anxiously awaited her reply.

She trembled violently until at last the answer came. 'Sir – I cannot,' wringing her small hands as the negative dropped from her parched lips. (53)

Despite volumes of verse, novels, and invective, Amanda McKittrick Ros never tired of the exuberant display of energy and emotion, as this quotation from her final work shows. After her death, T S Mercer, an ardent sympathiser with whom she corresponded over a long period, published a selection of her letters in *Bayonets of Bastard Sheen* (1949), and a sample of invectives aimed at critics.

Selected Works:

Irene Iddesleigh. Belfast: Privately published, 1897; London: Nonesuch, 1926; New York: Boni & Liveright, 1927. Novel.

Delina Delaney. Belfast: Privately published, 1898; London: Chatto & Windus, 1935. Novel.

Poems of Puncture. London: Arthur H Stockwell, 1913. Poetry.

Fumes of Formation. Belfast: R Carswell, 1933. Poetry.

Helen Huddleson, edited with an introduction and final chapter by Jack Loudan. London, Chatto & Windus, 1969. Novel.

Notes

1. Details of her life can be found in Frank Ormsby's introduction to his valuable *Amanda McKittrick Ros Reader, Thine in Storm and Calm* (Belfast and St Paul: Blackstaff Press), 1988.

2. *Helen Huddleson,* 48.

Rowley, Rosemarie

Born: Ireland, 1942
Educated: Ireland.

Rosemarie Rowley was born in Dublin and started writing poetry as a child. She took a degree in English, Philosophy, and Irish at Trinity College, Dublin in 1969, wrote a Master's thesis on Patrick Kavanagh in 1983, and completed a course in feminist theology in Milltown Park. She has worked as a teacher in Birmingham and has also had positions with the BBC, the Irish Film Industry, the European Parliament in Luxembourg, the Dublin Institute of Adult Education, and writers' workshops. She lives in Dublin with her son and is a member of the Irish Green movement.[1]

Religious images take on new, fresh life and meaning in several of Rowley's poems, for example, in 'The Unfortunate Cup of Tea'.

Was it her fault he picked at nourishment,
And threw the dishes at her?
Swallowed tweedy-looking pills,
That almost stopped his heart?

What was she wondering about all the time,
When swords of light had crossed,
Illuminating the dark ages
Like a cathedral?

The swords of light made a bridge of light,
An airfield for lost travellers to land on,
While he slept on, doubtless glad
He was causing much anxiety.[2]

Works:
The Broken Pledge and Other Poems. Dublin: Martello, 1985. Poetry.
The Sea of Affliction. Dublin: Rowan Tree, 1987. Poetry.
Flight into Reality. Dublin: Rowan Tree, 1989. Poetry.

Notes
1. Introduction in *The Broken Pledge and Other Poems*, 1.
2. In *The Broken Pledge*, 43.

Ryan, Margaret Mary
Born: Ireland, c 1855; Died: 1915
Educated: Ireland.

Margaret Mary Ryan published poetry in journals as 'MR' and '*Alice Esmonde*'. Her volume of poetry is published under her own name.[1]

Works:
Songs of Remembrance. Dublin: M H Gill, 1998. Poetry.

Notes:
1. see *Pillars of the House*. A A Kelly, ed. Dublin: Wolfhound Press, 1988, 57-58.

Ryan, Mary
Born: Ireland, 1945
Educated: Ireland.

Mary Ryan was born in Roscommon and attended Convent of Mercy schools in Castlerea and Castlebar until the family moved to Dublin. The Loreto Convent in North Great Georges Street was her first Dublin school, followed by a four-year spell at boarding school in Loreto Convent in Balbriggan, 1958-62. She took her BA and Higher Diploma in Education at University College, Dublin, and taught in England until 1968, when she returned to Ireland and worked for two years in RTE. In 1972 she took up Law, graduated BCL in 1975, was admitted as a solicitor in 1976, and has been practising since. Her practice is at home, which gives her the freedom to write. She is married and has two sons.

Growing up in Ireland, she notes, inevitably shaped one's perspective: 'Most of all perhaps has been the sense of outrage at the indignity offered women; the sense that so much powerful reality was denied recognition or visibility, brushed aside, hidden and wasted.' In her own life, she responded to 'the insults to the feminine in Catholic dogma and liturgy', and lived 'the passion for political independence and the anger at the history of Ireland'. She was fortunate to have parents who were open to dialogue, a grandfather 'passionately interested in poetry', and a grandmother 'resentful of male dominance'.[1]

Ryan has published several short stories and to date two novels; a third is almost finished. *Whispers in the Wind* (1990) tells the story of Kitty Delaney, an adventurous young woman married to a teacher in the west of Ireland during the War of Independence. Unknown to Kitty, her husband and many of the local men are involved in the struggle; the novel charts their skirmishes, escapes, arrests, and torture against the background of her increasing irritation at the limits placed on women. Poor women, such as Kitty's maid Eileen, are easy prey for both the Black-and-Tans and the local Volunteers. When the 'witch' Mrs Finnerty offers Eileen a 'remedy' for her pregnancy, Eileen reacts in shock at the 'sin', but Mrs Finnerty laughs, 'That's men's religion, girl! Do you think the real God is dependent on you for this life — that there are no other wombs in the world?'[2] Kitty too comes to distrust the church: when the parish priest remonstrates with her about her absence from Confession, she replies: 'Maybe when the Host is consecrated by a woman, Father, when a woman hears my Confession — I'll be able to call it my religion.' (428)

Works:
Whispers in the Wind. Dublin: Attic Press, 1990. Novel.
Glenallen. Dublin: Attic Press, 1991. Novel.
Into the West. London: Headline, 1992. Novel.

Notes
1. Personal communication.
2. *Whispers in the Wind*, 228.

— S —

Sadlier, Mary Anne (*née* Madden)
Born: Ireland, 1820; Died: 1903
Educated: Ireland.

Mary Anne Madden was born in Cootehill, Co. Cavan. She emigrated to Canada in 1844, where she met and married a Catholic publisher, James Sadlier. She had a long career in Canada and New York as a Catholic journalist and novelist. She wrote historical fiction and romantic tales of the Irish in America.

Selected Works:
The Confederate Chieftains: A Tale of the Irish Rebellion of 1641. London, Glasgow: Cameron & Ferguson, 1859. Novel.
The Fate of Father Sheehy: A Tale of Tipperary in the Olden Times. Dublin, London: James Duffy, 1864. Novel.
The Blakes and the Flanagans: A Tale Illustrative of Irish Life in the United States. New York: P J Kennedy, Excelsior Catholic Publishing House, 1896. Novel.
New Lights; or, Life in Galway. New York, Montreal: D & J Sadlier, 1885. Novel.
The Old House by the Boyne. Dublin: Gill, 1910. Novel.

Salkeld, Blanaid (*née* ffrench Mullen)
Born: India, 1880; Died: Ireland, 1959
Educated: Pakistan, India.

Blanaid Salkeld was born to Irish parents in Chittagong, India, now Pakistan. Her childhood was spent in Ireland, but she lived in Bombay, India, after her marriage to an English civil servant. Widowed, she returned to Ireland when she was twenty-eight, joined the Abbey Theatre company, wrote several plays, and published several volumes of poetry. She also published translations of Hindustani folk songs and poems from Russian. She began the Gayfield Press in 1937 with her son, Cecil ffrench Salkeld, who became a well-known Irish artist. Her granddaughter, Beatrice, married Brendan Behan.

'Evasion', as so much of Salkeld's poetry, reflects the dramatist's and actor's eye.

The old woman has forgotten her face:
a chance mirror met, to avoid disgrace
she blinks her glance with lightning wit;
no recognition reflects in it.

The maid at the dresser drops the delph
as someone enters; she is all thumbs —
but the old woman holds on to herself,
sucking her gums.

If I didn't shrink — I am so diminished,
the old one thinks, I feel cold shy
of strange members that seem never finished
casting off and losing that thing was I.
She turns objective, for shame — in case
she might have to acknowledge her latest face.[1]

Works:
Hello, Eternity! London: Elkin Mathews & Marot, 1933. Poetry.
The Fox's Covert. London: Dent, 1935. Poetry.
... the engine is still running. Dublin: Gayfield, 1937. Poetry.
A Dubliner. Dublin: Gayfield, 1943. Poetry.
Experiment in Error. Aldington, Kent: Hand & Flower, 1955.
    Poetry.

Notes

1. In *New Irish Poets*, edited by Devin A Garrity (New York: Devin-Adair, 1948), 167.

Sayers, Peig
Born: Ireland, 1873; Died: 1958
Educated: Ireland.

Peig Sayers was born into a family of Irish-speaking story-tellers in Dunquin, Co. Kerry. In its language and customs, this family was more Irish than most Irish families of the time, yet the Sayers family was originally from England, and Protestant until Peig's grandfather became a Catholic. As a young woman, Peig married Pádraig O Gaoithín, a man from the Blasket Islands, off the south-west coast of Ireland, and lived most of her life on the Great Blasket Island, where she raised two daughters and four sons.

Only three miles off the mainland, the Great Blasket Island is separated by a wild stretch of the Atlantic, and trips to the mainland in curraghs, tarred canvas canoes, were few and often dangerous. Although the Islands can be idyllic in summer, they are lonely, bleak spots in winter, the first land to feel the fierce Atlantic storms. Winters, she notes, hemmed the islanders in 'like a flock of sheep in a pen, buffeted by storm and gale, without shade or shelter but like a big ship in the middle of a great sea, cut from the land without news coming to us or going from us.'[1] On those long dark nights, the ancient Irish tradition of story-telling was the all-important source of entertainment. Already in her lifetime this tradition was fading, as indeed was life itself on the bare Blasket Island. But the story-tellers did more than entertain: in the tales they passed on by the kitchen hearth, the traditions, fears, superstitions, beliefs, and history of a nation were preserved.

Peig Sayers' father, brothers, and son were all story-tellers. Peig's stories give us a valuable perspective on women's lives. Seosamh O Dálaigh, a collector of folk-tales, describes the evenings in Peig's house: the supper over, the rosary said, Peig took her pipe and her place by the fire, and the family and neighbours gathered into the circle to discuss the day's news, which often served as a lead-in to the stories. O Dálaigh collected 375 of Peig's tales: most of these had been passed on to Peig, but many in *Peig* (1935; her autobiography) and in *An Old Woman's Reflections* (1962) are stories of her own life or of the lives of her neighbours. These are unusual also in being written by Peig herself who was encouraged to write them by her editor, the playwright Máire Ní Chinnéide. Both these works are translated into English, and *Peig* is considered a modern Irish classic, one of three to emerge from the Blasket Islands, essential for every student of Irish literature.

The translations attempt to reproduce the Irish idiom, as well as the simple, evocative poetry and humour of Peig's words. The repetitions and rhythm will remind readers of Synge's stylised rendition of the speech of the Aran Islanders. Of the man proposed as a match for a young girl, for example, 'He was yellow, he didn't walk nicely, he was stoop-shouldered — there was no fault in the world but he had.' Or again, 'It wasn't a sulk the grey mare put up when she came to the edge of the cliff, but to carry her four hooves with her, clean over.' The expectation is set up in the negative, then removed: 'There wasn't in the boat of me only two feet.' When a relative complains of the fox stealing her hens, 'The twister (fox) is too cute for me. He takes a bite with him on his visits always. They're (hens) gone from Kate down here, too,' Peig gives the story a typically humorous turn. 'It's a great thing that he didn't make ye envy each other!' she retorts.[2] Robin Flower calls Peig 'a natural orator, with so keen a sense of the turn of phrase and the lilting rhythm appropriate to Irish that her words could be written down as they leave her lips, and they would have the effect of literature.'[3] We can appreciate the simplicity and rhythm in the translation: 'My spell on this little bench is nearly finished,' Peig tells us, the bench being both the story-teller's and the woman's, for 'I am now at tight grips with the years.'[4]

Works:

Peig. Máire Ní Chinnéide do chuir i n-eagar (Baile Atha Cliath: Comhlucht Oideachais na hÉireann), 1936; *Peig: The Autobiography of Peig Sayers of the Great Blasket Island*. Translated by Bryan MacMahon. Dublin: Talbot Press, 1973. Memoir.

Machnamh Sean-mhná, Máire Ní Chinnéide do chuir i n-eagar, 1939; rpt. 1980; *Peig Sayers: An Old Woman's Reflections*. Translated by Seamus Ennis and Introduced by W R Rogers. London: Oxford, 1962. Memoir.

Notes:

1. *Peig Sayers: An Old Woman's Reflections*, 49.
2. *Peig Sayers: An Old Woman's Reflections*, 9, 11, 53, 38.
3. *The Western Island or The Great Blasket* (New York: Oxford, 1945), 50.
4. *Peig Sayers: An Old Woman's Reflections*, 128.

Scanlan, Patricia
Born: Ireland, 1956
Educated: Ireland.

Patricia Scanlan was born in Ballygall in Dublin, educated in Our Lady of Victories Primary School in Ballymun and Dominican Convent, Eccles Street, Dublin. She worked with Dublin Public Libraries from the time she left school in 1974, and is currently on a five-year career break. Unmarried, she enjoys 'practising' motherhood on her 'three beautiful nieces', and recently bought a house in Ballygall, which she thoroughly enjoys decorating.[1]

Always keen on writing, she entered many short story competitions but never won a prize or had her work published until Poolbeg accepted her *City Girl* manuscript in 1989. The novel was entered in a competition run by

Cosmopolitan, and when it didn't win a prize, she sent it to a London publisher who returned it, recommending her to consult an agent. She credits Maeve Binchy with advising her on agents, and Gemma O'Connor for helpful advice on editing. 'I wanted to write about modern Irish women,' she notes. 'I wanted to portray their lives, their ambitions. I wanted to show that Irish women are vibrant, glamorous and sexy and as cosmopolitan as American, French, English, and other women. ... I think I struck a chord! Recently we celebrated the sale of 100,000 of my books here in Ireland, a figure achieved in less than eighteen months!'[2] A second book, *Apartment 3B,* appeared in 1991, a third, *Finishing Touches,* in 1992, and *City Girl* was launched in the USA in June 1992.

City Girl and *Apartment 3B* were instant bestsellers. They both feature women who achieve success, social and financial, by their own talents and determination. They are both set in contemporary Ireland, and Scanlan enjoys detailing luxury clubs, stores, restaurants, and homes. The heroines shop on Grafton Street, meet in the Gresham, dine in the Westbury, drink in O'Dwyer's, take vacations in Portugal, and are driven in BMWs by wealthy boyfriends. Despite a brief visit to Ballymun flats, housing for the poor, the scene is usually one which many Irish readers might aspire to. Romance plays its part, but friendships between women are stronger than the romances they yearn for.

Works:
City Girl. Dublin: Poolbeg, 1990. Novel.
Apartment 3B. Dublin: Poolbeg, 1991. Novel.
Finishing Touches. Dublin: Poolbeg, 1992. Novel.

Notes
1. Personal communication.
2. Personal communication.

Shane, Elizabeth
Born: Ireland, 1877; Died: 1951
Educated: Ireland.

Born Gertrude Elizabeth Herone Hine, Elizabeth Shane lived in Belfast and wrote poetry and plays. The poems, or tales, she suggests were 'written for my own and my "Mate's" pleasure,' not for publication.[1] Shane's view of the islands and islanders is idyllic, as in this picture of Kitty in 'The Singer'.

> Kitty has hair like the sun-kissed corn,
>> Red-gold – red-gold;
> She is fresh as the buds that on April morn
>> Unfold – unfold;
> Her voice is as sweet as a bird's might be,
>> It rings – it rings;
> She opens her red lips deliciously
>> As she sings – she sings.

Works:
Tales of the Donegal Coast and Island. London: Selwyn and Blount, 1921. Poetry.
Collected Verse. Revised J F Donovan. Dundalk: Tempest, 1945.

Notes:
1. Introduction to *Tales of the Donegal Coast and Island*, 13.
2. In *Tales of the Donegal Coast and Islands*, 68.

Sheridan, F D
Born: Ireland, 1929
Educated: Ireland.

Born in Dublin in 1929, F D Sheridan completed her education at University College, Dublin, and then travelled throughout Europe. Her first volume of stories, *Captives*, was published by Co-op Books in 1980.

Captives tells of many kinds of captivity: from the Italian woman caught in an arranged marriage, the Italian children shunned because their mother is designated 'unfaithful', to the poor, and the keeper who himself is the captive. 'The Keeper' is the most ironical story in the collection. Dan locks an image of his perfect, submissive woman in his mind for years. When he finally finds this woman, she is married to a man Dan has seen with another woman. He decides to tell her of her husband's betrayal and give her the presents he has bought over the years for the perfect wife-to-be. But the woman is cold and hard, not the soft perfection he has imagined, and the angry Dan accuses her husband of killing her.

'The Empty Ceiling' comments allegorically on the political situation in Ireland, as a widow isolates herself from the 'jungle' of her island, creating visions of beautiful embroidered silk. 'The use of silk has, I suspect, acted as a filter and golden moths are susceptible to passing birds as I have been susceptible to guilt these past years of relative inactivity, coinciding with the horror of my island. Partly assuaged only because I see no solution and how can I work for something I do not even see?'[1]

Works:
Captives. Dublin: Coop Books, 1980. Short Stories.

Notes
1. *Captives*, 27.

Sheridan, Frances (*née* Chamberlaine)
Born: Ireland, 1724; Died: 1766
Educated: Ireland.

Frances Chamberlaine was born in Dublin, taught to read and write in secret by her brother because her formidable father, the Rev Dr Philip Chamberlaine, disapproved of education for women. She married the stage manager, Thomas Sheridan, in 1747, and the couple lived in poverty in London and Dublin. She continued to write novels and plays while bringing up her four children, two of whom, Richard Brinsley and Alicia Lefanu became well-known writers. Indeed, both are said to have included scenes from their mother's work in their own. The family moved to France to escape creditors, and she died there, at Blois, in 1766.[1]

In London, Frances Sheridan numbered Samuel Johnson, David Garrick, who directed her acclaimed play, *The Discovery*, and Catherine Macauley among her friends. Samuel Richardson encouraged her writing, and to him she dedicated her successful, anonymous novel, *Memoirs of Miss Sidney Bidulph*, two volumes, published in 1767, reprinted in 1987. In diary form, the novel includes many long letters from Sidney to her friend Cecilia, to whom she confides everything. The uneven romance between Sidney and Orlando is the main plot, but stories of friends and relatives are also woven into the long novel. Although she employs all the contrivances of eighteenth-century novels, Sheridan introduces a more realistic heroine than Richardson's Pamela. According to her grand-daughter Alice, Frances had a romantic friend, the poet Elizabeth Pennington. Frances took her in and they moved to Bath, from London,[2] for health reasons. Apparently, Elizabeth died in Frances' arms.

Works:
Memoirs of Miss Sidney Bidulph. 1761; rpt. London: Pandora, 1987. Novel.
The History of Nourjahad. London: J Dodsley, 1767. Novel.

Notes
1. Sue Townsend, 'Introduction', in *Memoirs of Miss Sydney Bidulph*. Pandora edition. See also *Dictionary of Irish Literature*, Robert Hogan, ed. (Westport, Conn.: Greenwood Press, 1979), 604-605; and *A Biographical Dictionary of Irish Writers*, Anne M Brady and Brian Cleeve, eds. (Mullingar: Lilliput Press, 1985), 220.
2. Alicia Lefanu, *Memoirs of the Life and Writings of Mrs Frances Sheridan* (1824), 89-91, 97.

Shorter, Dora Sigerson
Born: Ireland, 1866; Died: 1918
Educated: Ireland.

Dora Mary Sigerson was born in Dublin, the eldest daughter of the historian George Sigerson and of Hester Varian, who wrote one novel. She and her friends, Katherine Tynan and Alice Furlong, wrote of Irish themes during the Literary Renaissance. She married the English critic Clement Shorter in 1895 and moved to England.[1]

She published many volumes of verse; 'Sixteen Dead Men' — like many of her poems — celebrates Irish resistance and sacrifice.

Sixteen dead men! What on their sword?
'A nation's honour proud do they bear.'
What on their bent heads? 'God's holy word;
All of their nation's heart blended in prayer.'[2]

Works:
Verses. London: E Stock, 1893. Poetry.
The Fairy Changeling and Other Poems. London & New York: J Lane, 1898. Poetry.
Ballads and Poems. London: J Bowden, 1899. Poetry.
The Father Confessor, Stories of Danger and Death. London: Ward, Lock, 1900. Short Stories.
The Woman Who Went to Hell, and Other Ballads and Lyrics. London: De La Mare, 1902. Poetry.
As the Sparks Fly Upward. London: Alexander Moring, 1904. Poems and ballads.
The Country-House Party. London: Hodder & Stoughton, 1905. Novel.
The Story and the Song of Black Roderick. London: Alexander Moring, 1906.
The Collected Poems of Dora Sigerson Shorter. London: Hodder & Stoughton, 1907. Poetry.
Through Wintry Terrors. London: Cassell, 1907. Novel.
The Troubadour and Other Poems. London: Hodder & Stoughton, 1910. Poetry.
New Poems. Dublin & London: Maunsel, 1912. Poetry.
Do-Well and Do-Little. London: Cassell, 1913. Fairytale.
Love of Ireland, Poems and Ballads. Dublin & London: Maunsel, 1916. Poetry.

Madge Linsey and Other Poems. Dublin & London: Maunsel, 1916. Poetry.

Sad Years and Other Poems. London: Constable, 1918. Poetry.

A Legend of Glendalough and Other Ballads. Dublin & London: Maunsel, 1919. Poetry.

A Dull Day in London, and Other Sketches. London: Eveleigh Nash, 1920. Short Stories.

The Tricolour. Dublin: Maunsel & Roberts, 1922. Poetry.

Twenty-one Poems. London: Ernest Benn, 1926. Poetry.

Notes

1. *Dictionary of Irish Literature*, Robert Hogan, ed. (Westport, Conn.: Greenwood Press, 1979), 612-13.
2. In *The Tricolour*, 6.

Slade, Jo
Born: England, 1952
Educated: Ireland.

Jo Slade was born in 1952 in Berkhamsted, Hertfordshire. She attended school at Laurel Hill Convent in Limerick; studied art in Limerick College of Art and the National College of Art in Dublin; attended Trinity College, Dublin and Mary Immaculate College, Limerick. Married to the painter Richard Slade, and mother of two sons, she is a poet and painter.

Slade's poetry has appeared in many journals and newspapers; her first volume of poetry, *In Fields I Hear Them Sing* was published in 1989. The poems are magical and mysterious: image follows image in quick succession, and the vivid natural scenes seem enchanted as they echo ancient tales, myths, and taboos. An implied kinship between nature and women suggests nothing of the traditional images of mother earth, but rather witch-like, men-frightening power.

The long title poem reveals this relationship, as well as the enchanted nature, in memorable images. The persona recalls the 'two strong mountain women' who came to the village of her childhood, and of whom it was said, 'they'd never die/But carry on even when/The crows had picked them/And village dogs had licked/And chewed their bones.' In contrast to the women, the persona's brothers wrestled and vied for village attention, 'riding down/The wide road their high boots like/The slick hairs of a black cat'.

The women came singing. Once the villagers get used to the women, the men jeer at their 'independent ways', but the persona visits and they tell her 'what it is to be a woman'. When she tells her father what the women have told her,

> He kept me inside our house.
> For weeks I watched from my window
> Autumn tint the trees in blood colours.
> Days dragged on
> My mother told me they'd gone,
> That on their breath men smelt a burning.
> Now I think back
> And I wish those women were here
> In this place and I wish the other people
> Had seen it then the way I saw it
> But they didn't.
> Still in fields I hear them sing,
> Across grass their shadows linger.[1]

A second volume of poetry, *The Vigilant One*, is due to be published shortly.

Works:
In Fields I Hear Them Sing. Galway: Salmon Publishing, 1989.
 Poetry.

Notes
1. In *In Fields I Hear Them Sing*, 20-23.

Smithson, Annie M P
Born: Ireland, 1987; Died: 1948
Educated: Ireland, England.

Annie M P Smithson was born in Dublin and trained as a nurse in London and Edinburgh. Returning to Ireland in 1901, she was sent to Ulster, where she first experienced the problems of Irish nationalism and unionism. To the distress of her family, she became a Catholic and became involved in the republican movement when she was thirty-four. She worked as a volunteer for Sinn Féin in the 1918 general election, and taught members of Cumann na mBan to care for the wounded in the Civil War in 1922. Arrested and imprisoned, she was forced to retire from the Queen's Nurses Committee, but worked privately for the poor of Dublin.

All nineteen of Smithson's novels, many of which have been reprinted, were bestsellers. Romantic and dramatic, they present young Irish Catholic women as pure, honest, and courageous, young men as honourable. This fact probably contributed to their popularity, since a majority of the Irish audience might identify with Smithson's heroines. Coincidence and preposterous demands play a large part in all her work. In *Nora Connor*, for example, Catholic Nora promises her Protestant husband Duke to keep her marriage secret. When Duke goes away then, initially to visit his ill mother, and later to a foreign war, Nora is left to bear the 'shame' of her pregnancy alone. A series of incredible coincidences result in Duke's thinking Nora has forgotten him, though Nora always keeps faith; eventually the pair are happily reunited. The conclusion is vintage Smithson:

> Duke held his girl wife in his arms and kissed the slim finger on which he had just slipped the wedding ring which was never more to leave it. 'Sweetheart, can you forgive me?' he asked. Nora opened her eyes in astonishment. 'Why, there is nothing to forgive, Beloved' she said.[1]

Works:
Her Irish Heritage. 1917; rpt. Cork: Mercier, 1988. Novel.
By Strange Paths. Dublin: Talbot; London: Unwin, 1919. Novel.
The Walk of a Queen. 1922; rpt. Cork: Mercier, 1988. Novel.
Carmen Cavanagh. Dublin: Talbot, 1925. Novel.
The Laughter of Sorrow. Dublin: Talbot; London: Simkins, Marshall, 1925. Novel.
Nora Connor. 1925; rpt. Cork: Mercier, 1988. Novel.
These Things, the Romance of a Dancer. London: Unwin, 1927. Novel.
Sheila of the O'Beirnes. Dublin & Cork: Talbot, 1929. Novel.
Traveller's Joy. Dublin & Cork: Talbot, 1930. Novel.
For God and Ireland. Dublin: Talbot, 1931. Novel.
Leaves of Myrtle. Dublin & Cork: Talbot, 1932. Novel.
The Light of Other Days. Dublin & Cork: Talbot, 1933. Novel.
The Marriage of Nurse Harding. 1935; rpt. Cork: Mercier, 1989. Novel.
The White Owl. Dublin & Cork: Talbot, 1937. Novel.
Wicklow Heather. Dublin & Cork: Talbot, 1938. Novel.
Margaret of Fair Hill. Dublin & Cork: Talbot, 1939. Novel.
The Weldons of Tibradden. Dublin: Talbot, 1940. Novel.
Katherine Devoy. Dublin: Talbot, 1941. Novel.
By Shadowed Ways. Dublin: Talbot, 1942. Novel.
Tangled Threads. Dublin: Talbot, 1943. Novel.
The Village Mystery. Dublin: Parkside, 1945. Novel.
Paid in Full. 1946; rpt. Cork: Mercier, 1990. Novel.

Notes
1. *Nora Connor*, 146.

Somerville and Ross:

Somerville, E O
Born: Corfu, 1858; Died: 1949
Educated: Ireland, England, France

Martin, Violet
Born: Ireland, 1862; Died: 1915
Educated: Ireland.

These writers are considered together because they shared such a close and warm life-long friendship and were also literary partners: Edith Somerville continued to publish her novels under both their names after Violet Martin's death.

Born in Corfu, Edith Oenone Somerville was a member of the Somerville family of Drishane House in Castletownshend, Co. Cork. Her cousin, Violet Martin, belonged to the Martin family of Ross House, in Ross, Co. Galway. Their mothers were first cousins, two of seventy grandchildren of Charles Kendal Bushe and Nancy Crampton. Castletownshend itself was filled with the many Somerville, Townshend, and Coghill cousins, and Somerville and Ross did not meet until 1886. Edith Somerville attended Alexandra College, Dublin, and was allowed to follow her cousin Egerton Coghill to Dusseldorf and Paris to pursue her first interest, painting. Violet Martin was educated at home by her aunt and a former hedge schoolmaster, James Tucker. While the cousins in Castletownshend comprised a varied and large social group, the Martins had no such extended family at Ross. The young Martins and the children from their estate were brought together, however, for classes with the Martin tutors, and there were several Protestant/Catholic marriages in the Martin family.[1]

A deep friendship and an extraordinary literary partnership resulted from the cousins' first meeting. Many years after Violet Martin's death, her cousin described the collaboration:

Our work was done conversationally. One or the other
— not infrequently both, simultaneously — would state

a proposition. This would be argued, combatted perhaps, approved or modified; it would then be written down by the (wholly fortuitous) holder of the pen, would be scratched out, scribbled in again; before it found itself finally transferred into decorous Ms. it would probably have suffered many things, but it would, at all events, have had the advantage of having been well aired.[2]

As for the friendship, Edith would write her brother after Violet's death, 'My share of the world has gone with Martin and nothing can ever make that better.'[3]

The world of Somerville and Ross is that of the Big House at the end of the nineteenth and beginning of the twentieth centuries. Deep affection and loyalty to this world pervades their work, but also keen awareness and resentment of its gender injustices. Their own work was hampered constantly by their mothers' insistence that they give up the 'nonsense' and attend to women's real duties: entertaining and visiting. The treatment of Charlotte, the title character in *The Real Charlotte* (1894), the novel which receives the most critical acclaim, reveals the authors' conflicting loyalties. Charlotte is a plain, unscrupulous, vulgar, and insensitive woman, who schemes to acquire the land and man she loves equally. She embodies traits the authors despise, but yet they muse near the end of the novel:

It is hard to ask pity for Charlotte, whose many evil qualities have without pity been set down, but the seal of ignoble tragedy had been set on her life; she had not asked for love, but it had come to her, twisted by the malign hand of fate. There is pathos as well as humiliation in the thought that such a thing as a soul can be stunted by the trivialities of personal appearance, and it is a fact not beyond the reach of sympathy that each time Charlotte stood before her glass her ugliness spoke to her of failure, and goaded her to revenge.[4]

Suffragists themselves, unmarried, and women whose work supported their family homes, Somerville and Ross were bitterly aware of the discriminatory codes that valued only particular women and denied all women economic opportunity.

Somerville and Ross picture the dying society of ascendancy Ireland fully and with humour. Their canvas is always wide and detailed, bringing even minor characters to life. In *The Real Charlotte*, we see the interwoven lives of many members of society: landlords, tenants, agents, soldiers, and trades-people, and of all classes in society from the ascendancy to the middle-class and would-be ascendancy down to the working-class. The effects of national and social history are played out in these lives, the land situation in *The Real Charlotte*, the consequences of marriages between members of different classes and religions in nineteenth-century Ireland in *The Big House of Inver* (1925). Despite the gravity of the topics, the novels and the stories of the Irish R M (originally published in British magazines, but collected and published in two volumes in 1889 and 1908), are full of humour, sometimes directed at particular characters, but more often at the grotesque or ridiculous situations that bedevil their society.

Besides many short stories, travel books, and novels, Edith Somerville was active as an artist and illustrator: 'Retrospect', painted in 1887 and rejected by the Paris salon, is an arresting study of introspection; her works are in private collections and in the collection of Queen's University, Belfast. A splendid rider, she was Master of the West Carbery Hunt, trained and sold horses, and took an active part in making the estate productive in the twentieth century.

Selected Works:
An Irish Cousin. London: Bentley, 1889. Novel.
Naboth's Vineyard. London: Blackett, 1891. Novel.
Through Connemara in a Governess Cart. London: Allen, 1893.
    Travel Book.

In the Vine Country. London: Allen, 1893. Travel Book.

The Real Charlotte. 1894; rpt. London: Quartet, 1977. Novel.

Beggars on Horseback. London/Edinburgh: Blackwood, 1895. Travel Book.

The Silver Fox. London: Lawrence and Bullen, 1898. Novel.

Some Experiences of an Irish R M. London: Longmans, Green, 1899. Short Stories.

Some Irish Yesterdays. London: Longmans, Green, 1906. Memoirs.

Dan Russel the Fox. London: Methuen, 1911. Novel.

Irish Memories. London: Longmans, Green, 1917. Memoirs.

Mount Music. London: Longmans, Green, 1919. Novel.

An Enthusiast. London: Longmans, Green, 1921. Novel.

The Big House of Inver. London: Heinemann, 1925. Novel.

French Leave. London: Heinemann, 1928. Novel.

Sarah's Youth. London: Longmans, Green, 1938. Novel.

Happy Days. London: Longmans, Green, 1946. Memoirs.

Notes

1. For their life and work, see their own account, *Irish Memories*; John Cronin, *Somerville and Ross* (Lewisburg, PA.: Bucknell, 1972); Hilary Robinson, *Somerville and Ross: A Critical Appreciation* (New York: St Martin's Press, 1980); Maurice Collis, *Somerville and Ross: A Biography* (London: Faber and Faber, 1968); and Gifford Lewis, *Somerville and Ross: The World of the Irish R M* (Harmondsworth, Middlesex: Penguin, 1985).
2. Robinson, 85.
3. Robinson, 20.
4. *The Real Charlotte*, 276-77. Quartet edition.

Strong, Eithne
Born: Ireland, 1923
Educated: Ireland.

The list of Eithne Strong's public achievements is daunting, surpassed only one suspects by her personal achievements. Born to teachers in the 'western bog country' of Limerick, an area that was 'really a *breac-Ghaeltacht*', she attended a school whose curriculum was taught through Irish, and there she learnt to enjoy 'the making of poetry' in traditional Irish metres, as well as 'extra-curricular' attempts at English poetry. When she came to Dublin in 1942, she joined the Irish language movement, and published her first poetry in Irish in *An Glór*, 'a brave little publication, produced on a shoestring with volunteer labour'. Although intensely Irish, she always experienced a pull to the outer world; in Limerick, this pull was nourished by emigrants who brought back stories from America and England; in Dublin, by her own response to European influences, particularly psychoanalysis, a suspect subject in Dublin in the 1940s.

In 1943, she married the poet Rupert Strong, and in due course there were nine children, the youngest mentally handicapped. Although her writing, as she notes with typical generous understatement, 'was curtailed in this period', it was a time of 'experimental living, of immense activity, complex relationships and deepening experiences. A large family can be a microcosm of human conflict in general. Then, too, the reality of mental handicap meant difficult, new territory, one to which I had hitherto been entirely indifferent. ... Dealing realistically with mental handicap in a close relative can help to jettison some of the rubbish in oneself, can be cathartic and lead to wider sympathies, more genuine attitudes. To a writer, all is grist.'

In 1961, she published her first collection in English and thereafter 'combined family responsibility with freelance journalism, a four-year degree course at Trinity College, Dublin, writing for a second collection of poetry, a first collection of short stories and a novel'. She also taught in a Dublin school for twelve years, worked in creative writing workshops, and has given scores of readings in Ireland, England, Denmark, France, North America and Finland. The writers she admires are too numerous to list; she praises the upsurge of women poets in contemporary Ireland and enjoys Joyce and Yeats — selectively.[1]

Strong's poetry is characterised by a generosity of spirit humour, and attention to the most ordinary as well as the extra-ordinary. 'I have a great liking', she writes, 'for the ridiculous,/the way it makes/a fatal hole in solemnity,/letting in/the light of laughter./ ... Let us enjoy the banana skin/bringing dictators to the ground.'[2] 'Flesh — the Greatest Sin' focuses on a particularly Irish streak of meanness which deprives a young woman of any self-confidence or delight in herself: 'sure 'tis a blessing/to be ugly:/you're better off/than to be/always preening — /that leads to mortal sin.' 'Dance to Your Daddy' images the relentless circle of poverty and children, so often the fate of pregnant girls in Ireland.[3] A poem like 'Bottoms' moves from the persona's scrubbing the bottom of the pan to the flash of bottom on the corner TV and to all the bottoms, babies, basins, buses 'slizzing past/with a contemptuous fart/diminishing the air,' all the way to 'the posterior of a thought/I do not care to face.'[4]

Strong's poetry and fiction in Irish and English are widely anthologised.

Works:

In Irish
Cirt Oibre. Baile Atha Cliath: Coiscéim, 1980. Poetry.
Fuil agus Fallaí. Baile Atha Cliath: Coiscéim, 1983. Poetry.
Aoife fé Ghlas. Baile Atha Cliath: Coiscéim, 1990. Poetry.
An Sagart Pinc. Baile Atha Cliath: Coiscéim, 1990. Poetry.

In English
Poetry Quartos. Dublin: Runa Press, 1943-45. Poetry.
Songs of Living. Dublin: Runa Press, 1961. Poetry.
Sarah, in Passing. Dublin: Dolmen Press, 1974. Poetry.
Degrees of Kindred. Dublin: Tansy Books, 1979. Novel.
Patterns. Dublin: Poolbeg, 1981. Short stories.
Flesh — the Greatest Sin. Dublin: Runa Press, 1980. Poetry.
My Darling Neighbour. Dublin: Beaver Row Press, 1985. Poetry.
Let Live. Galway: Salmon Publishing, 1990. Poetry.

Notes
1. Personal communication.
2. 'Yellow Joke', in *Wildish Things*, Ailbhe Smyth, ed. (Dublin: Attic Press, 1989), 110.
3. In *Pillars of the House*, A A Kelly, ed. (Dublin: Wolfhound, 1988), 114, 115.
4. In *Sleeping with Monsters*, 115.

Sweetman, Elinor Mary
Born: c 1860
Educated: Ireland.

A A Kelly notes that details of Sweetman's life are 'hard to come by.' She lived in Offaly and published three volumes of verse. [1]

Works:
Footsteps of the Gods and other poems. London: George Bell and Sons, 1893. Poetry.
Pastorals and Other Poems. London: J M Dent, 1988. Poetry.
The Wild Orchard. London: Herbert and Daniel, 1911. Poetry.

Notes:
1. See *Pillars of the House*, A A Kelly, ed. Dublin: Wolfhound Press, 1988, 68-70.

Swift, Carolyn
Born: England, 1923
Educated: England.

Carolyn Swift was born Carol Samuel in London, and educated in London and Sussex. Employed by the British Council from 1941-46, she joined Anew McMaster's Company for a season at the Gate Theatre, Dublin, in 1947, as assistant stage manager and understudy. After acting in several plays, and working as stage manager, she wrote her first play, *The Millstone*, in 1951. Since then, she has written many plays, revues, scripts for television and radio, educational scripts, adaptations, lyrics, short stories, children's books, and theatre memoirs. She is a member of numerous organisations, including the board of the Abbey Theatre, Dublin, the Irish Film Board, the Society of Irish Playwrights, Irish Actors' Equity, and Writers' Guild of Great Britain. Her plays and her lyrics have received awards.

In 1947, she married Alan Simpson, the Irish theatre director in London, and they had three children. With her husband she founded the Pike Theatre in Herbert Lane, Dublin, and she acted as company director, script editor, and co-director or assistant director for all productions. The productions included the world premiere of Brendan Behan's *The Quare Fellow*, the first unabridged production in English of Samuel Beckett's *Waiting for Godot*, the first English language production of an Ionesco play, *The Bald Prima Donna*, and a production of Tennessee Williams's *The Rose Tattoo*, which was threatened with prosecution as 'an indecent and profane production'.[1]

Carolyn Swift has never been afraid to speak her mind. Although she has no non-Jewish blood, she was proposed to the Ireland-Palestine Friendship Society (Al-Sadaqa) by a Palestinian and seconded by a Syrian. Three plays reflect her personal urge to fight injustice. *The Millstone* was part of a successful campaign to get legal adoption in Ireland, and she herself played the part of the twelve-year-old child.[2] *Resistance* (1977) exposes fascism, and *Lady G* (1987) reappraises Lady Gregory's contribution to poetry and theatre. The 'country speech' in Yeats's plays came from Lady Gregory's pen, we hear, as did the tale itself in *The Pot of Broth*. Lady G. wrote the sonnets published by Wilfred Blunt as 'A Woman's Sonnets', actually the love letters of Augusta Gregory to Wilfred Blunt. Indeed, the sentiments Grania experiences for the ageing Finn once she meets the young and handsome Diarmuid, are those Augusta experienced for her elderly husband when she met the young and handsome Wilfred Blunt. Carolyn Swift was left, as was Lady Gregory, to face and fight the law over plays, when the persons regarded as the senior partners (W B Yeats and Alan Simpson) were absent.[3]

The list of Swift's work is long. It is to be hoped her plays will soon be published; in the meantime, I shall simply note her theatre biography, which details the author's personal life and the life of Dublin theatre from 1946-58, and a sample of her books for children.

Works:
Stage by Stage. Dublin: Poolbeg, 1985. Theatre Memoirs.

Children's Books:
Robbers in the House. Dublin: The Children's Press, 1981.
Robbers in the Hills. Dublin: The Children's Press, 1982.
Robbers in the Town. Dublin: The Children's Press, 1983.
Robbers in the Theatre. Dublin: The Children's Press, 1984.
Bugsy Goes to Limerick. Dublin: Poolbeg, 1988.
Robbers on TV. Dublin: Poolbeg, 1989.
Robbers on the Streets. Dublin: Poolbeg, 1990.
Bugsy Goes to Cork. Dublin: Poolbeg, 1990.
Irish Myths and Tales. Dublin: Poolbeg, 1990.
Bugsy Goes to Galway. Dublin: Poolbeg, 1991.
The Secret City. Dublin: Kildanore, 1991.
Myths & Tales from Europe. Dublin: Poolbeg, 1992.
The Mystery of the Mountain. Dublin: Kildanore, 1992.
Robbers in a Merc. Dublin: Poolbeg: 1992.

Notes
1. Personal communication.
2. Personal communication.
3. Maureen Charlton, *Appraisal*, RTE 1, 23 August, 1987.

— *T* —

Taylor, Alice
Born: Ireland, 1938
Educated: Ireland.

Alice Taylor was born in Newmarket, Co. Cork, and attended Dromanarigle School, St Mary's Secondary School, and Drishane Convent in Co. Cork. 'Growing up in the silence and wide open spaces of the countryside made me', she notes, 'aware of the beauty and strength of nature and the power of God. Even today I am never so completely at peace within myself or so within my own being as when I am sitting in the corner of a hilly meadow down by the river on the home farm. I have always wanted to pour the wonder of the land through my writing and maybe that is why I love the writings of Patrick Kavanagh.'[1] She lives in Inishannon, Co. Cork, with her husband, four sons, and one daughter; she writes memoir/stories and poetry.

Brandon in Kerry first published her volume of poems and three volumes of memories of a childhood spent in the Irish countryside. Vignettes of family life and of eccentric or memorable local characters, and memories of the duties, customs, and events of the past are separated into four-to-six page titled sections in each volume. Although the narratives move through the year's events, and we learn more of important characters as we read on, each section is also complete in its own right. The author's mother, 'who lit a candle in all our hearts', as the dedication in *Quench the Lamp* notes, is lovingly and vividly recalled. 'My mother never lost her faith in the goodness of human nature. If anybody wronged her she invariably excused them, reasoning that they would not have done it if there was any alternative open to them.' Despite her belief, however, she knew how to administer a put-down: when her daughters think they've 'outmanoeuvered her' with their complicated arguments, she smiles and says, 'For a stupid woman, how did I have two such clever daughters?'² Wise as well as gentle, she reassures her daughter who cannot understand the teacher's insistence that the description of the 'sex life of a cow' be deleted from her essay on farm life, 'People from a different background do not always understand.'³

All the memories shimmer with the poignancy of youth and a way of life that is past, but beautifully preserved in Taylor's prose. 'Going to school in the winter mornings through the grey frosty fields had its own beauty. The bushes and briars took on unearthly shapes of frozen rigidity and the trees glittered with outstretched arms like graceful ballerinas; underfoot the grass crunched beneath our strong leather boots. The muddy gaps through which the cows waded up to their knees in gutter were now strangely transformed into frozen masses of intriguing shapes. In their frozen state you could dance from one strange pattern formation to another or try to crack the black ice with the tipped heel of your boot and create your own strange designs.'⁴

Works:

To School Through the Fields. Kerry: Brandon, 1988: New York: St Martins Press, 1990; London: Century Publishers, 1991. Memoir/Stories.

An Irish Country Diary. Kerry: Brandon, 1988. Memoir/Stories.

Close to the Earth. Kerry: Brandon, 1989. Poetry.

Quench the Lamp. Kerry: Brandon, 1990; New York: St Martins Press, 1991; London: Century Publishers, 1991 (*To School Through the Fields* and *Quench the Lamp* in the one volume).

The Village. Kerry: Brandon, 1992. Memoir/Stories.

Notes

1. Personal communication.

2. 'Holiday Hens', in *To School Through the Fields*, 62.
3. 'To School Through the Fields', in *To School Through the Fields*, 92.
4. *To School Through the Fields*, 94.

Tighe, Mary (Née Blackford)

Born: 1772; Died: 1810
Educated: Ireland.

Mary Tighe was educated by her mother, who founded the Dublin House of Refuge for Unprotected Female Servants. She married her cousin Henry Tighe. Her long poem, *Psyche, or The Legend of Love* (1795) was published privately in 1805, and re-issued many times after her death. John Keats was deeply influenced by *Psyche*, and Donald H Reiman suggests that Shelley must have known it also, as it received a great deal of publicity from 1811-1816.[2] *Psyche* is dedicated to the poet's mother:

> Oh, thou! whose tender smile most partially
> Hath ever bless'd thy child: to thee belong
> The graces which adorn my first wild song,
> If aught of grace it knows: nor thou deny
> Thine ever prompt attention to supply.
> But let me lead thy willing ear along,
> Where virtuous love still bids the strain prolong
> His innocent applause; since from thine eye
> The beams of love first charm'd my infant brast,
> And from thy lip Affection's soothing voice
> That eloquence of tenderness express'd,
> Which still my grateful heart confess'd divine. [3]

Works:

Psyche, or The Legend of Love. 1805; Facsimile introduced by Donald H Reiman. New York and London: Garland Publishing, 1978. Poetry.

Notes:

1. Spelled in various sources: Blackford, Blatchford, and Blachford.
2. 'Introduction', *Psyche, or The Legend of Love*, Garland Facsimile, ix.
3. In *Psyche*, 5.

Thurston, Katherine Cecil
Born: Ireland, 1875; Died: 1911
Educated: Ireland.

Katherine Thurston was born in Cork. She married the English novelist and playwright, Ernest Temple Thurston in 1901. Her second novel, *John Chilcote, MP* (1904), a bestseller in the USA, Britain and Ireland, was dramatised by her husband, and twice made into a movie. She was much in demand as guest and speaker after this success. Her sense of humour and colourful lifestyle attracted much publicity. She was divorced from her first husband and due to remarry the month her body was discovered in Moore's Hotel in Cork. There was speculation as to the cause of death, but the official verdict was suffocation as the result of an epileptic fit.

Katherine Thurston wrote six novels; of these *John Chilcote, MP* (1904), a political thriller, fast-paced and packed with sensational incidents and characters, was the most popular. *The Fly on the Wheel* (1908) and *Max* (1910) are, however, richer and more original novels. *The Fly on the Wheel* moves more slowly and explores the mundane world of Catholic, middle-class Waterford. The society Thurston depicts mirrors in many ways the Limerick society of Kate O'Brien's novels: newly-arisen, it guards itself jealously from any intrusions of questionable ideas or characters.

Although kind Waterford matrons welcome the beautiful, penniless, but educated, Isabel Costello to their teas and parties, they make it very clear that she will not be accepted as wife to any of their sons.

It's not only women who guard the boundaries of society. When she arrives in Waterford, Isabel is engaged to the young Frank Carey, whom she has met in Paris. But Stephen Carey, his brother, intervenes to break that engagement. Stephen, the eldest son of a builder determined that his sons would enter the middle-class through professions and the priesthood, has had to take over the duty of educating his brothers when his father's business collapsed. Determined and ruthless, Stephen tells Isabel he will refuse to pay Frank's allowance, thus preventing his completion of his medical degree, unless she writes and breaks the engagement. Stephen voices the early twentieth-century wisdom about men and women: 'if a woman likes to make a poor marriage she does it with her eyes open and she finds compensations; it's the man who does it blindly, and it's the man who sinks under it.'[1]

Despite the sometimes stereotypical treatment of Stephen Carey, *The Fly on the Wheel* is an incisive, bitterly humorous, analysis of the Irish Catholic middle-class at the beginning of the century. It could be considered an early critique of patriarchy, as Janet Madden-Simpson argues in the afterword to the Virago 1987 reissue, noting that Stephen does not give up Isabel, with whom he has fallen in love, because of moral commitments or personal consideration for his wife. He refuses to leave Waterford with Isabel because such a flight would blight his own sons' future in the petty, uncharitable world of the Irish middle-class.[2]

Works:
The Circle. Edinburgh: Blackwood, 1903. Novel.
John Chilcote, MP. Edinburgh: Blackwood, 1904. Novel.
The Gambler. London: Hutchinson, 1906. Novel.
The Mystics. Edinburgh: Blackwood, 1907. Novel.
The Fly on the Wheel. 1908; rpt. London: Virago, 1987. Novel.
Max. London: Hutchinson, 1910. Novel.

Notes
1. *The Fly on the Wheel*, 80-81.
2. 'Afterword', *The Fly on the Wheel*, 329-344.

Tracy, Honor

Born: England, 1913
Educated: England, Germany, France.

Honor Tracy was born in Bury St Edmunds, Suffolk, educated at a private school in England and a school in Dresden, and studied for two years at the Sorbonne in Paris. From 1946 to 1953, she was a special correspondent to the *Observer*, next Dublin correspondent to the *Sunday Times*, and then foreign correspondent to the BBC's *Third Programme*. She contributed short stories to Seán O'Faolain's review, and to *Vogue*, *Mademoiselle*, and *Harper's Bazaar*.

Her first book, *Kakemono* (1950), was an account of the American occupation of Japan. She followed this with a collection of essays and was to return again to nonfiction. She is chiefly known, however, as a satirical humorist, who brings her wit to bear on the vagueness of the upper class and the irresponsibility of the working class. In *The First Day of Friday* (1963), for example, Michael Duff enters the dining room to partake of the early breakfast he had ordered the evening before from the housekeeper Attracta. Nothing is ready; the previous evening's supper of rabbit pie is still on the table, and the kitchen is deserted. He accosts his mother in the dining room:

'Attracta must go, Mother,' he said gently.
'Yes, darling, of course.' They often talked like this together. 'Certainly we are having rabbit pie rather often. And it is not a breakfast dish.' 'I told her,' he said piteously.

'I told her, last night, last thing, that breakfast would have to be ready today. She said, "May God strike me dead, Master Michael, if I should fail you."

'Those people drag the Almighty into everything,' Mrs Duff observed. 'Plums and custard too, I see. It seems only yesterday that we had them.'

'Is she wicked, Mother? Or merely an imbecile?' It was the perennial question.

'I rather think that it must be religion,' Mrs Duff said. 'I imagine Attracta has gone to her chapel. They invariably do so when they are needed.'[2]

Honor Tracy made a home in Dublin and in Achill Island, Co. Mayo.

Selected Works:
Kakemono. London: Methuen, 1950. Sketches of life in Japan.
The Deserters. London: Methuen, 1954. Novel.
The Straight and Narrow Path. London: Methuen; New York: Random House, 1956. Novel.
The Prospects are Pleasing. London: Methuen; New York: Random House, 1958. Novel.
A Number of Things. London: Methuen; New York: Random House, 1960. Novel.
A Season of Mists. London: Methuen; New York: Random House, 1961. Novel.
The First Day of Friday. London: Methuen; New York: Random House, 1963. Novel.
Men at Work. London: Methuen; New York: Random House, 1967. Novel.
The Beauty of the World. London: Methuen, 1967. Novel.
Settled in Chambers. New York: Random House, 1968. Novel.
The Butterflies of the Province. New York: Random House; London: Eyre Methuen, 1970. Novel.
The Quiet End of Evening. New York: Random House; London: Eyre Methuen, 1972. Novel.

Notes
1. Author Introduction, *The First Day of Friday*.
2. *The First Day of Friday*, 7-8.

Treacy, Maura
Born: Ireland, 1946
Educated: Ireland.

Maura Treacy was born in Co. Kilkenny in 1946, and educated at the Convent of Mercy, Ballyragget, and Presentation Convent, Kilkenny. Her stories and articles have been published in magazines and journals in Ireland, the USA, and several European countries; many have been broadcast on RTE Radio 1. 'The Weight of the World' won the Listowel Short Story Award in 1974; and she received bursaries from the Arts Council in 1983 and again in 1989, and a grant from the American-Irish Foundation in 1987. She lives in Kilkenny.[1]

Treacy's first collection of short stories, *Sixpence in Her Shoe and Other Stories* (1977), spans many aspects of women's lives in Ireland, from childhood to old age. The first story, 'A Time for Growing', is set in rural Ireland, where the hard work of growing beet meets with scant reward. Treacy takes us into a small child's mind as she tags along with her older brother and sister or father. Treacy treats children's and teenagers' problems seriously, showing the troubling, even if brief, depth of their anxieties. This first story is shadowed by the old woman's warning to the children about their father, 'He'd want to mind himself better than he does. I was looking at him there yesterday; he has himself killed going.'[2] Treacy suggests the child's first ill-defined sense of mortality as she watches her father stop work, a hand on his chest, and stand, 'tall and dark as a shadow against the bright wailing sky'.(13)

Many stories suggest the limits to women's aspirations and possibilities. The girls who seem to be having such a good time at the football match and in the pub in 'The Followers', for example, are simply adapting to suit their male escorts. In the pub, Pheenie sitting beside the silent Celia feels 'she had to say something. One silent woman was an enigma, or could be, if there was a man watching with the acquired imagination to think so; two or more tight-lipped women in a corner looked like the hatching of a campaign of opposition.' (82)

One reviewer called *Scenes from a Country Wedding* (1981) a 'compulsive novel'.[3] Treacy details, carefully and fully, all the domestic concerns and encounters, as the Heaslip family, friends, and relatives gather to celebrate the wedding of Desi Heaslip and his childhood sweetheart. There are no dramatic turns, no surprises, but the reader is absorbed and cares about the characters, perhaps because Treacy renders them so authentically.

Works:
Sixpence in Her Shoe and Other Stories. Dublin: Poolbeg, 1977. Stories.
Scenes from a Country Wedding. Dublin: Poolbeg, 1981. Novel.

Notes
1. Personal communication.
2. 'A Time for Growing', in *Sixpence in Her Shoe*, 13.
3. Bernard Share, 'Universal Feel', *Irish Press*, November 1981.

Troy, Una Walsh (Elizabeth Connor)
Born: Ireland, c 20th century
Educated: Ireland.

Elizabeth Connor and Una Troy are names used by Una Walsh, who was born in Clonmel, Co. Tipperary. In the 1940s, she wrote plays — several performed by the Abbey Theatre — and also writes short stories and novels.

'The Apple', a delightful story republished in *Woman's Part*, stages Mother Mary Aloysius's 'sin', as she succumbs to the temptation to visit her old home.

The back door was open. There was one green pane of glass in the four cramped panes of that crooked window. When you looked through it, you looked into a new world where the sea had come in and covered everything and you were living safely, a mermaid on the sea-floor. There was a picture of a dog and a child hanging over your bed. The back door was open. A board was loose by the window; it squeaked when you stood on it; you could press it up and down with your foot and frighten yourself by pretending there was a mouse in the room. You weren't really frightened of that mouse. It was a pet one; its name was Florrie. The back door was open. There were three nails where clothes hung ... The back door was open.[1]

Finally, at forty-nine, Mother Mary Aloysius grows up, when she deliberately chooses desire over security.

Works:
We Are Seven. London: Heinemann, 1955. Novel.
Maggie. London: Heinemann, 1958. Novel.
The Workhouse Graces. London: Heinemann, 1959. Novel.
The Other End of the Bridge. London: Heinemann, 1960. Novel.
Esmond. London: Hodder & Stoughton, 1962. Novel.
The Brimstone Halo. London: Hodder & Stoughton, 1965. Novel.
The Benefactors. London: Hale, 1969. Novel.
Tiger Puss. London: Hale, 1970. Novel.
The Castle that Nobody Wanted. London: Hale, 1970. Novel.
Stop Press! London: Hale, 1971. Novel.
Doctor, Go Home! London: Hale, 1973. Novel.
Out of Everywhere. London: Hale, 1976. Novel.
Caught in the Furze. London: Hale, 1977. Novel.
A Sack of Gold. London: Hale, 1979. Novel.
So True a Fool. London: Hale, 1981. Novel.

Notes
1. In *Woman's Part, An Anthology of Short Fiction By and About Irish Women 1890-1960*, Janet Madden-Simpson, ed. (Dublin: Arlen House, 1984), 166.

Tynan, Katharine
Born: Ireland, 1861; Died: 1931
Educated: Ireland.

Katharine Tynan was born in Dublin to Andrew and Elizabeth Tynan, the fourth daughter of eleven children. In 1868 the family moved to Whitehall, Clondalkin, Co. Dublin, when Clondalkin was still in the countryside. Katharine Tynan loved this home and there developed her interest in and love of nature. She attended Siena Convent in Drogheda, and in 1874 returned to Whitehall to become her father's companion. Her memories of her father are always affectionate— she believes he formed her tastes and opinions — while she dismisses her mother as a pretty but narrow woman, neither an intellectual companion for her father nor for herself.

As hostess in her father's home, she met many literary people, including Yeats. She began writing poetry in 1878 and published two volumes of verse before her poetry appeared in *Ballads and Lyrics* (1891), the first joint effort of the Irish literary revival. She married Henry Albert Hinkson in 1893 and lived in England, where she began her journalistic career and where her five children were born. Hinkson was appointed resident magistrate for Co. Mayo in 1911, and the family returned to Ireland. Despite her own family's republican sympathies, Tynan and her husband identified themselves as British subjects and saw the Rising as a rebellion which did not merit their support. Her husband died in 1919, and she moved again to England and began years of travel, often with her daughter Pamela. She died in London in 1931.[1]

Katharine Tynan's literary output is immense: she began her career with poetry and moved on to biography, journalism, novels, short stories, and autobiography. Her work includes 105 novels, twelve short story collections, three plays, eighteen poetry collections, two poetry anthologies, seven books of devotions, twelve collections of memoirs, essays, and criticism and two biographies. Her early journalistic pieces often focussed on social problems that affected women, and the novels continue this interest.[2] The novels — and the journalism — were very popular. She addresses women's rights in the novels and in 1914 went to Rome to observe the International Women's Congress. Much of her poetry is religious and expresses an orthodox Catholic view of life, but much also reveals her very personal love of nature. Christ as lamb is a frequent image.

> All in the April evening,
> April airs were abroad;
> The sheep with their little lambs
> Passed me by on the road.
>
> The sheep with their little lambs
> Passed me by on the road;
> All in the April evening
> I thought on the Lamb of God.[3]

Or again:

> He sleeps as a lamb sleeps,
> Beside his mother.
> Somewhere in yon blue deeps
> His tender brother
> Sleeps like a lamb and leaps.[4]

The mother of God is one of the maternal images which occur frequently:

> She looked to east, she looked to west,
> Her eyes, unfathomable, mild,
> That saw both worlds, came home to rest, —
> Home to her own sweet child.
> God's golden head was at her breast.
>
> What need to look o'er land and sea?
> What could the winged ships bring to her?
> What gold or gems of price might be,
> Ivory or miniver,
> Since God Himself lay on her knee?[5]

Despite the quantity of work (or perhaps *because* of the quantity — necessary to support her family), Katharine

Tynan is not usually ranked with the greatest of the Irish literary revivalists.

Selected Works:
Louise de la Valliere. London: Kegan Paul, 1885. Poetry.
Shamrocks. London: Kegan Paul, 1887. Poetry.
Ballads and Lyrics. London: Kegan Paul, 1891. Poetry.
Cuckoo Songs. London: E Mathews & J Lane, 1894. Poetry.
The Way of a Maid. London: Lawrence & Bullen, 1895. Novel.
A Lover's Breast-Knot. London: E Mathews, 1896. Poetry.
The Wind in the Trees. London: G Richards, 1898. Poetry.
Innocencies. London: A H Bullen, 1905. Poetry.
Twenty-One Poems. Selected by W B Yeats. Dundrum, Dublin: Dun Emer, 1907. Poetry.
Flower of Youth. London: Sidgwick & Jackson, 1915. Poetry.
Lord Edward. London: Smith, Elder & Co, 1916. Study of Lord Edward FitzGerald.
The Wandering Years. London: Constable & Co, 1922. Autobiography.

Notes
1. For details of life and work, see Herbert Sussman, *Katharine Tynan*, Twayne's English Series (Boston: Twayne, 1979).
2. *Dictionary of Irish Literature*, Robert Hogan, ed. (Westport, Conn.: Greenwood Press, 1979), 666. For extended list of works, also see this entry.
3. 'Sheep and Lambs', *Twenty One Poems*, 1.
4. 'Lambs', *Twenty One Poems*, 3.
5. 'Mater Dei', *Twenty One Poems*, 2.

— U —

Uí Dhiosca, Una
Born: Ireland,1880; Died: 1958
Educated: Ireland, Switzerland.

Una Bean Uí Dhiosca or Una Bean Uí Dhiocs was the name used by Elizabeth Rachel Leech after her marriage to Ernest Reginald McClintock Dix. She was born in Clontarf, Dublin. She was sent to school in Neuchatel in Switzerland as a very young girl, after which she attended Alexandra College in Dublin. She qualified as a teacher and spent three years in Canada: her novel, *Cailín na Gruaige Duinne* (1932), is based on her experience there. She had been interested in the Irish language since her youth. She met her husband in an Irish college in Co. Galway. After her marriage she began writing and became active in areas of current and international affairs.

She founded an organisation called *Na Cairde Gael*, which fostered interest in the League of Nations, and she was president of the Irish branch of War Resisters International. On the death of her husband she moved her family from Rathfarnam to Co. Kildare and became involved in rural development, the co-operative movement, Muintir na Tíre and the Irish Countrywomen's Association.[1]

Works:
Cruadh-chás na mbaitsiléirí no is éiginteach do dhuine agaibh pósadh.
   Baile Atha Cliath: Oifig Díolta Foilseacháin Rialtais, 1931.
   Play.

Cailín na Gruaige Duinne. Baile Atha Cliath: Oifig Díolta Foilseacháin Rialtais, 1932. Novel.

An Seod do-fhághala. Baile Atha Cliath: Oifig Díolta Foilseacháin Rialtais, 1936. Novel.

Notes

1. Beathaisnéis a hAon 1882-1982, D Breathnach and M Ní Mhurchú. Clóchomhar 1986.

Uí Fhlatharta, Máire

Born: Ireland, 1930
Educated: Ireland.

Born Máire Ní Eoin in Carraroe, Co. Galway, in 1930, Máire Uí Fhlatharta was the first of the four children of Séamus and Máire Mac Eoin. She attended the local National School, Scoil Mhic Dara, and when she was fourteen, moved to the Vocational School in Carraroe. She left school in 1946, having achieved second place in the entrance exam to the Department of Posts and Telegraphs, and went to work in the General Post Office in Galway. She met John Flaherty in the Post Office and they were married thirty-three years ago. They have no children, which they missed very much in their early years, but now delight in the attention of nieces and nephews. She is manager of a Credit Union in Galway.[1]

The love of place and language, evident in her work, seems almost a birthright from her parents: 'My father and mother worked hard on their rock-strewn acreage,' she writes. 'They loved every stone of it. They wasted very little of it; every little patch was tilled and sown and reaped, year after year. Like our neighbours, we were not very well off, but we shared with one another whatever we could spare of our own produce. Consequently, we were never hungry. In those days, your neighbour was your greatest asset, and we were blessed with good neighbours.'[2]

She writes in Irish, her first tongue. She admires the scholarly work of Yeats, Pearse, Gore-Booth, and Mhac an tSaoi, but sees her own work as unscholarly, in the manner of Raftery the Poet, though without his malice. She writes about patriots, writers, and ordinary everyday people, about beautiful places and events. 'I attribute my love of words, stories, folklore, to my father's and mother's love of their heritage. I was weaned on the heroism of Fionn MacCumhaill and the tall dark Ullóir Mac an Rí. Our house was a house of music and song. My parents were both blessed with beautiful singing voices, a great love of life, a great love of their Maker.'[3] She has published one volume of poetry with her brother, Tomás Mac Eoin, and has much she would like to publish, including a novel, when time allows. Humour and goodwill enliven her work. She believes the poem in honour of Seán O Riada is her most important verse. The last stanza follows:

O bhás go críoch – ní críoch do Sheán –
Séideann a anáil ó neamh orainn
De bharr na splaince a d'fhadaigh sé ar leaca Fáil
Faoi íobairt álainn an Aifrinn.
Ní críoch ach athfhás do phréamha a ghrá
A scaipeann faoi bhláth i measc Gael inniu.[4]

Works:
Loscadh Sléibhe. With Tomás Mac Eoin. Indreabhán, Conamara: Cló Iar-Chonnachta, 1989. Poetry.

Notes
1. Personal communication.
2. Personal communication.
3. Personal communication.
4. 'Seán O Riada', in *Loscadh Sléibhe*, 30.

— V —

Varian, (née Tracy) Elizabeth W

Born: Ireland c 1835; Died: nd
Educated: Ireland
An early socialist from Co. Antrim, Elizabeth was known as 'Finola'. Her social beliefs are expressed in her poetry which was published in 1874. She was also a regular contributor to *The Nation*.[1]

Selected works:
Never Forsake the Ship and other poems. McGlashan & Gill, Dublin, 1874. Poetry.

Notes:
1. From A A Kelly's *Pillars of the House*, 50.

— W —

Waddell, Helen
Born: Japan, 1889; Died: 1965
Educated: Ireland, England.

Helen Waddell was born to Irish parents in Tokyo and was brought to Ireland when her family returned there in 1900. She was educated at Victoria College and Queen's University, Belfast, and later at Oxford College.

Waddell is best known for the quality, scope, and volume of her scholarly work. *The Wandering Scholars* (1927), a study of the scholars of Chartres, Orleans, and Paris in the twelfth century, received the A C Benson Silver Medal from the Royal Society of Literature. She translated *The History of the Chevalier des Grieux and of Manon Lescaut*, and was elected first woman member of the Royal Society of Literature, and the Irish Academy of Letters. She published one novel, *Peter Abelard* (1933) and two plays, *The Spoiled Buddha* (1919) and *Abbe Prevost* (1933).[1] Her fiction reflects her scholarly interests: *Abbe Prevost*, for example, is the romantic drama of the love of Abbe Prevost for Lenki and her betrayal. Lenki is Abbe Prevost's Manon Lescaut: it is she who inspires him to write of the love that would bring a soul from heaven.

Selected Works:
The Spoiled Buddha. Dublin: Talbot, 1919. Play.
The Wandering Scholars. London: Constable, 1927. History.
The History of the Chevalier des Grieux and of Manon Lescaut, by Abbe Prevost d'Exiles. Translation. London: Constable, 1931. Translation.

Abbe Prevost. London: Constable, 1933. Play.
Peter Abelard. London: Constable, 1933. Novel.

Notes
1 *Dictionary of Irish Literature*, Robert Hogan, ed. Westport, Conn.: Greenwood Press, 1979, 671-74.

Walshe, Dolores
Born: Ireland, 1949
Educated: Ireland, The Netherlands.

Dolores Walshe was born in Dublin and educated at University College, Dublin, and Trinity College, Dublin, where she read History, English, Ethics and Politics. She also attended the Institute of English Studies in Holland. She has lived in many places: Dublin, Belfast, New York, Amsterdam, and San Rafael, California, and worked at a variety of jobs: office work, teaching, fund-raising for UNICEF's Third World programmes, suicide counselling. She now lives in Dublin with her husband and two daughters.

She began writing in 1986. 'Living outside Ireland, experiencing many other cultures' helped shape her perspectives and the concerns of her work.[1] Much of her work is about racism, and in 1990 her poetry was read in the Gaiety Theatre, Dublin, at the Mandela concert, in Stockholm, and in Wembley Stadium, London, to mark the Mandela visit. Her poetry was also read at the Yeats International Festival in 1990, and at the Peacock Theatre, Dublin, in 1991. She speaks Irish and Dutch and draws from these cultures to enrich her writing in English. She admires dramatists and is herself a successful playwright and has also published short stories, poetry, and a novel. Salmon Publishing, Galway, will publish her first volume of short stories in 1993.

In 1987, she won first prize in the O Z Whitehead Society of Irish Playwrights/SIP/PEN playwriting award;

in 1989, she again won this award, a joint winner this time around; and in 1992, she won joint second prize in this competition for her fifth play, *Seeing an Angel in Hades*. In 1991 she won the Irish Stage and Screen/Andrew's Lane Theatre Playwriting Award, and in 1992, she won the Writers' Week Listowel/Bank of Ireland Full-Length Play Award for her fourth play, *All Kinds of Trinity*. In 1988 her play was shortlisted in the international section of the Royal Exchange/Mobil Playwriting competition in Manchester. She was awarded an Arts Council Bursary in 1990 and commissioned to write a play by the Royal Exchange Theatre, Manchester. Not only have her plays won prizes, they have also been successfully staged: the first play, *In the Talking Dark*, in 1989 by the Royal Exchange Theatre, the second, *The Stranded Hours Between*, was read at the Riverside Studios, London, by Bristol Express Theatre Company as part of their policy of helping new writers, and in 1991 *A Country In Our Heads* ran for four and a half weeks as part of the Dublin Theatre Festival at the Andrew's Lane Theatre.

Her poetry and fiction have also been recognised. In 1988 she won a poetry competition held by RTE, Radio One, and in 1991 she received the Jerusalem Bloomsday Award from the James Joyce Cultural Centre, Dublin, for a short story.

As we might expect, the scenes and dialogue in the poems and short stories of this playwright are dramatic. In 'East of Ireland', the persona confronts Rhein, her German lover, a painter, with the fact of her pregnancy. '"What d'you think?" I pushed my plate of food aside. "I think nothing." He swirled the wine in his glass, his eyes watchful under hooded lids, a cat in a cage waiting for a child to stretch its hand between the bars.'[2] Pressed by the woman to answer, he retorts: '"It is a thing. A parasite. Feeding on you. I will tell you something." He turned to look at me, the words erupting from the hard rim of his mouth. "It will not feed on me."' (84)

Works:
Where the Trees Weep. Dublin: Wolfhound, 1992. Novel.

Notes
1. Personal communication.
2. 'East of Ireland', in *Wildish Things*, Ailbhe Smyth, ed. Dublin: Attic Press, 1989, 84.

White, Agnes Romilly
Born: Ireland, 1872; Died: 1945
Educated: Ireland.

Agnes Romilly White was the daughter of a rector and lived at Dundonald, Co. Down, from 1890 to 1913. The life of the village is the subject of her two comic novels.

Works:
Gape Row. 1934; rpt. Belfast: White Row Press, 1988. Novel.
Murphy Buries the Hatchett. London: Selwyn & Blount, 1936. Novel.

White, Victoria
Born: Ireland, 1962
Educated: Ireland.

Victoria White was born in Dublin and attended the local Protestant National School, St Andrew's College, and Trinity College, Dublin. She studied Italian and English, gaining a First in English. Her master's thesis, also in Trinity, was entitled 'Sylvia Plath and the Body'. She worked in the University of Pavia, Italy, teaching English, and now works in Dublin as writer and journalist. She has published one volume of short stories, *Raving Autumn* (1990), and has completed a novel set in contemporary Dublin against the background of the abortion debate.[1]

White's stories move across centuries and continents, from the recollections of a neighbour of Mary Magdalene, through those of a nineteenth-century missionary in Queensland, to the anger of a mother on welfare in Dublin. On the surface, the characters seem very different, but in each case White reveals — carefully and sensitively — the exceptional beneath the mundane. The desire for sex and/or love plunges many characters into misery. Although Margaret's 'courage, imagination, passion' are equated with the mystery of her pregnancy in the first story, her gifts prove to be only burdens. Alison's pregnancy in 'Eva' is seen as the mechanical result of mechanical action: 'They smoked their cigarettes together nervously, they went through with sex as if it were the cruellest penance in God's creation.'[2] In another story, Aisling pays for her celebratory evening of extravagance and love with fierce anger and remorse the morning after, as she realises the month of deprivation to come. The misery of her mad night of love with an old friend is summed up by her madness in leaving the electric fire on all night.[3]

Works:
Raving Autumn. Dublin: Poolbeg, 1990. Stories.

Notes
1. Personal communication.
2. 'Eva', in *Raving Autumn*, 163.
3. 'Electricity', in *Raving Autumn*, 137-142.

Wilde, Lady (Jane Francesca Elgee)
Born: Ireland, c.1824; Died: 1896
Educated: Ireland.

Jane Francesca Elgee was born in Wexford; in 1826, she claims, but her biographers suggest 1824. Writing under the pen-name Speranza, she contributed a great many patriotic verses and impassioned essays to *The Nation*; she also retold many Irish folktales and myths. In 1851, she married William Wilde, and the couple kept open house at their home in Merrion Square, Dublin. She moved to London after her husband's death in 1876 and died there during her son's imprisonment.

Selected Works:
Poems. Dublin: Duffy, 1864. Poetry.
Ancient Legends, Mystic Charms, and Superstitions of Ireland. 2 vols. London: Ward & Downey, 1887. Stories.
Ancient Cures, Charms and Usages of Ireland. London: Ward & Downey, 1890. Stories.
Notes on Men, Women, and Books. London: Ward & Downey, 1891. Non-fiction.

Woods, Una
Born: Ireland, c 20th century
Educated: Ireland.

Una Woods was born and reared in Belfast, and attended Queen's University for a year. She worked in London for some time, married and lived in Dublin for six years. She now lives in Belfast with her two children.

Her work has been published in several anthologies; her first novella, *The Dark Hole Days* (1984), set in Belfast in the midst of the Troubles, brims with horror, as shadow, illusion, and reality threaten and push the characters toward madness. The unemployed Joe and Colette record their nightmare lives in diaries, until tragedy forces them together. Reminiscent of Kafka characters, Joe writes from his space beneath the floor:

> Life goes on, one dark hole day after another. Things that worry me. 1, No money now and she's finding it very tough on her pension. 2, When she races out for my fresh baps in the morning or to do any shopping, for that matter — what if she's knocked down, if she just

doesn't come back and I don't know what's happened to her – what do I do? 3, If she gets ill in the house. 4, If I get ill. It can't be healthy down here and never getting fresh air. 5, No hope of a girl.[1]

Her writing resists categorisation, which sometimes makes publication difficult. 'My writing moved inward,' she notes,

> because there was nowhere for it to progress but closer to its source. Writing for any other reason is of no interest to me. I have to keep trying to maintain the writing at the point from where I believe it originated. I want to write at this point rather than *about* anything. I call this point the 'point of being'. It was the point of being alive because it was the point of the possibility of the fulfillment of what being alive meant ... I move no further in my work than the moments when I most lived. And since I most lived in possibility my writing dwells in suspended moments; in the effect of small light changes on expectation and hope; in the atmosphere of say the dusk falling on the city road and its implication for the whole of future life. [2]

The following extract from 'Edge of Lull' may suggest this quality of suspension.

> This dull quiet. From where this dull quiet recognised its birth. Shadow birth dull quiet on that road. And on. On for all dull quiet. For example a closed door. Enough for all dull quiet a closed door. Or nothing happening. All dull quiet nothing happening. Another. Yes it remembers. The dull quiet recognises a friend in an empty chapel. Smell of an old woman's clothes. Yes. Enough for dull quiet the smell in the shadow.[3]

Works:
The Dark Hole Days. Belfast: Blackstaff, 1984. Novel.

Notes
1. *The Dark Hole Days*, 60.
2. Personal communication.

3. In *Wildish Things*, Ailbhe Smyth, ed. Dublin: Attic Press, 1989, 199.

Wykham, Helen
Born: c 1933
Educated: England.

Helen Wykham is the pen-name of the novelist Pamela Evans. She was born around 1933, grew up in Ireland, and took her degree in archaeology from Newnham College, Cambridge. Married, she lives in Wales and has three children.

Mary Rose Callaghan believes that Wykham's first novel, *Ribstone Pippins* (1974), 'though marred, shows quite remarkable talent, catching beautifully and comically the intensity and sexual confusion of adolescence.'[1] She finds the second, *Cavan* (1977), less successful.

Works:
Ribstone Pippins. Dublin: Allen Figgis/London: Calder & Boyars, 1974. Novel.
Cavan. London: Marion Boyars, 1977. Novel.

Notes
1. *Dictionary of Irish Literature*, ed. Robert Hogan (Westport, Conn.: Greenwood, 1979), 696.

Wynne, Frances
Born: Ireland 1866; Died: 1893
Educated: Ireland.

Born in Co. Louth, Frances Wynne lived in London after she married her cousin, the Rev Henry Wynne. Her poetry was published after her death. [1]

Works:

Whisper and other poems. London: Elkin Matthews, 1908. Poetry.

Notes:

1. See *Pillars of the House*, A A Kelly, ed. Dublin: Wolfhound Press, 1988, 82.

— *Y* —

Young, Ella

Born: 1865; Died: 1951
Educated: Ireland.

Born in Fenagh, Co. Antrim, Ella Young is known primarily as a children's writer and poet. As a member of George Russell's Hermetical Society she was encouraged to further her research in Irish folklore. Her writings reflect the influence of the Celtic Revival, a movement in which she had many friends. Her poetry was published in Ireland, England, New Zealand and American periodicals. *The Rose of Heaven* was illustrated (decorated) by Maud Gonne Mac Bride.[1]

She wrote for Sinn Féin and organised gun-running for the IRA. On returning to Dublin from Achill in 1916 she was black-listed and fled to Connemara. She returned to Dublin again in 1919. In 1925 she lectured in the USA, and settled in California where she studied Indian and Mexican Folklore.[2]

Selected Works:
The Coming of Lugh. Dublin: Maunsel, 1905. Poetry.
Poems. Dublin: Maunsel, 1906. Poetry.
The Rose of Heaven. Dublin: The Candle Press, 1920. Poems
Marzilian and other Poems. California, Oceano, 1938. Poetry.
Flowering Dusk. New York: np, 1945. Memoir.
Smoke of Myrrh. USA: privately published, 1950. Poetry.
The Unicorn with Silver Shoes. New York: McKay, 1968. Children's
    Stories.

Notes:
1. A A Kelly, *Pillars of the House.*
2. *Dictionary of Irish Literature*, Robert Hogan, ed. (Westport, Conn.: Greenwood, 1979).

— *Index of Names* —

···· ···· ····   ···· ···· ····   ···· ···· ····

Work by the following is included in the titles listed below:

Aine Ní Ghlinn, Angela Bourke, Anne Enright, Anne Le Marquand Hartigan, Biddy Jenkinson, Carolyn Swift, Clairr O'Connor, Deirdre Brennan, Dolores Walshe, Eavan Boland, Eiléan Ní Chuilleanáin, Eilís Ní Dhuibhne, Eithne Strong, Elaine Crowley, Evelyn Conlon, Frances Molloy, Gerardine Meaney, Ivy Bannister, Leland Bardwell, Linda Anderson, Liz McManus (née Elizabeth O'Driscoll), Maeve Binchy, Maeve Kelly, Máire Mhac an tSaoi, Máiríde Woods, Mary Beckett, Mary Dorcey, Mary Maher, Mary Morrissy, Mary O'Donnell, Medbh McGuckian, Moy McCrory, Moya Cannon, Moya Roddy, Nuala Ní Dhomhnaill, Paula Meehan, Rita Ann Higgins, Rita Kelly, Róisín Sheerin, Roz Cowman, Sara Berkeley, Trudy Hayes, Una Woods.

- *Wildish Things: An Anthology of New Irish Women's Writing,* Ailbhe Smyth (ed), 1989.   £15.99/£7.99
- *Virgins and Hyacinths: An Attic Press Book of Fiction,* Caroline Walsh (ed), 1993.   £7.99

- *Ride on Rapunzel*: Fairytales for Feminists, 1992.   £6.99

Attic Press books may be ordered direct, with payment in advance to:
4 Upr. Mount Street, Dublin 2, or by Fax - (1) 6616176 - with full Visa/Access /Mastercard details. Let us know if you would like a complete list of our titles.